Embedded Systems Engineering

C R Sarma
Associate Professor
Department of Electronics and Communications Engineering
G. Narayanamma Institute of Technology and Science
Hyderabad

Universities Press

UNIVERSITIES PRESS (INDIA) PRIVATE LIMITED

Registered Office
3-6-747/1/A & 3-6-754/1, Himayatnagar,
Hyderabad 500 029 (A.P.), India
e-mail: info@universitiespress.com

Distributed by
Orient Blackswan Private Limited

Registered Office
3-6-752, Himayatnagar, Hyderabad 500 029 (A.P), India

Other Offices
Bangalore / Bhopal / Bhubaneswar / Chennai
Ernakulam / Guwahati / Hyderabad / Jaipur / Kolkata
Lucknow / Mumbai / New Delhi / Patna

First published 2011
Reprinted 2013

Cover and book design

ISBN: 978 81 7371 676 8

Typeset in Garamond 12/14 by
Techastra Pvt. Ltd., Hyderabad 500 029

Printed at
Graphica Printers
Hyderabad 500 013

Published by
Universities Press (India) Private Limited
3-6-747/1/A & 3-6-754/1, Himayatnagar,
Hyderabad 500 029 (A.P.), India

Contents

	Preface	**vii**
1	**Embedded Computing**	**1**
1.1	Embedded Systems and Human Intelligence	1
1.2	Complex Systems and Microprocessors	2
1.3	The Embedded System Design Process	7
1.4	Formalisms for System Design	16
1.5	Design Example: Automatic Cooking Oven	17
1.6	A few Brief Examples of the Possibilities of Embedded Systems	24
	Self Evaluation Questions	29
2	**The 8051 Architecture**	**30**
2.1	Introduction	30
2.2	8051 Microcontroller Hardware	31
2.3	Input/Output Ports and Circuits	38
2.4	Internal and External Memory	42
2.5	Counter and Timers	45
2.6	Serial Data Input/Output	47
2.7	Interrupts	49
	Self Evaluation Questions	53
3	**Concepts in Assembly Language Programming**	**55**
3.1	Introduction	55
3.2	Assembly Language Programming: The Process	58
3.3	Programming Tools and Techniques	61
3.4	Programming the 8051: Data Transfer and Logical Instructions	64
	Self Evaluation Questions	69
4	**Arithmetic Transfer Control Instructions**	**71**
4.1	Arithmetic Operations	72
4.2	Logic Instructions	75
4.3	Flags Affected by Instructions	76
4.4	Bit Manipulation Instructions	79
4.5	Jump and Call Instructions	80
4.6	Examples of Binary and Decimal Arithmetic Operations	83
	Self Evaluation Questions	86

5 Application Programming 88
- 5.1 Developing Applications 88
- 5.2 Display 89
- 5.3 The Keyboard 105
- 5.4 Conversion and Interfacing of Different Data Types 110
- 5.5 Multiple Interrupts 117
- Self Evaluation Questions 120

6 Real–Time Operating Systems 122
- 6.1 Real-Time Processing 122
- 6.2 What is a Real-Time Operating System? 123
- 6.3 The Mode of Operation of an RTOS 125
- 6.4 Differences Between a Desktop OS and an RTOS 129
- 6.5 More about Tasks and Task States 129
- 6.6 Blocked States, Semaphores and Messages 134
- 6.7 Semaphores and Shared Data 135
- 6.8 Message Queues, Mailboxes and Pipes 137
- 6.9 Timer Functions and Events 139
- 6.10 Events Management 139
- 6.11 Inter-Task Communication 140
- 6.12 Interrupt Routines in an RTOS Environment 140
- Self Evaluation Questions 141

7 Basic Design Using a Real-Time Operating System 143
- 7.1 Designing with Real Time Operating Systems: Criteria for using RTOS 143
- 7.2 Designing with Real Time Operating Systems: Points to be considered 144
- 7.3 Hard Real-Time Scheduling Considerations 145
- 7.4 Saving Memory and Power 145
- 7.5 An example of an RTOS: μC-OS (Open Source) 146
- 7.6 Embedded Software Development Tools: Host and Target Machines 150
- 7.7 Linker/Locators for Embedded Software 151
- 7.8 Getting Embedded Software into the Target System 155
- 7.9 Debugging Techniques: Testing on a Host Machine 157
- Self Evaluation Questions 158

8 Introduction to Advanced Architectures 159
- 8.1 ARM and SHARC 159
- 8.2 Bus Protocols: I2C Bus and CAN Bus 165
- 8.3 Networked Embedded Systems 170
- 8.4 Internet-Enabled Systems 170
- 8.5 Design Example: Elevator Controller 171
- Self Evaluation Questions 174

Appendix A: Instruction Set of 8051 175

Appendix B: 8051 Timer Programming 183
B.1 Initialising a Timer 183
B.2 Reading the Timer 184

Appendix C: 8051 Counter Programming 185
C.1 Limits to Reading Counters 185
C.2 Frequency Measurement: Tachometers 185

Appendix D: 8051 Serial Programming 186
D.1 Setting the Serial Port Baud Rate 186
D.2 Writing to the Serial Port 187
D.3 Reading the Serial Port 188

Appendix E: 8051 Interrupt Programming 189
E.1 Serial Interrupts 189
E.2 Common Problems with Interrupts 191

Appendix F: Keil IDE Project, Build, Debug 193
F.1 The Keil Integrated Design Environment 193

Index 198

Preface

This book is a result of decades of my work in embedded systems—design, development, teaching and training—both hardware and software. I have been working in this field since 1977, when, as the Chief of Research & Development in Sri Siddheswari Electronic Equipments, I was told by our Chief Executive, Mr C S N Sarma, that the company was getting a license to make microprocessor-based equipment. We began production of microprocessor based systems, most of which were all ROMable and dedicated applications. Sounds just like the embedded systems of today, does it not? Yes, the only difference is that the systems of those days were larger in size. A typical board containing the equivalent of a 40-pin 8051 microcontroller needed one each of a 40-pin CPU, a 24-pin ROM, a 24-pin RAM, a 40-pin I/O chip plus half-a-dozen TTL (74 series) ICs! Clearly, such an assembly is too large in size to be embedded in appliances of everyday use, and could not be called 'Embedded Systems', although, functionally they played a similar role. In those days, such systems were of the type that could be kept in a railway engine or an astronomical observatory to act like a computer for controlling the equipment. We have come a long way in miniaturisation and integration since then.

In the year 2000, my father, Mr C M Sarma, a retired executive director of LIC, suggested to me that I should consider writing a book on the subject of embedded systems, putting to good use the experience I had gained working in the field. This book, which follows the ones I have written earlier on microprocessors, microcontrollers, computer networks and network programming, has been a great source of satisfaction to me, for, the contents, offered as a course to the 2005 batch of computer science engineering students at GNITS, Hyderabad, has been extremely well-received. That, I consider as the icing on my cake.

This book can be used as courseware by most universities that offer embedded systems in their curriculum. The first chapter deals with the methodology of embedded systems and their evolution. The second chapter leads to an understanding of microcontrollers and the architecture and internals of i8051. The third chapter dwells on concepts of assembly language programming, followed by a description of the data transfer instruction set of i8051. Further assembly language instructions of i8051 are explained in the chapter 4. Interfacing i8051 to peripheral device is an important aspect of embedded systems design and development. In chapter 5, the reader gets an exposure to popular interfaces and their programming aspects. Here, one of the important development tools for embedded systems—the RTOS—is introduced. The concepts essential for single-user multitasking is explained in the chapter that follows, i.e., chapter 6, while chapter 7 proceeds further to examine the elements of designing with RTOSs and the use of open-source RTOS.

Introduction to other advanced-architecture microcontrollers forms a part of chapter 8. This chapter looks at the popular interfaces like I2C and CAN, followed by networked embedded systems and Internet-enabled services. Finally, in this chapter, a framework for a multiple-elevator control system is discussed.

Like I mentioned earlier, this book is the result of almost three decades of exposure I have had to embedded systems and draws largely from the practical work I have carried out in my small private lab. Writing this book has not been easy, for, I have had difficulty in determining how simple the subject needs to be made for the reader. To this end, intensive interactions with my trainee colleagues in Rendezvous on Chip, Hyderabad, and the students of GNITS have provided me valuable feedback; the same has been an impetus to me to author the book. I have tried to keep the discussions simple and tried to explain concepts and features of embedded systems as lucidly as possible. I would greatly appreciate feedback from readers on my endeavour.

I have had an army of people supporting me in bringing about this book, which makes it nearly impossible to acknowledge each one of the warriors individually. I thank all of them whole-heartedly. However, I should like to mention a few. First and foremost, I would like to thank the 2005 batch of students at GNITS CSE department for their active participation in the classroom and laboratory during the embedded systems engineering course I had offered them. It was truly a learning experience, and I have gained considerably in the course of intensive interaction with the students. I am indebted to my father, C Markandeya Sarma for inspiring me, to my mother, C Annapoorna, and to the rest of my family for their help and support. I am thankful to my publisher, Universities Press, and the editorial and sales team who interacted with me— Mr Madhu Reddy, the director, and Jebah S David, Sreelatha Menon, Shubashree Desikan and Umakanth Kontham. Special thanks are also due to Vandana Sathpathy and Gayatri Adarasupally of the 2005 batch at GNITS.

I would like to share with the reader some of my memorable experiences during the course of writing of this book. A part of the manuscript was delivered to the publisher hours before my departure to the US, and I was at it till the eleventh hour, making final changes and fine-tuning the contents. Mr Umakanth, who I would like to call the catalyst to this book project, came to collect the manuscript late in the night, knowing fully well the situation I was in and sensitively giving me as much time as possible. I edited the draft of chapters 7 and 8 on a cruise ship in the US, surrounded by my friends and relative who were having a great time, while I drowned myself in work on the mid-deck, having even a greater time! It was lucky that the cruiser had AC outlets for charging my laptop. I continued working on it even on my way to a casino—the bright 17" LCD screen of my laptop was visible to all motorists on the freeway. There were many more such dramatic moments over a period of 28 hrs I spent on the draft manuscript, including the fact that I did not sleep even a wink in order to meet my commitment to the publisher.

Having shared the above, I conclude with wishing the reader well. For all your feedback and interactions, please mail me at rschivukula@yahoo.com, crsarma@ieee.org.

C R Sarma
www.crsarma.com

1 Embedded Computing

The study of embedded systems is a multidisciplinary subject requiring skills from electronics, computer engineering and signal processing, to name a few. To delve into its complexity, it is therefore important to understand the various concepts involved. In this chapter we arrive at an understanding by comparing computing machines with human beings and thereby understand how to develop embedded systems.

1.1 Embedded Systems and Human Intelligence

Computation is a very important aspect of the everyday functioning of any intelligent entity. Here, when we use the word *entity*, we refer to all living and nonliving beings that have a predefined functionality. Of all such entities, biological forms such as humans, animals and plants, insects, microorganisms are a significant part of the whole. Notice that these are all entities that show a property called scalability, both of size and functionality. For example, a newborn human baby has very simple functions: breathing, suckling, crying, sleeping and so on. Apart from this, the baby performs essential metabolic activities that are needed for energy acquisition and maintenance. The infant depends heavily on its caregivers for everything and is often unable to even communicate the demands of its body and its desires except by wailing or smiling.

Given time, most babies grow in size and also learn many essential skills and become more independent. This is an example of how a living object shows scalability in physical and intellectual activity. The property of scaling is characteristic of all living objects and is observed in all biological systems ranging from the largest and most complex animals to the smallest and simplest microorganisms. Although nonliving entities may have definite functionality properties, these are not scalable, unlike living entities.

Human beings have always had a keen desire to use their intellect and creativity to make machines to help them consolidate their position in this world. Through their efforts to create appliances, tools, gadgets, prime movers and land, sea or air transportation vehicles, the human race has achieved enormous advancement in technology. Yet, it was realised in the end of the last century that there was something crucial that still remained to be tackled—the matter of intelligent design! By intelligent design, we mean the technology of building machines that can think and make decisions and spare humans the necessity of having to supervise the way machines do their work, even in small tasks. In other words, to make machines that are intelligent and almost on par with human beings.

To design such a machine, it is necessary to build into it, the capacity for computation, which would enable it to make simple, or even complex, decisions without the intervention of a human being. If machines had computational skills and could take independent decisions, they would be autonomous, that is, they can then function independently, just as we humans can!

The advances in electronics and development of computer systems which took place around the middle of the twentieth century made this dream seem realisable. The technological leaps that were seen in the field of microprocessors in the last quarter of the twentieth century revolutionised the computer industry by bringing down the size, power and cost of all computer parts. This was chiefly due to the development of integrated circuits.

1.2 Complex Systems and Microprocessors

1.2.1 Brief History of Microprocessors and Microcontrollers

The history of electronic computing begins with the invention of the thermionic valve also called a vacuum tube by Lee Forest. The vacuum tube was used in electronic communication and extensively served the telecommunication equipment in World War II. There was a parallel development of circuits involving vacuum tubes in the field of binary computing. The foundations for binary computing were already well laid by predecessors like Lady Ada, Charles Babbage, Boole and others.

The first electronic general-purpose digital computer named the Electronic Numerical Integrator and Calculator (ENIAC) was so huge that it was much bigger than an office room, consumed kilowatts of energy, dissipated a lot of heat, and worst still, frequently broke down. It was developed in the year 1945 by J.W Mauchly, used about 17000 vacuum tubes and weighed tens of tons. Thus began the electronic computing era and this was the first mainframe!

The next major invention in this field was the transistor and it made digital computing progress by leaps and bounds. It was invented in the year 1947 by three scientists at Bell Labs in USA. The scientists, Bardeen, Brattain and Shockley, were awarded the Nobel Prize for Physics in 1956. Shockley later left Bell Labs and started his own enterprise, Shockley Semiconductor Laboratory, to make transistors. Robert Noyce and Gordon Moore joined him. On parallel lines, two other companies also started manufacturing transistors. One of them, Motorola, was already manufacturing radio communication equipment and they used these to modernise their products and also sell the transistors as individual devices. The other company was Fairchild Semiconductors which was formed in the year 1957 by Noyce (who left Shockley Semiconductor Laboratory with a group of engineers). This company was a subsidiary of Fairchild Camera and Instruments.

It was in Fairchild Semicondutors that Jack Kilby and Robert Noyce invented the Integrated Circuit, nowadays commonly called IC or chip. The concept of the chip came about from the fact that transistors are made using substrates on which the respective P-NN-P junctions were grown, doped and linked as in circuits. This evolved in such a way that multiple transistors could be grown on the same substrate and packaged such that the connections for these are available through leads brought outside the package.

Later Noyce left Fairchild Semiconductors in 1969 and started INTEL Corporation along with his former colleague Gordon Moore to make integrated circuits for use as memory, or in short memory chips. This company, INTEL was named as a shortened form of Integrated Electronics. Fairchild and Motorola were already well into semiconductor processes and INTEL had just started making memory chips from a process called MOS adopted from Fairchild.

It was during this time that INTEL was contacted by a Japanese company, BUSICON, for manufacturing a chip set for desk top calculators. Ted Hoff, an employee of INTEL, was the one who developed this chip set. It so happened that Busicon, declined to buy the chip set and Intel was faced with issues of development costs and no users. They thought that while a calculator has a CPU which consists of a control unit and an arithmetic unit, and the classical computer CPU consisted of a control unit and the arithmetic logic unit, the chip set developed had a combination of both and it was of a much smaller size. So they called it a micro processor unit like CPU and decided to bring it out themselves. The author remembers that in 1970s they used to be referred to as MPUs (micro processor units). In the late 1970s they were referred to as microprocessors.

This chip set, a four-bit device, was called the i4004 family and turned out to be a great success. Almost at the same time, Fairchild brought out their PPS 4, a 4-bit microprocessor.

1974 saw the evolution of the i8008, an 8-bit microprocessor, Fairchild came out with PPS 8, another 8-bit. At about the same time, Motorola brought out its 8 bit microprocessor, the M6800.

INTEL came out in quick sucession with the 8-bit, 8080 and the 8085. The former was an improved 3-chip architecture of 8080 which needed only a ± 5 volts supply and the latter was a single chip single 5 volt supply version of 8080.

Motorola and Intel then came out with their 16-bit versions, MC68000 and the i8086, which were patronised by APPLE and IBM computers.

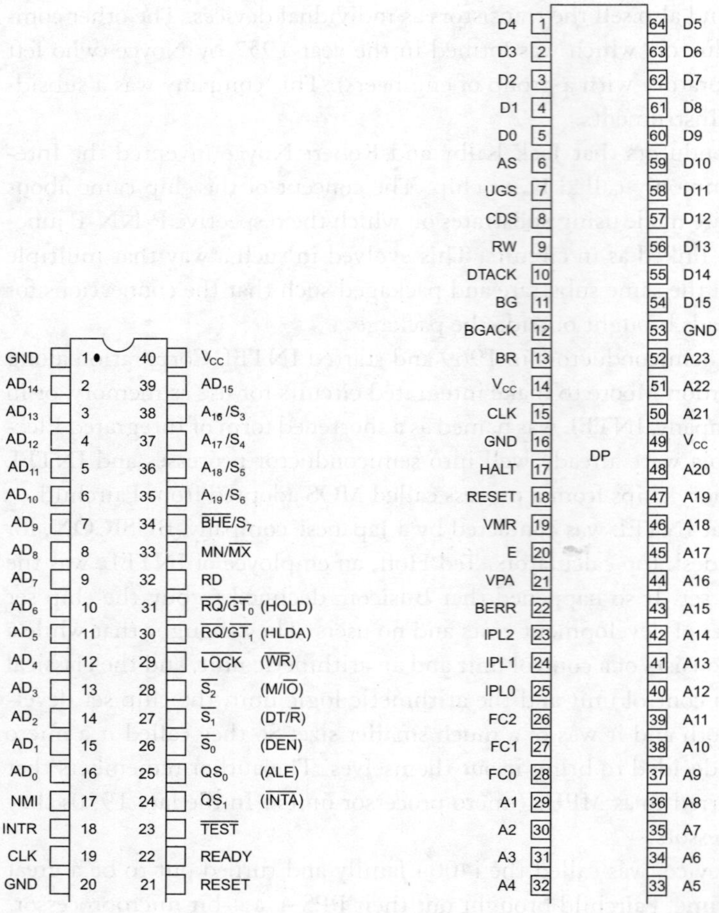

Fig. 1.1 *Microprocessors of the 1980s: (a) 8086; (b) 68000*

Figure 1.1 shows two of the most popular microprocessors of the 1980s. A comparison of the two is given below.

8086	68000
40 pin	64 pin
Data bus: 16 bits	Data bus: 16 bits
Address bus: 20 bits	Address bus: 24 bits
Memory addressing: 1mega byte	Memory addressing: 16 mega byte
Hardware select single processor/multiprocessor	Multiprocessor ready
1 level interrupt (no priority)	8 level priority interrupt
Dual address space (memory/IO)	Single address space (memory)

To built a computer system with a microprocessor like the ones shown in Fig. 1.1, more ICs are needed like

1. Bus drivers
2. ROM
3. RAM
4. Address decoders and latches
5. I/O devices (serial, parallel ports)

It was possible to load microprocessor chips with more and more features due to the advances in very large scale integration capabilities. These chips now had all the blocks as in classical computer models and they were called single chip microcomputers. It was found that these single chip microcomputers had an interesting issue. They could not be used as general purpose computers because general purpose computers needed large RAM for processing, which was not available on board these chips. But there are certain applications where the ROM and RAM available on these chips were enough for functionality. These applications are control applications and hence the chips were renamed as microcontrollers (Fig. 1.2).

Fig. 1.2 *Contemporary microcontrollers: (a) Intel 8051; (b) Motorola 6805*

A comparison of the two microcontrollers commonly used today is given below:

Intel 8051	Motorola 6805
Four 8-bit I/O ports or two 8-bit I/O ports and 8/16 multiplexed data/address bits	Two I/O ports and 8/16 multiplexed data/ address bus

1.2.3 Microprocessors versus VLSI

Why did microprocessors come to be preferred to analog systems? The answer to this can be seen in the way microprocessors satisfied the practical requirements that rose during the 1940s war. Let us read the following with reference to the history of technology described in the previous section.

Phase lock loop techniques (which compares the output phase with the phase of an incoming reference signal and adjusts itself until both are aligned) evolved in the 1940s. They were first used during World War II to monitor the trajectories of bombs flying with the help of gyroscopes and control systems. The control system circuits were made of thermionic valves and had a fixed value of transfer function (a function which shows the relationship between output and input). The advent of transistors followed by integrated chips reduced the size and power consumption of these control systems by a large factor; however, the method of computation remained the same. Digital circuits were also available as integrated chips (ICs); however, once the circuit had been designed, further scalability and changeability could not be provided.

It was in the mid-1970s and early 1980s that microprocessors came into being. These consisted of an arithmetic logic unit, or ALU, and a control unit on a single IC reducing the size of the computers from being room-sized to something that could sit on a desktop. It was during this period that the concept of embedding a computer within the equipment for controlling it, to improve functionality and efficiency, came about. The microprocessor thus found applications within systems in a need-based manner; these systems typically used to be called custom-designed systems, tailor-made systems and so on. On its own, the microprocessor was of no use, as it did not have the random access memory, read-only memory, and input–output devices (the RAM, ROM and I/O, respectively) that were needed for its functioning. In the classical model of a computer these are the building blocks—thus the expression 'computer as a component' was born.

The late 1980s and 1990s brought about tremendous advancement in integrating large number of circuits (very large scale integration—VLSI design) and FPGA (Field-Programmable Gate Array, a device which can be configured by the user) and CPLD (Complex Programmable Logic Device, similar to the FPGA) technology was born. They revolutionised the development and prototyping of Application-Specific Integrated Circuits (ASICs). VLSI-based systems are very densely populated and fast in their execution as they process directly at the speed of the semiconductor. These capabilities of the FPGA or CPLD ASICs chips were very popular and initially it seemed as if using these, rather than microprocessors, would be the right approach to embedded systems. This proved false as VLSI devices have applications that are fixed when they are sent for fabrication—though they are also programmable, this is the major difference between the VLSI and the microprocessor. That is, the user programmability of VLSI devices is closed after the IC has been fabricated. For instance, a washing machine can be endowed with user-programmable features by using a VLSI device; however, these features cannot be upgraded as the device lacks the property of being scalable. This is where a computer can be of great use, as it is user programmable. The microprocessor being the CPU, will execute the program as written in the ROM; updation of data variables in the RAM for user-programmability can be done through the I/O blocks. The microprocessor is a VLSI and a part of an embedded system. Therefore it is more right to say that VLSIs are used in embedded systems than embedded systems are VLSIs.

1.3 The Embedded System Design Process

1.3.1 Issues in Designing Embedded Computing Systems

Designing, developing, testing and installation are the essential steps in creating embedded systems. Since an embedded system is an integral part of a larger system, using the correct method of installation and testing are crucial. Some of the issues to be dealt with are presented here. This is not a final list but only a set of guidelines. Each embedded system will have its own set of issues, as it has been made to suit a larger equipment with a specific purpose of improving or enhancing the equipment's functionality.

1. Ensuring that the system will work without any performance deterioration in a variety of environmental, mechanical, electrical and user-related conditions *requires a very complex testing methodology*. This is more so as the embedded system is to work as part of the equipment it is embedded into and so has to be tested along with it. One aspect to keep in mind is to increase the mean time between failures (MTBF) and that is achieved by keeping the component count to an optimal minimum as the MTBF decreases with increase in number of components. The computation of MTBF is done by summing up the MTBF values of each component. There are tables that give the MTBF of all varieties of components. Even a soldering joint has got its own MTBF rating.

2. It is important to know the state in which the embedded system is currently executing. If the system is waiting for a switch to close and the switch is not closing, it will appear as if the embedded system is not working. There are no keyboard or display screens through which the system can respond or update the state information. Conclusions about working conditions can be deduced only by observing the electrical signals on the buses and interfaces. This brings up the issue of *limited controllability and annunciation (observation).*

3. Consider the development of an embedded system for the control panel of an elevator to be used in a small, ten-storeyed building. The system would, after completion, have to be

installed on the terrace in the motor room of the elevator. The system has to be developed and tested under controlled conditions to observe the software and hardware responses of the inputs and outputs to or from the elevator. The elevator is the system whose functionality is being enhanced by the embedded system under development. The development centre for this cannot be located on the terrace of a building, as sophisticated equipment like oscilloscopes, logic state analysers, soldering stations, work benches and work stations are required. These are available in the research and development laboratory. The ten-storeyed building cannot be installed in the laboratory, nor can the laboratory be installed in the building. This brings about a *constraint in the development environment* and needs careful consideration. Embedded systems are used nowadays in all areas of product development, and it is difficult or next to impossible to have a realistic test set up for each and every application being developed.

1.3.2 Methodology

Methods help us in evolving a systematised design process. These allow the designer to keep track of the tasks performed and their proper order; checking that nothing is missed; generalising techniques that can later be documented as process documents; leading ultimately to computer aided design wherein the computer takes as input the design approach and gives out the final design. This is possible only if the entire process is divided into smaller manageable-size tasks that can be performed one after the other, in a sequence.

Embedded systems are usually designed by a team of designers working on different stages of the system. Methods help make inter-designer communication easy and comfortable as the designer knows the input that will be received and the type of output that has to be passed on to the designer of the next stage. Coordination among the various processes in the design is thus made simple.

1.3.3 Design Steps

In this section, the various steps to be taken in the design of embedded systems are discussed. The requirement for an embedded system originates from the manufacturers of those machines whose functionalities have to be enhanced in order to beat the competition. This comes about in two ways: (1) by adding extra features to their machines, (2) cutting costs by using software to perform operations thus removing the hardware that is no longer needed. An example of the second requirement is the application of the dual beam spectrophotometer. The dual beam spectrophotometer uses two optical beams: one for the sample under estimation; and the other for the reference sample. The outputs from these two are computed to evaluate the optical density of the sample with respect to the reference. In the application, the optics, beam source and optical sensor related to only one of the two beams were retained. The second beam and its associated optics were removed. The scanning for the reference was done by bringing the reference into the beam's path and storing the data in memory. This was followed by the sample being brought into the beam's path and storing the data in a different memory location. The embedded system then reads the reference and sample values from memory for each data point of the scan range, computes the optical density, stores it in another memory location and plots the analysis on the screen (VDU). When satisfied with the analysis, the scientist or user can get the spectrum plotted on a printer. This reduces the component count of the spectrophotometer, as the double optics, beam source and optical sensors were eliminated by using the system memory. Further instead of using a sophisticated X–Y plotter, a commonly available dot matrix printer was used, thereby reducing the repetitive costs considerably. *Thus the design requirement is generated by the user, in this case, manufacturer of the spectrophotometer.*

The user's engineering department then evolves the specifications, which list out all the functional requirements of the controlling system and the types of input and output available for sense and control and the type of interaction with the embedded system that is desired. The specifications evolved by the developer would also be supported by a writeup. This write-up describes in detail the functioning of the system after it is embedded and also indicates the technical constraints suggested by the specifications. The user and the developer deliberate on the writeup and the specifications resulting in the final work document. This work document, besides describing the functionality, also makes clear the mechanical, electrical, interfacing and software specifications of the system being embedded. The designer of the embedded system is now ready to discuss the design process with a team of engineers. The design process could be approached either, top–down or bottom–up. Table 1.1 describes the different stages involved in the development of an embedded system using the top–down approach. We will also illustrate it with an example.

Table 1.1 *Stages involved in the development of embedded systems using the top–down approach*

Stages	1	2	3	4	5
Process	User requirement	Evolving the specifications	Structure and architecture	Modules and components	Integrating the system

A manufacturer of automobiles wants to incorporate an anti-skid braking system in the automobiles they manufacture. The way to ensure that the vehicle does not skid while braking is known from past experience. For example, while travelling on a slippery road, if the automobile needs to be stopped, then instead of applying the brakes continually for a long time, they could be applied for a short duration, released for the next short duration, applied again and so on, until the automobile comes to a halt. The automobile manufacturer is not an embedded-system designer, and so an organisation specialising in embedded systems is invited for a discussion on anti-skid braking. After a reasonable depth of interaction, the user requirement sheet is prepared as visualised by the embedded-system specialist. This forms the first of the five stages in the process of developing the embedded anti-skid braking system through a top–down approach. Next, the design team sits together and draws out a specification. Here the speed of the automobile, number of braking cycles and their duration is computed and the specifications are chalked out; this is the second stage. The third stage is where the technical aspects of the design are understood. For example, in the measurement of speed, the road speed, engine speed and the revolutions per minute (RPM) of the wheel are taken into consideration. The structural framework of the design is made and the style in which to execute (the architecture) it is decided. The structure is clear, as RPM measurement of all the four wheels and the engine is to be done. The architecture part consists of decisions about whether the measurement is through optical means/electrical pickup/magnetic pickup/Hall effect sensors/ or a simpler reed switch–magnet approach; what are the alarms or announcements to be generated for the driver's comprehension and so on. The design and choice of modules for various inputs and outputs comes under stage three, along with individual performance tests. Finally, stage four is where the microprocessor is used for integrating the modules/components as the embedded system. *This now is the top–down design procedure.*

Often the embedded systems to be developed need not be mass produced. There could be an inventory of components purchased in large quantities for price advantage. This brings about the reverse approach, *the bottom–up approach*, to system design: Choose the available devices (stage 5); build the modules or components required for various sub operations (stage 4) and so on, till the user requirements are met with, as in stage 1.

1.3.4 Metamorphosis of the Embedded Design Process

The hardware for the application to be embedded is finalised after several design iterations and the board is designed and ready for testing with the application program. A provision is made in the design for the transfer of the program from a development system to the application board under development. This can be done in many ways, for instance, through a serial port or a LAN and the program stored in the RAM to be executed. The ROM on the application board has a minimum program called the monitor which facilitates interaction with the board through a serial or LAN interface. This application board is called the target. A larger general-purpose system is used in order to develop the application program and simulate or debug it. The bug-free program is transferred to the target board through a cable (serial or Ethernet) for testing. The larger system, which is used as the development system, is rich in development resources. The resources that are generally expected to be on a development system are editors, cross-compilers, cross-assemblers, linkers, loaders, simulators, debuggers, file-converters, down-loaders, up-loaders and, sometimes, in-circuit emulators (ICE). The development system should have all, or most, of these and plenty of storage space (disc) and workspace (RAM), a video display unit and a PROM programmer. Since the development system hosts a number of tools for the development of the embedded application, it is called the host system. The application board and the development system together form a work-station environment called the *host–target development environment*. After sufficient tests with simulated input–output conditions, the target board can be field-tried on the equipment where it is to be embedded.

The following sections will clarify the metamorphosis taking place in the process of development. A typical target board is shown in Fig 1.3, containing the microprocessor XMIT420, which is the CPU, RAM for workspace and downloaded program, the ROM with the monitor program for interaction with the host through the serial/LAN port, the application interface and the user console. The application interface usually is different for different applications and so is the user console.

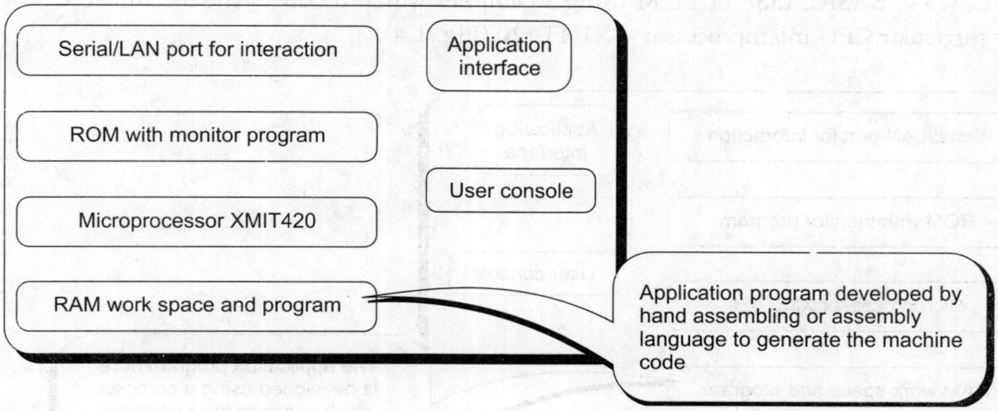

Fig. 1.3 *An embedded system board with CPU, ROM, RAM and I/O called the target board*

1.3.5 Case Studies

The following cases need careful study.

Case 1: Application software developed using machine code or assembly language

Consider the case where the software has been developed using the language of the processor: the machine code or assembly language the system showed in Fig. 1.3 is a good example. The scenario is this: the software for this application has been tested thoroughly before the embedded system was installed. After installation, all the initial bugs were cleared and a few rarer ones that popped up after several weeks and months were also cleared. The embedded system has been in use for quite some time, to the users' satisfaction.

One fine day, the CPU is declared obsolete. When this happens, the CPU may be available as a changed and upgraded version or not available at all. In the latter case, a newer CPU is to be used. The software which was thoroughly tested in the field for such a long time can no longer be used, as the instruction set of the newer processor will be different. Even if this were not the case, the enhanced CPU specifications would change the execution times, code size and dependencies. This means that the software has to be developed again for this newer CPU and has to be tested again thoroughly before installation. After installation, the initial bugs have to be cleared and the software may take its own time to prove itself on the field. This causes hiccups in the continuity of delivery of a field-tested application, which can affect the confidence of the user. *The question is: what could have been done to avoid this break?*

Case 2: Application software developed using C or some other high-level language

Consider the situation where the application program is developed in a higher-level language like C, C++, BASIC, LISP or PL/M using a compiler which produces the machine code for that particular CPU microprocessor—XIMT420 (Fig. 1.4).

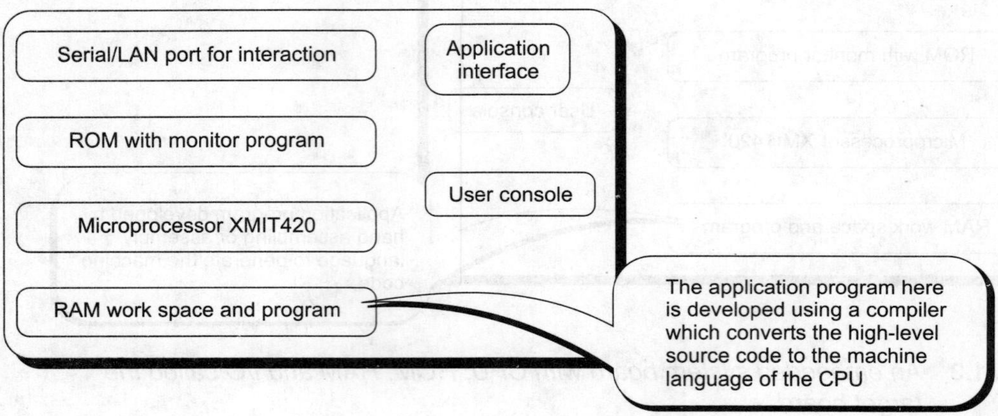

Fig. 1.4 *An embedded system board with software developed using high-level language*

The machine code is generated using a compiler. In this case if the CPU is declared obsolete or there is a need for a change in CPU, the source code at the high level need not change. The compiler can be changed so that it produces the machine code for the changed CPU while keeping the tested source code unaltered. This does not cause a hiccup, only a slight jerk in the continuity of the delivery process.

The current trend to reduce costs is to utilise general-purpose user application interfaces that are made by specialist manufacturers. The customer may ask for a change from the existing application or user interface to one that is available at a specialist manufacturer. The developer has to comply with the change and so brings about the software change. This causes a further disturbance in the continuity for delivery. *How does one deal with this?*

Case 3: Application software developed using C or some high-level language and device drivers for the application and user interfaces

In this case, the application software does not interact with the application interface directly. The application software interacts with a file-like procedure called a device driver (Fig. 1.5).

The device driver communicates with the application software on one side and interacts with the application or user interface on the other side. This means that if there is an application interface from manufacturer x to be used, then the corresponding device driver is to be supplied by the manufacturer of the interface for the CPU used in the application board. This makes the interface transparent to the application program, and all it does is communicate with the device driver as if it is the interface. In case the application interface is to be changed to another, say, application interface #zz, then the only thing to do is replace the device driver #x with device driver #zz for the new interface. This is valid for the user console as well. So there is no need for further repetitive testing. *What happens if the customer specifies an application board of their own choice?*

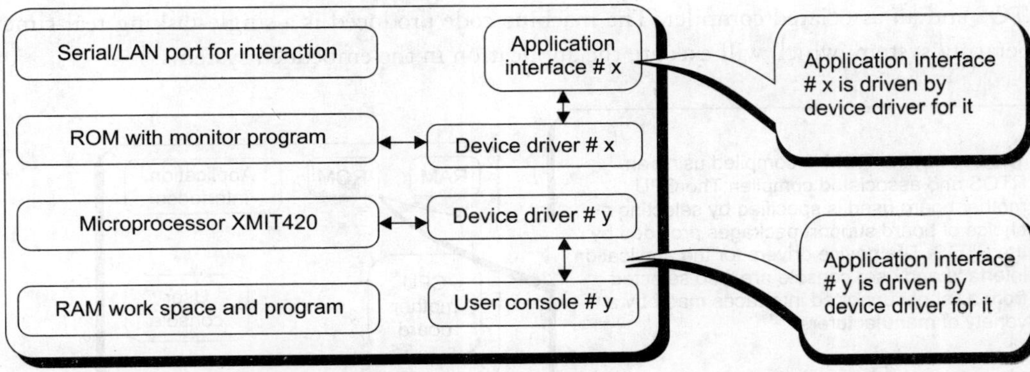

Fig. 1.5 *An embedded system board with software developed using high-level language and device drivers*

Case 4: The mother board has to be changed

The current trend is for manufacturers to specialise in a specific board and mass produce the same so as to reduce prices. Take for example, the case of the very popular personal computer (PC) which is used in large volumes. The standardisation brought in the design of the PC helped streamline the engineering processes, making it possible to quickly assemble the PC. The skills needed are minimal and maintenance is very simple. For example, if the keyboard fails, simply go to a PC hardware store and buy a replacement; this works out to be cheap and fast. Similarly, if the CPU is to be upgraded, then get a mother board with the new CPU and fit it. It seems so easy! Many times, it is desirable that the CPU board of the embedded system be bought from a standard manufacturer as it would be less expensive than making it in house. Since these modules are thoroughly tested to ensure reduction in service cost, they are reliable for use in embedded systems. When this is the case, there should be a way to use the same tested software, application or user interfaces with one of these standard CPU modules.

The use of these boards in embedded systems gives the developer a wide range of choice in CPU and general purpose I/O. To achieve this objective, operating systems are used.

Operating systems come with a variety of device drivers and can be deployed on to a variety of popular CPU boards. This makes it very convenient to maintain and support the embedded product. Further, operating systems provide multitasking which facilitates modular programming; however, the operating systems normally used in desktop computers are too huge in size and monolithic. In an embedded system, the operating system resides in the memory and so affects the footprint. Special operating systems are used with smaller footprints called real-time operating systems (RTOS). The RTOS are not like desktop operating systems (UNIX, MS WINDOWS, Mac, to mention a few) as they are not stand-alone applications. They come with a variety of device drivers and board support packages covering a very wide range of application interfaces and CPU boards (Fig. 1.6). The developer just needs to specify the device drivers and the board support package (BSP) used and compile the executable code with the RTOS and an associated compiler. The machine code produced is a single-tasking real-time operating system, which will execute the application in the embedded systems.

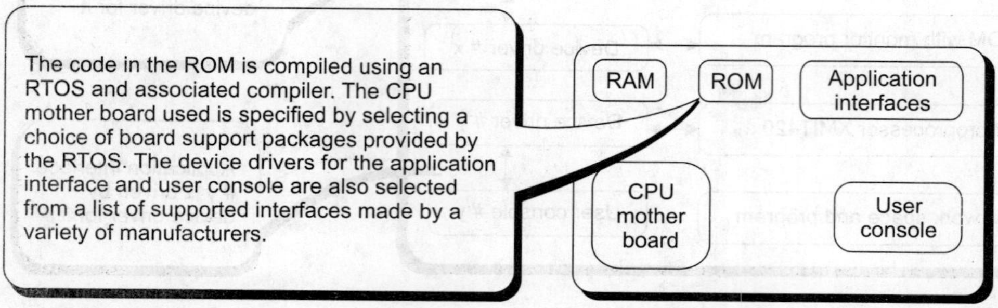

Fig. 1.6 *An embedded system board using a readymade CPU board*

So in this fourth case it is clearly seen that by using readymade CPU boards, the cost of the system is reduced. In addition, if the CPU has to be upgraded or changed, then the appropriate CPU board is purchased from the manufacturer. The same is true for the application interface and user console, which are purchased from regular manufacturers. Further, the software is implemented using a RTOS which on being compiled with the source code and the associated compiler, produces an executable code to be ROM-ed. The CPU board is specified to the RTOS through the board support package included in the RTOS. The device drivers are also provided for many interfaces by the RTOS and the required ones are selected before compiling the code.

This makes the embedded system robust and changes in the CPU or interface effect the delivery and testing times only marginally.

1.3.6 Points to Consider when Developing an Embedded System

1. The device to be embedded should be designed such that it does not occupy any more space than necessary; it should be tiny enough to fit into the system in which it is to

be embedded. This makes it necessary for the designer to ensure that the hardware to be used in the system being embedded should have the *optimal size and shape*. This is in addition to constraints arising from having to minimise manufacturing costs and maximise effectiveness in achieving performance guarantees. Hardware usually adds to the cost of the product. Designing a product with less hardware takes much more time than the designer may have on hand, whereas using more hardware increases the manufacturing cost. It helps if software could be used to perform a task in place of a piece of hardware, as it does not add to the recurring cost of the equipment.

2. In their anxiety to complete the design before schedule, designers may tend to run the hardware at higher speed using a clock with a higher frequency. This may cause other problems and rarely does it solve the delivery-time issue. So deadlines must always be met by adopting *judicious planning and careful implementation* and not by tampering with the machinery.

3. Many embedded systems are mobile or portable, and when they are used on the move, they cannot work on power supplied from the electricity boards. These systems need batteries to power them. This brings about more issues, like the reduction of the power consumed by the system and also the capability to charge the battery at a rapid rate. Digital systems consume less power at lower clock rates, and this could be used to reduce power consumption; however, this slows down the system performance. Keeping in mind the performance of the system, the designer must optimise various components that are used and remove noncritical components. Some devices, like microprocessors and microcontrollers, have *power-management features* and can operate in different power-consumption modes. These modes are active mode (2.8 mA), idle mode (0.8 mA) and power-down mode (1 μA). The values within parentheses indicate the current consumption at the rated working voltage. These are typical values to indicate the level of power drawn in each mode.

4. *Scalability* and *changeability* should be features of the embedded system. The hardware component of the embedded system may have to be used over a long period of time. This can be explained taking the example of a cell phone with a multiline character display and a 12-key telephone key pad. If this phone were to be upgraded to a graphic display, the older display has to be removed from the connector and the newer graphic display inserted in the same connector. However, this is hardware scaling only. In addition to this, the software also has to be upgraded. This could be done easily if the initial design of the cell-phone hardware took into consideration these factors. Then, the same generation of phone can be scaled up to graphic display and the display can be interchanged between multiline and graphic using the software to program.

5. One of the important issues to keep in mind is the *reliability of the equipment*. This is to be estimated by observing the equipment after rigorous testing for any deterioration in electrical, mechanical, software or performance features. It is to be estimated beforehand,

as it is not practical to wait until a breakdown happens in order to fix the bug. The characteristics of the component and their use in the system are also to be considered. If a power dissipating device is not properly cooled, it brings about deterioration in soldering and hence the mechanical and electrical properties of the printed circuit board change. The deterioration in soldering causes the joint to often turn dry, which in turn causes connection loss in the circuit. The copper tracks in printed circuit boards provide connection paths and therefore, the deterioration of the joint may also cause loose contacts or provide extraneous electrical paths causing cross-talk or power drain.

6. The main feature of an embedded system should be that it is *compact* enough to be implanted into the equipment and that it enhances the features of this equipment. This results in the high density of components in the e.mbedded system making it cramped, delicate and sometimes difficult to work with.

1.4 Formalisms for System Design

The embedded system design philosophy differs from that adopted for software used in desktop machines. Primarily, the software on desktop applications are stand-alone, meaning, that the software and the computer together form the entire system, whereas in embedded applications, the software and the computer are part of a larger system.

This difference between stand-alone applications and embedded-system applications brings about considerable conceptual variation.

Stand-alone systems application

In this, there is a desktop computer containing application software. The application software is developed keeping in mind the user application. The user is therefore the end customer for the application developer. Let us assume that BIZPRO is a company which provides a package for inventory management to a customer base, Z. This is a straightforward procedure for satisfying the customer database.

Embedded systems application

In this case, a computer with suitably small footprint contains the application software. This application software is used for operating a larger equipment/system. This larger equipment or system developer is the customer of the embedded-system developer. In turn, the larger equipment or system developer would satisfy its customer who is the actual user. Let us assume that an elevator manufacturer by name LOTUS has a customer base, X. If LOTUS wants to add intelligence to its elevators, it contacts an embedded-system developer, EMBSYS, to develop the control. So for EMBSYS, the customer is LOTUS, who uses EMBSYS's product to cater to LOTUS's customer base, X. The issue of satisfying the customer base, X, comes a while later. The initial issue is one of achieving a satisfying interplay of the control made by EMBSYS and the larger equipment or system made by LOTUS. After this is achieved, the user interaction with the entire system is to be satisfied. It is therefore essential that EMBSYS gets a proof of concept of their embedded system's performance in the larger equipment/system of LOTUS.

Development cycle for stand-alone applications

Algorithm Soon after the first interaction with the customer or user, the developer should write down the steps to be followed in the development process. These steps are included in the flow chart.

Flow chart This is done after the algorithm is approved by the customer/user indicating that the development thought process is in the required direction.

Development cycle for embedded-system applications

Simulation or modelling scale model The application is scaled down and made ready for evaluation to match the desired scaled-down specifications. This is usually done when the application is huge, and a proof of concept is desired before attempting to proceed with the end application.

Simulation or modelling using tools Simulation is supposed to be done before implementing the application in reality. This is to ensure that the bugs that could not be tracked down by executing the code mentally are cleared. After satisfying that the end result of the simulation is OK the code is generated.

Code generator There are certain tools available in RTOS which generate the code specified by the developer automatically. This is done for commonly used applications and is also sometimes called an Application Wizard.

1.5 Design Example: Automatic Cooking Oven

Developing of a design is illustrated using the example of an automatic cooking oven.

STEP 1: Evolve the functionality of the target system as an algorithm

This is the initial step where the user (customer) and the developer of the product understand each other and come to an agreement about the requirements of the customer. This also sets the guidelines for the entire team to follow so that they can work in a well-coordinated manner.

Automatic Cooking Oven

In the design of the automatic cooking oven the functionality is as follows.

This equipment will be heated to cook a cooking material of volume 2 litres. The highest temperature, to be developed is 150 ºC. It should take atmost 5 minutes to reach that temperature, given the maximum capacity. The user can choose or cancel the temperature and time to cook.

A suitable number of seven-segment displays to indicate the temperature and time are needed. The heating should be done using heating elements of nichrome, which are separated from the oven's compartment by a heat-conductive plate that is electrically insulated. The accuracy of the temperature measurement should be about 1ºC. The oven should be programmable with respect to time to switch off, temperature–time gradient and cut-off temperature. It should display the temperature and time elapsed. The program inputs are to be given using a keyboard. An appropriate number of keys should be provided with labels such as TEMP, TIME, MINUTES, HOURS, ENTER, CANCEL, 0–9 and so on. The heating must be stopped once the required time is reached.

STEP 2: Make the specifications clear

This step is essentially meant for the purpose of deciding the standards that the product is to follow (whether it is ISO, BIS or something else). The technical specifications are enumerated.

Automatic cooking oven:

Specifications

1. Maximum power consumption: 4.5 kW
2. Temperature display: 3-digit display
3. Time-elapsed display: 4-digit display
4. Keyboard input
5. Heating element: 4 kW
6. Relay control of heating element
7. Operating voltage: 230 V AC ± 10 per cent
8. Peak current: 30 amps
9. Idle current: 100 mA
10. Enclosure: Aluminum body with metallic heat- and scratch-resistant paint, with a front-door opening out to the left, transparent window on the door for inspection with quartz heat-resistant glass of thickness 3 mm.

Step 3: Create an operational flow chart

A flow chart is now made as to how the system is to be operated. This consolidates the type of input or output and the computation process needed, the type and nature of inputs to the system—like the keyboard, the number of keys, switches for interaction and so on. The output may be desired to be displayed using LED or LCD; seven-segment or fourteen-segment or dot matrix 5 × 7 or customised. The alarm output may be had as a combination of visual and audio signals. There could be a mechanical actuation for opening doors or drawers.

Automatic cooking oven

The flow chart for an automatic cooking oven is shown in Fig. 1.7.

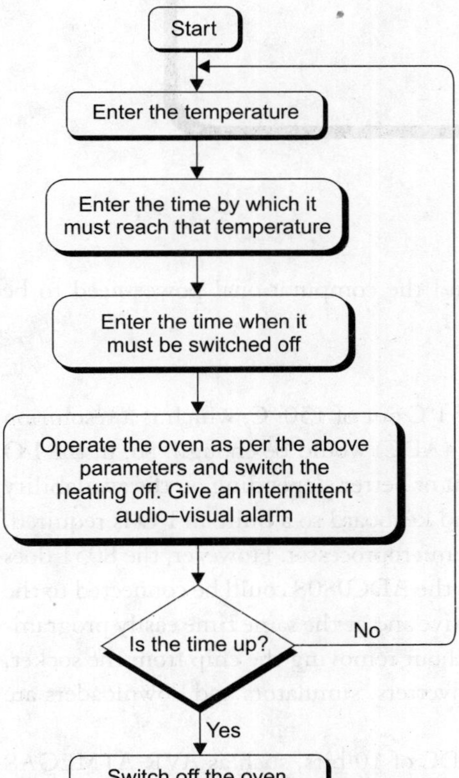

Fig. 1.7 *Flow chart for operation*

Step 4: Make a clear system block diagram keeping the user in view

A system block diagram is an overall representation for the hardware as Step 3 is for software Automatic cooking oven. The block diagram for this system is shown in Fig. 1.8.

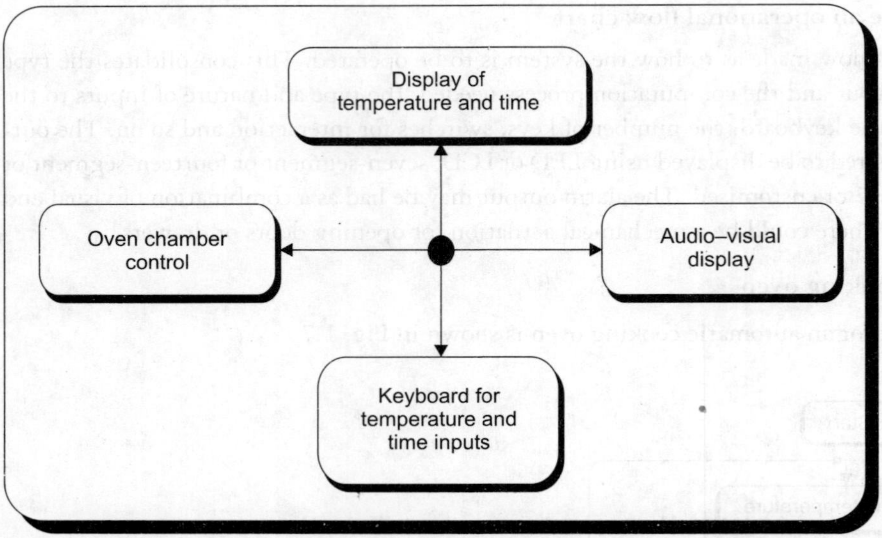

Fig. 1.8 *Block diagram to show the hardware*

Step 5: Choose the CPU microcontroller

To choose the microcontroller, I/O requirements and the computational power need to be known.

Automatic cooking oven:

The temperature is to be measured to an accuracy of 1°C out of 150 °C, which is a resolution of 1/150 and so an 8-bit analog-to-digital converter (ADC) would be enough. So, in the I/O for the oven, an ADC is required which could be 8-bit or better, depending on the availability and the price. Further, the outputs need a display and keyboard so a built-in I/O is required. The choice of CPU is now relatively easy—the 8051 microprocessor. However, the 8051 does not have an ADC built in, though an 8-bit ADC like the ADC0808 could be connected to the spare I/O bits. The 8051 is locally available, inexpensive and at the same time easily programmable. The programming can be done in-system without removing the chip from the socket. Tools such as assemblers, compilers, linkers, file-converters, simulators and downloaders are easily available and inexpensive.

Quite a few choices are available with built-in ADC of 10 bits, such as AVR ATMEGA8 and the PIC 16F877; however, the tools for supporting these and their availability and price are factors to be considered. Given these choices, the developer's familiarity and comfort in using the tools plays the major role. The modules in Fig. 1.8 are to be used as reference in choosing the CPU (microprocessor/microcontroller).

Step 6: Design the interfaces for the various blocks

Automatic cooking oven:

First list out the interface needed:

1. The 3-digit numeric temperature and the 4-digit time display counters
2. The 8-bit analog-to-digital converter
3. Keyboard for input
4. The relay control for heater on/off and oven power on/off
5. Audio–visual alarm

Now that the list of interfaces needed has been made out, the design can be done individually.

The 3-digit numeric temperature and the 4-digit time display counters This interface needs 3 + 4 seven-segment displays. The choice of display is seven-segment, as only numbers are to be displayed. The display should be self-luminescent so that LEDs are the best choice. Such digital arrays of LEDs are discussed in detail in Chapter 5. In advance, we can mention that the circuit in Fig. 5.5 would be a good option. The first four digits from the left could be used for time. The fifth digit from the left may be removed and the sixth, seventh and eighth digits be used to display the temperature.

The 8-bit analog-to-digital converter The construction and working of the analog-to-digital convertor (ADC) will be explained in detail in Chapter 5. The ADC 00808 in Fig. 5.10 can be interfaced in our design here.

Keyboard for input Similarly, Fig. 5.9 shows a 16-key keyboard, which is quite suitable for the input of numbers 0 to 9, leaving 6 for the purpose of selecting temperature-setting and time-setting modes.

The relay control, heater on/off and oven power on/off Here a solenoid driver IC like ULN2803 may be used to drive the relay and the audio–visual alarms. This is needed because the port of the microcontroller does not have the current drive necessary to operate the relays and solenoids. Relays and solenoids are similar except for the fact that relays are used for making an electric switch operation whereas solenoids drive mechanical parts, as in the case of door openers.

Audio–visual alarm The circuit in Fig. 5.1 may be used for both the audio and visual alarm. The lamp circuit will be connected to the solenoid driver ULN2803 output and the corresponding input goes to the port bit. The same is true for the audio. The audio output is usually an intermittent buzzer readily available. This buzzer could be connected through the ULN2803 as the LED was—only thing is that the buzzer is now in place of the LED and the ULN2803 input goes to another free bit of a port.

Step 7: Make a flow chart for the interface modules and the main module

Display temperature module

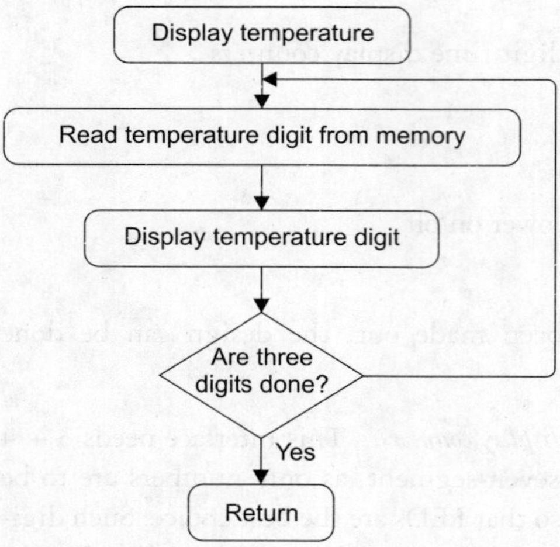

Display time module

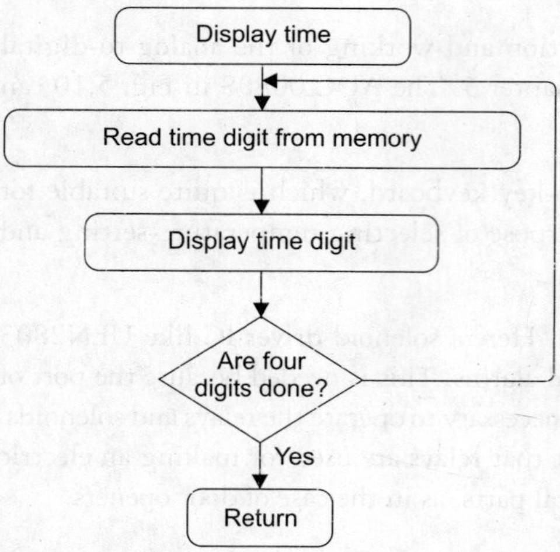

Similarly the modules for keyboard, relay control and alarm may be made.

Step 8: Create software modules for controlling the interfaces

Follow the flow charts carefully as they will give an idea of the structure of the program and datactures to be used. Based on that code the software modules are created.

STEP 9: Create the main module

Based on STEP 3, the operational flow chart makes the code for the main module calling the interface modules and the process modules as and when expected.

STEP 10: Get the hardware of the application wired and ready for downloading the software

The circuit diagram given in Fig. 2.3 of Chapter 2 could be chosen as the CPU part of the circuit. The interface modules could be connected and thus make the circuit diagram complete. This diagram could be wired on a breadboard, soldered on to a general-purpose printed circuit board or given to the fabricator for making a circuit board of this circuit.

STEP 11: Simulate and test the interfaces using the respective software module

The software modules used for driving the interface are tested through a simulator. The simulators usually have the I/O simulation wherein the interface aspect could be tested.

STEP 12: Simulate and test the main program integrating the interface or sub modules

The main module is coded with the dummy interface modules being called in the main interface. The dummy modules return a test value which is used by the main program. Thus the main program is tested for its operation. As the interface modules were already tested in STEP 11, they can now be made to replace their respective modules.

STEP 13: ROM the code

The code is now ready to be copied to ROM for installing in the target board. The code is transferred to the ROM using a PROM programmer. Nowadays there are microcontrollers which have Flash ROMS and can be programmed without removing them from the target board. This is offered by many microcontroller manufacturers and is also available in 8051 compatible families, AT89S51 and so on.

STEP 14: Test the application for the specifications

The application is tested to see if it matches the specifications given in STEP 2

STEP 15: Verify the functionality

At this stage the functionality of the application is tested with the one evolved in STEP 1.

STEP 16: Goto STEP 5

If the application does not pass the verification in STEP 15 due to hardware, repeat from STEP 5.

STEP 17: Goto STEP 7

If the application does not pass the verification in STEP 15 due to software, repeat from STEP 7.

STEP 18: Trial production

A trial production of a number of pieces depending on costs is made now.

STEP 19: Beta Testing

Distribute them to closely observable captive users to check for bugs.

STEP 20: Release for production

If the target passes STEP 19, the application can be released for production. Otherwise, the entire process has to be reviewed from the bugs' point-of-view.

1.6 A few Brief Examples of the Possibilities of Embedded Systems

1.6.1 The Microcontroller Based Digital Security System Using a Variety of Sensors

A security system is an example of an embedded system. It consists of a microcontroller, sensors, magnets, read switches, a real time clock, wireless links, a speaker (or) alarm. The sensors are of different types—sensors which sense the movement of human beings in an area; ones which sense the movement (or) position of a doors and windows; and finally barrier interrupt sensors. A speaker is added to make appropriate announcements from the guard room. If no response is sensed by the pressing of a key switch, the system powers on a speaker with the help of a real-time clock. Some systems are even connected to the nearby police station through a wireless link.

Hardware required:

1. 89C52 microcontroller
2. Sensors
3. LCD panel
4. Real-time clock
5. Wireless link
6. Speaker

Software required:

1. Kiel software
2. Embedded 'C'

1.6.2 Multipurpose RFID Card Reader

Taking class room attendance is undoubtedly the most cumbersome management task given to lecturers. On an average, a typical class time period varies around 45 minutes. It is a big task to cover the huge syllabus in this course of short duration, let alone take attendance which costs 10 minutes. When seen in a big time frame, this accumulated 10 minutes from each period has a great impact on the completion of syllabus by the faculty.

The card reader tries to address this problem through the use of an upcoming technology–Radio Frequency Identification, popularly known as RFID.

1.6.2.1 RFID technology

RFID systems use radio frequency to identify, locate and track people, assets and animals. This system consists of 3 components—the reader (interrogator); the RFID tag; and the host computer. RFID tags come in three general varieties: *passive, active,* or *semi-passive* (also known as *battery-assisted*). The typical carrier frequency (reader's transmitting frequency) range from 125 kHz – 2.4 GHz.

1.6.2.2 RFID card reader

A card reader can be a passive RFID system where passive RFID tags are employed with no internal power supply. The carrier frequency is centered around 13.56 MHz based on its penetration capabilities and cost. The configuration is as shown in Fig. 1.9.

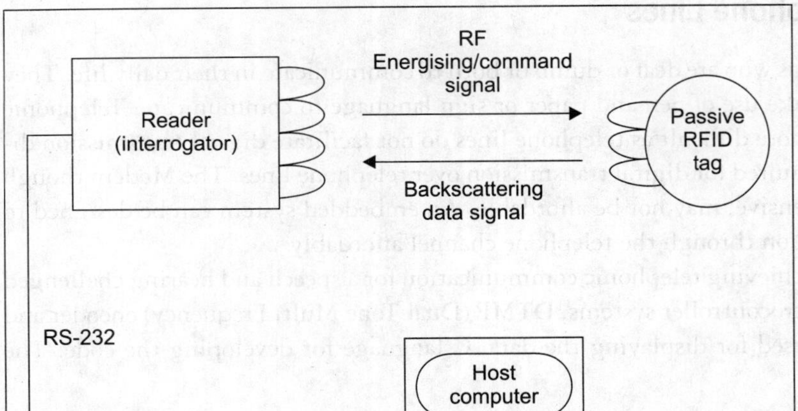

Fig. 1.9 *Simple configuration of RFID systems*

It transmits the carrier signal (13.56 MHz), receives the backscattered signal from the tag, and performs data processing. The reader also communicates with an external host computer. A basic block diagram of a typical RFID reader is shown in Fig. 1.10

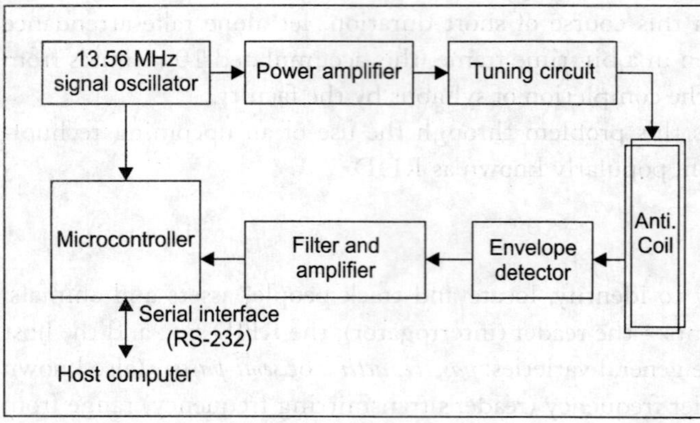

Fig. 1.10 *Functional block diagram of a typical RFID reader*

Apart from using the reader for taking attendance, it can be used extensively at medical stores, departmental stores, home security and military applications.

1.6.3 Two Way Communicator for Speech and Hearing Impaired over Telephone Lines

It is difficult for persons who are deaf or dumb or both to communicate in their daily life. They will either have to make use of pen and paper or sign language to communicate. Telephonic conversation is even more difficult as telephone lines do not facilitate digital transmission directly. A Modem is required for digital transmission over telephone lines. The Modem though not prohibitively expensive, may not be affordable. An embedded system can be designed to establish communication through the telephone channel affordably.

The hardware for achieving telephonic communication for a speech and hearing challenged person is based on microcontroller systems, DTMF (Dual Tone Multi Frequency) encoder and decoder. An LCD is used for displaying the data, C language for developing the code. The software used is Keil.

Methodology:

The basic components used are:

1. AT89S52 microcontroller
2. A 16 × 2 LCD

3. 8880 DTMF transceiver
4. PC keyboard

As shown in Fig. 1.11, the electronic communicator consists of an AT89S52 microcontroller and a 16 × 2 LCD which facilitates communication through the telephone line by using loop back technique. This communicator is then interfaced with a DTMF encoder/decoder which will transmit the ASCII code of the message typed by the user. The message is received at the remote end and decoded to form the original message. The whole system comes as a pair. Each one is set up at the sender and the receiver end.

The block diagram for the system is shown in Fig. 1.11.

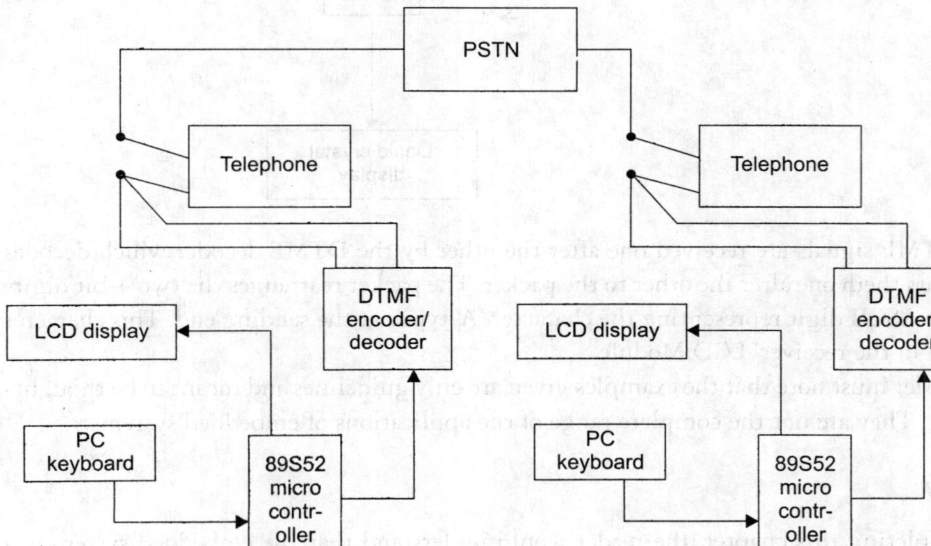

Fig. 1.11 *Block diagram of communicator. PSTN stands for public switched telephone network, the one normally used as the land line*

1.6.3.1 Example to illustrate the operation of the communicator

From the keyboard an ASCII character 'A' is typed— shown as <A> in the flow chart below— which is converted to hex code 41H. This hex code is now unpacked to two 4-bit numbers, that is 4 and 1, which is converted to DTMF code and transmitted through the telephone line (the type of whistling sounds one hears on digital/keyboard type telephones when keys are pressed is the DTMF code).

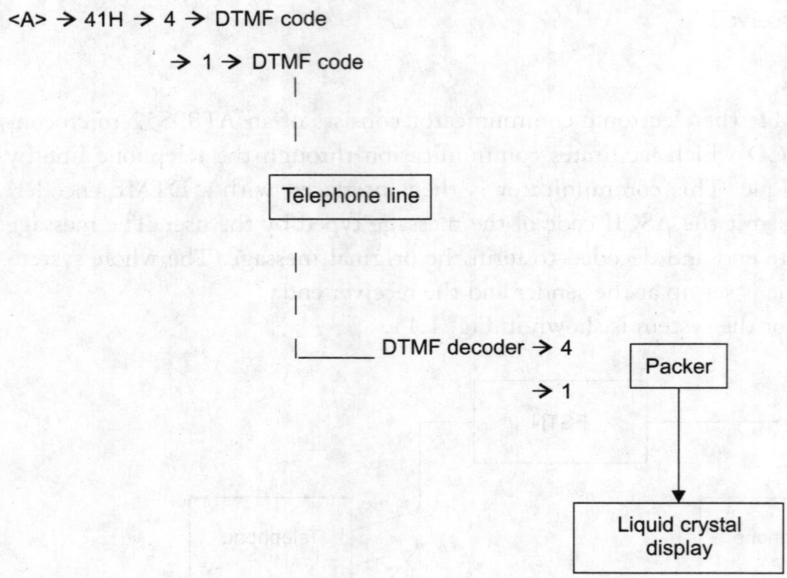

The DTMF signals are received one after the other by the DTMF decoder which decodes and presents them one after the other to the packer. The packer rearranges the two 4-bit digits to an 8-bit ASCII digit representing the character 'A' typed at the sending end. This character is updated in the receiver' LCD Module.

The reader must note that the examples given are only guidelines and meant to be thought-provoking. They are not the complete range of the applications of embedded systems.

Summary

After completing this chapter, the reader would understand that the embedded system is a dedicated system which is tailor-made to fit in an application, enhancing the functionality of that application. The application could be a new one or could be already existing. The concept of host–target systems for developing embedded systems is clear along with the need for high-level language, real time operating systems (RTOS) The design methodology and the top–down/bottom–up approach has been understood. Requirements such as power dissipation-consumption, MTBF, scalability, changeability and the need for transparency has been highlighted. The design example of an automatic cooking oven gives a run through over the whole process of developing a typical system.

The application of embedded systems is an art as shown by the other cursory examples of embedded systems. These are included only to show the variety of possibilities. These examples are real projects done by the author's students as part of their graduation course.The author has even developed an electronic rattle called eGilaka for his grandchild. This is viewable at http://www.instructables.com/id/Babys-sound-and-light-flower/. It is hoped that the same enthusiasm for applying the concepts they learn to requirements in real life, however small, will seize the readers too.

Self Evaluation Questions

1. What are the points to be considered for the design of embedded systems?
2. Reliability is an important issue everywhere and also in embedded systems. Explain the considerations for reliability to be made when developing embedded systems.
3. Explain the scalability and changeability aspects in embedded systems.
4. How is power related to embedded systems development?
5. In what way are the following associated with embedded systems:

   (i) Charles Babbage; (ii) Boole; (iii) Lady Ada; (iv) J W Mauchly; (v) Barttain; (vi) Shockley; (vii) Bardeen; (viii) Bell Labs; (ix) Jack Kilby; (x) Robert Noyce; (xi) Gordon Moore; (xii) Ted Hoff; (xiii) Intel; (xiv) Motorola; (xv) Fairchild; (xvi) Bell Labs
6. Compare the microprocessors from Intel and Motorola.
7. All microprocessors are VLSI products, yet all VLSI products are not microprocessors. Elaborate and comment on this.
8. What are the issues in designing embedded computing systems?
9. How does MTBF come into the scene in embedded system design?
10. What are the steps involved in the design of embedded systems? Explain clearly.
11. The embedded system design evolved over time. Explain the steps it has gone through.
12. Why is a high level language (eg. 'C') preferred over a low level language (eg. assembly language)?
13. How does a real time operating system make its entry into the development of embedded systems?
14. What are the steps involved in the actual development of a typical embedded system.

2 The 8051 Architecture

2.1 Introduction

Embedded system developers need to understand the hardware and software components of the system they are to develop. Developing an embedded system is like developing a living being with a body, capable of metabolic activities, and a brain, capable of retaining things in memory and issuing orders which the body will follow. In the embedded system, these elements are represented by the input/output, which is to be implemented as per the functionality of the system. Next, the role of the brain is played by the central control of the system which also has the memory to take care of both the functioning and the operation of the system. Next in line is the power source. Once the hardware, or the 'body' of the 'living being,' is defined, the operating system, or its 'mind,' with a functional program is to be installed. We have discussed in the previous chapter, the host–target development procedure, where the functional code is transferred from the host to the target through a cable. Once the performance of the target comes up to the level required, the cable is removed and the target is now ready for operation. The analogy of the target-embedded system to the development of a living being stops here, because unlike a living being, the created embedded system does not grow and further develop in size or functionality, by itself. Perhaps one day soon this will be possible.

All this explanation and the comparison of an embedded system to a living being is only to highlight the fact that an understanding of hardware and software is essential in order to be a good embedded systems developer. The initial step is to get to know the CPU of the embedded system, the microprocessor/microcontroller and the input/output (I/O) techniques to be adopted.

The microprocessor is a CPU in a VLSI(IC) and requires the RAM, ROM and I/O to be connected to it before it can be functional. In the development of CPU boards for embedded systems, a great deal of effort is spent in designing and engineering before they can become functional. The development of these boards takes about 70% to 90% of the total time available for developing the system, leaving only about 10% for development of applications. Microcontrollers have turned this upside down as it takes only 10% to 20% of the total time to make a CPU board, and the developer may spend the remaining 80% to 90% time in developing and perfecting the application to the satisfaction of the customer. Now, what is a microcontroller?

As microprocessors' ICs became populated with peripherals like I/O, RAM and ROM, the VLSI design density became higher and higher. These ICs containing entire blocks of the computer in them were called single-chip microcomputers. The functionality of these chips as general-purpose computers was limited, as the amount of RAM and ROM present in them was not sufficient for functions such as data processing which formed nearly 70% to 80% of computer applications. This was due to the fact that data processing applications need a lot of computer memory to store the data and the program code; memory which was not available in these single-chip microcomputers. However, soon it was found that the single-chip microcomputer could be used in control applications even with the restrictions on RAM and ROM size—controller programs not being data intensive was one of the main reasons. These devices were fortified by adding serial communication devices so that they could communicate with other computers, irrespective of size or type.

There are many varieties of microcontrollers available. The 8051 from the MCS51 family is the most common one. It is easily available and has a host of development tools, both priced and those under general public license (GPL) or freeware. It has been around for two decades now.

The understanding of the externals and the internals of this microcontroller will certainly be useful in understanding the development of embedded systems; however, this book will also discuss the development of application code used along with this microcontroller.

2.2 8051 Microcontroller Hardware

This microcontroller is a generic member of the MCS51 family of Intel. It is fabricated in n-channel metal oxide semiconductor (nMOS) or complimentary metal oxide semiconductor (CMOS) substrates. NMOS devices are faster but consume more power; the CMOS versions consume much less power and are not too slow. The nMOS version is referred to simply as 8051 whereas the CMOS version is denoted as 80C51.

2.2.1 8051 Specifications

- **40-pin dip IC package**
- **8-bit Harvard architecture CPU**: CPUs having Harvard-type architecture have two different paths for data flow—from the *code memory* and the *data memory*. In other words, the contents of the code memory (ROM) and the data memory (RAM) are accessed through separate paths even though they appear to occupy the same address space.

- **On-chip 4 kilobytes of ROM (code)**
- **On-chip 128 bytes of internal RAM (data)**
- **Three address spaces:** These are spread over 128 kilobytes and 128 bytes, as follows.
  1. The *internal data RAM*, consisting of 128 bytes, called the *data RAM*.
  2. The *code memory* of size 64 kilobytes which exists either as 64 kilobytes external memory only or as 4 kilobytes internal memory, which can contain the starting part of the code, and when the code exceeds this 4-kilobyte limit, an external additional memory of 60 kilobytes will be accessed, which is called the *code ROM*.
  3. Finally, the *external RAM* containing 64 kilobytes which is called *XRAM*.
- **On-chip 32-bit I/O port:** This is organised as four 8-bit ports, referred to as P0, P1, P2, P3.
- **Two 16-bit timers/counters**
- **Serial asynchronous port:** This is double-buffered and full-duplex.
- **Five-level interrupts:** These consist of two external interrupts; two time interrupts and one serial interrupt which is common for both transmitting and receiving.
- **Registers:** The following types of register are used:
  1. **PC:** program counter 16-bit;
  2. **DPTR:** data pointer 16-bit;
  3. **SP:** stack pointer 8-bit;
  4. **GPR:** general purpose registers, eight in number, identified as R0, R1, R2, R3, R4, R5, R6 and R7. These registers are actually internal data RAM locations. The first 32 bytes of the internal data RAM are also treated as four banks of 8 bytes each. The 8 bytes in each bank correspond to GPRs R0–R7. The locations of these banks are at the following sites.
     i. Bank 0 (00H to 07H): R0 to R7
     ii. Bank 1 (08H to 0Fh): R0 to R7
     iii. Bank 2 (10H to 17H): R0 to R7
     iv. Bank 3 (18H to 1Fh): R0 to R7

Effectively, the GPRs may be considered to add up to 32 in number using bank switching.

5. **PSW** (processor status word register): Bank switching is facilitated by the PSW register as shown in Fig. 2.1. The PSW is used to keep the current status of the processor in order to handle any abnormal conditions caused by the previous instructions. If the processor is executing a single task then it may also be called as a program status register.

6. **A:** This is an 8-bit register. It is called the accumulator register as it is associated with the Arithmetic Logic Unit (ALU) It is from here and the B register that the ALU takes inputs and gives its output.

7. **B:** This is an 8-bit register A, a general purpose register specifically meant for use with A in multiply and divide instructions.

The PSW is shown in Fig. 2.1 and its flags are explained below.

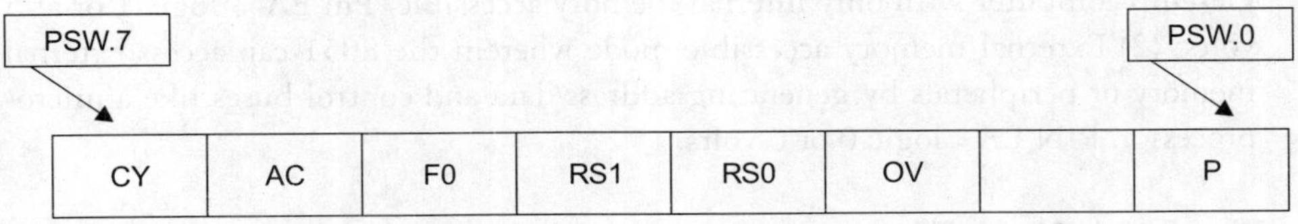

Fig. 2.1 *The 8051 processor status word register*

{PSW.7} Carry Flag (CY): Receives carry out from ALU

{PSW.6} Auxiliary Carry (AC) Flag: Receives carry out of PSW.3 of the Accumulator (A) register during addition operations

{PSW.6}: General purpose status flag **F0**

{PSW.5} and {PSW.4}: Register Bank selection **RS1 and RS0**

{PSW.3} OV: Overflow flag set by arithmetic operations;

{PSW.1}: User definable flag

{PSW.0} Parity Flag (P): the Accumulator parity set to 1. If number of ones in accumulator is odd, it is set by hardware.

- **Boolean Processor:** The Boolean processor is a 1-bit accumulator which is used exclusively for logical operations. For example, 'true' or 'false' like a 1 &&1 =1, there is no carry.
    - **Internal Data Memory:** The locations from 20H to 2Fh can be considered as 128 bits (20H to 2Fh is 16 bytes, each having eight bits). Boolean operations on this memory region consider the LSB of byte 20H as bit 00, MSB of byte 20H is treated as bit 07 and so on till the byte 2Fh MSB is treated as bit 127.
    - **Internal User Data RAM:** The locations 30H to 7FH are for the user; however, on re-setting, the SP is initialised to 07H which may be re-initialised by the user to some other, higher location in the internal data RAM, say 60H. Incidentally, the SP increments on a PUSH and decrements on a POP; this is to be noted.
    - **On-chip Oscillator:** This implies that a crystal need only be connected to the device pins.
    - **Dual Operational Modes:** (1) Mode where the 8051 behaves as a stand-alone single-chip computer with only internal memory accessible. Pin EA = logic 1 or at 5 volts; (2) External memory accessible mode wherein the 8051 can access external memory or peripherals by generating address/data and control buses like a microprocessor. PIN EA= logic 0 or 0 volts.

2.2.2 The 8051 Block Diagram

Studying the block diagram alongside the specifications gives a clearer idea of what 8051 has in store for the user. This block diagram is given in Fig. 2.2.

2.2.3 Pin Diagram of 8051

Shown in Fig. 2.3 are the pin assignments along with a comprehensive description. Referring to this diagram helps in understanding the minimum operational circuit diagram shown in Fig. 2.4.

The pin diagram in Fig. 2.3 will be of use to design a minimal microcontroller system. The circuit for this minimal microcontroller is given in Fig. 2.4 in which a practical circuit which can be used to blink a light-emitting diode is connected to Pin 25. Pin 25 is associated with Port 2 bit 4 and is also written as P2.4. As a standard practice, two capacitors are also connected to ensure oscillation. This is shown in the Fig. 2.4.

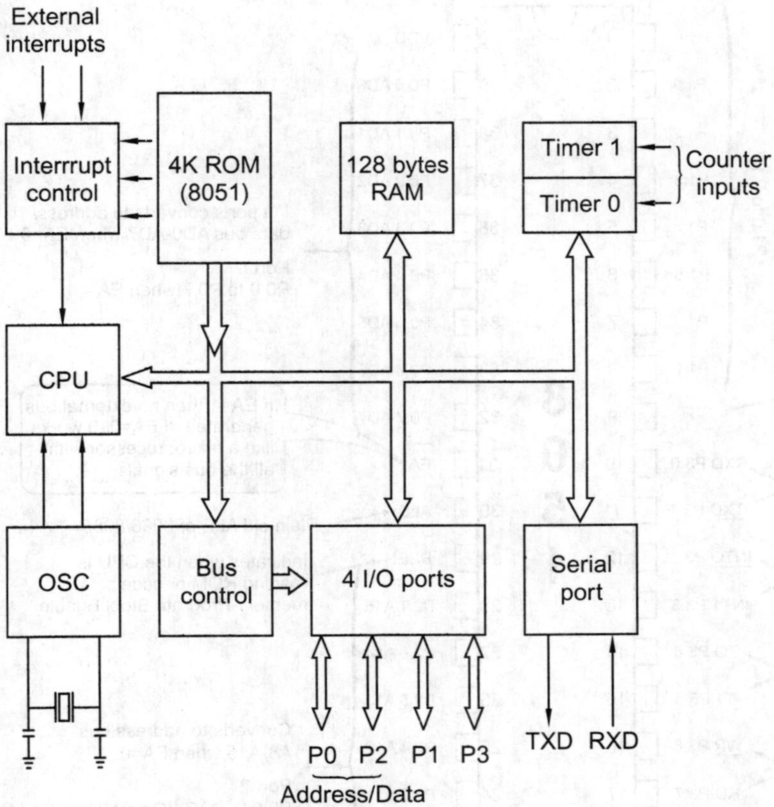

- CISC Harvard architecture
- 8-bit CMOS (low power) CPU
- 12 MHz clock
- 40 pin DIP IC
- Boolean processor
- accesses 64K program memory
- accesses 64K read write memory
- 4k internal ROM + 128 bytes RAM
- 32 IO bits in 4 ports
- Fully buffered serial UART RS232C
- Programmable baud rate
- 2 16-bit timer / counters
- Power control
- 5 interrupt levels
- Built oscillator: needs only crystal
- Single 5 volt supply
- Generates external address/data/ control busses for external IO/ memory interfacing apart from the internal peripherals
- Variations of 8051
  - 80C51: Masked ROM
  - 87C51: UVEPROM
  - 80C31: ROMless
  - 89C51: Flash ROM
  - 89C2051: 20 pin, 1 KbROM, battery operated
- In-system programmable -89S51–89C51 with ISP programmability and additional data pointer

Fig. 2.2 *Block diagram of 8051*

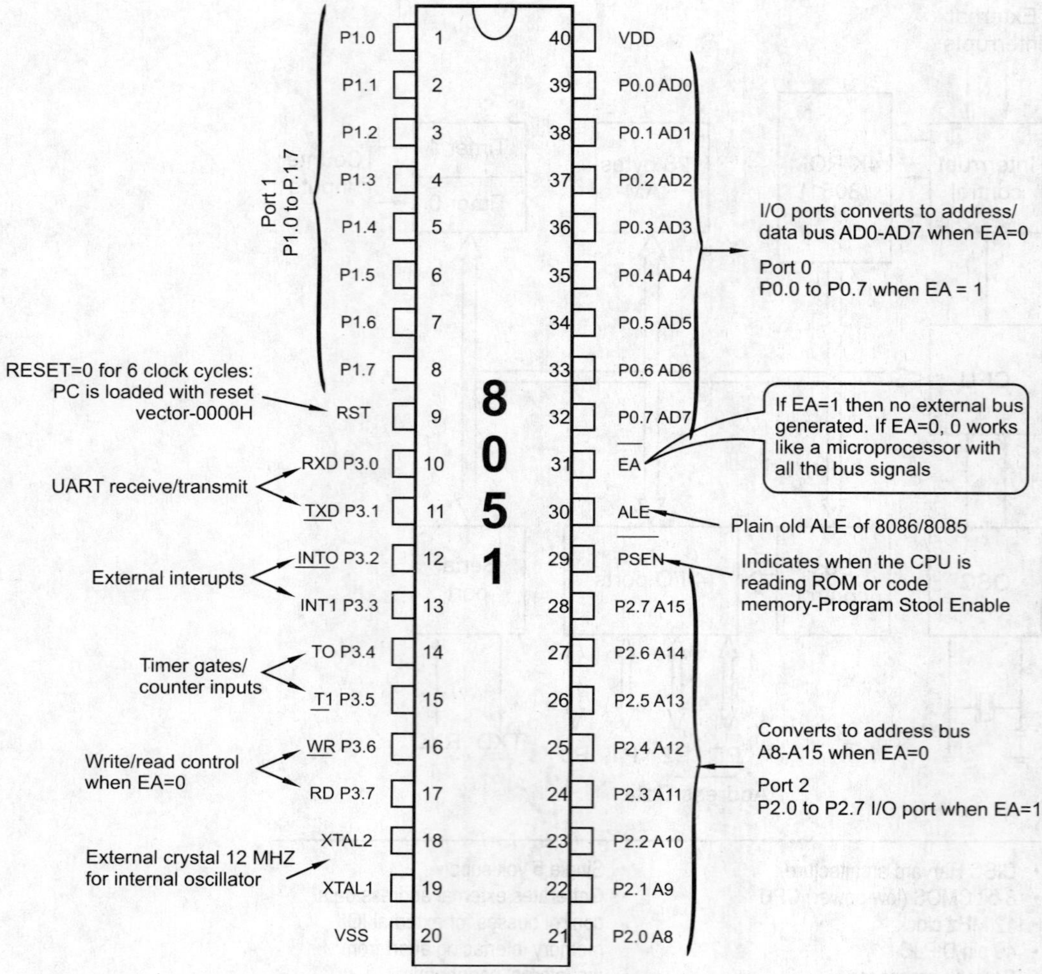

Fig. 2.3 *Pin diagram of 8051 giving the pin assignments*

The entire process of building an embedded system hardware + debugging errors + simulating + downloading to the microcontroller can be experienced in the circuit shown in Fig. 2.4. It thus gives an idea of all the development tools used from end to end.

The algorithm for the application is

STEP 1 Include the header file for the microcontroller
STEP 2 Make Pin 25 low (0 volts)
STEP 3 Delay 1 second
STEP 4 Make Pin 25 high (5 volts)
STEP 5 Delay 1 second
STEP 6 Repeat from Step 2

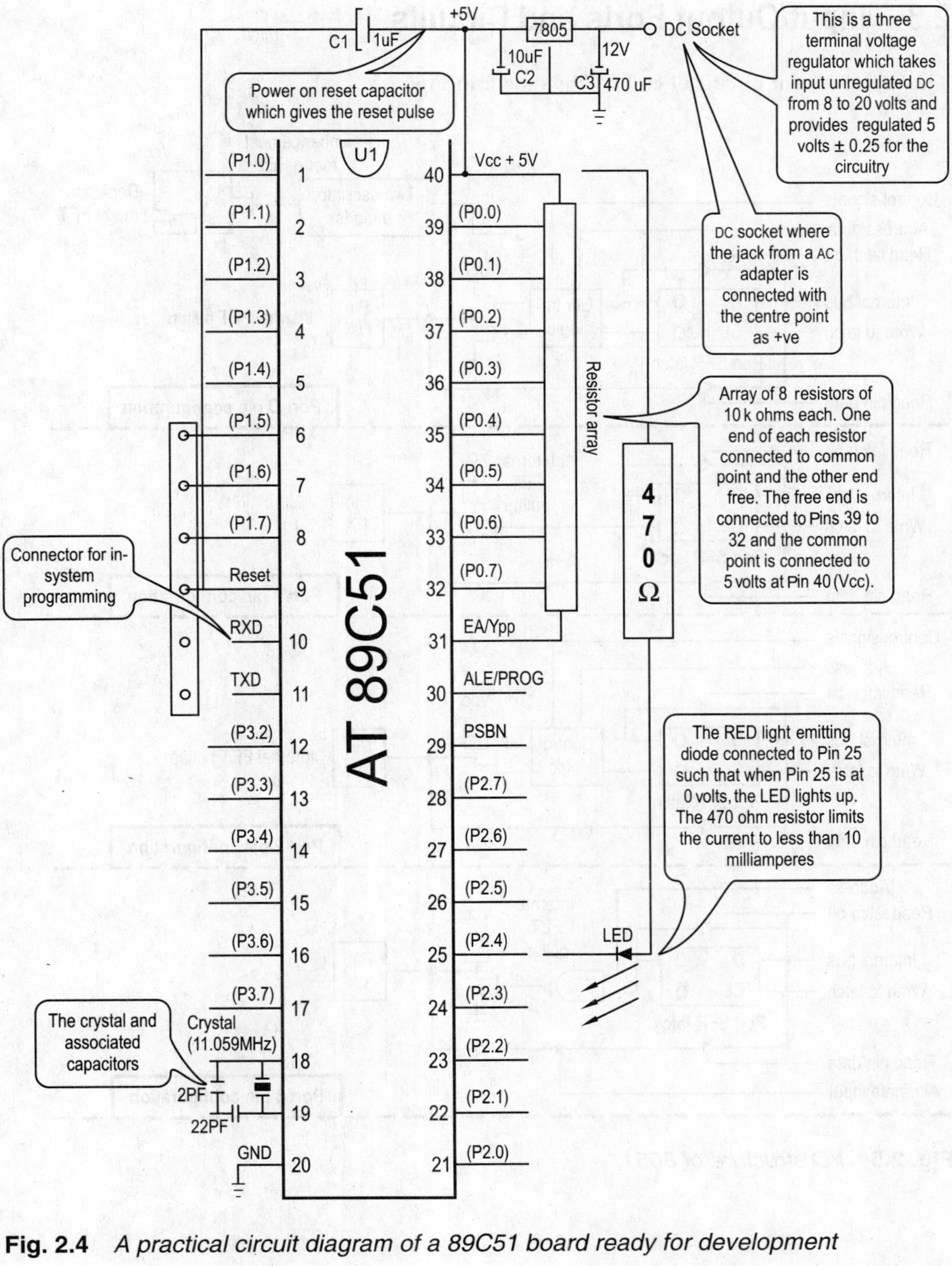

Fig. 2.4 *A practical circuit diagram of a 89C51 board ready for development*

2.3 Input/Output Ports and Circuits

The input/output circuit of an 8051 is shown in Fig. 2.5.

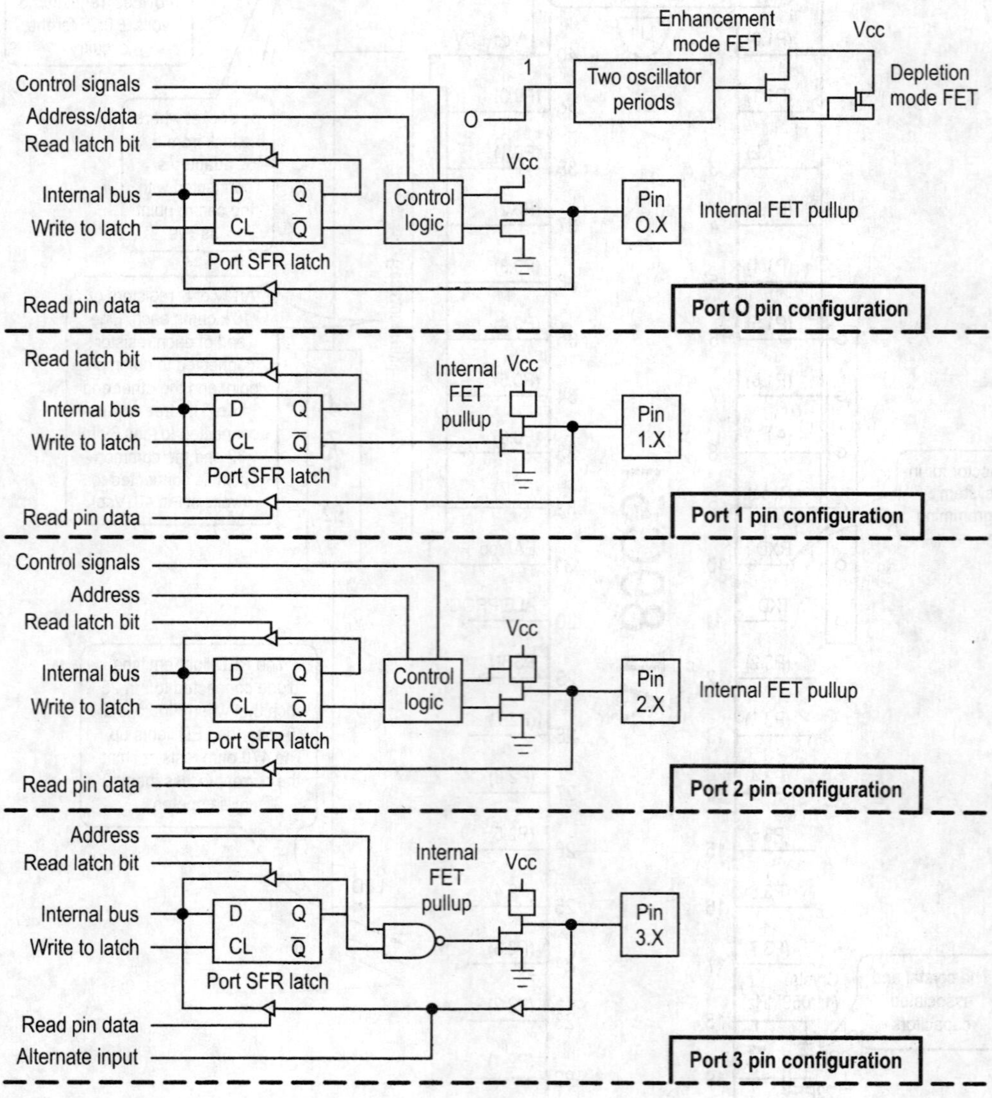

Fig. 2.5 *I/O structure of 8051*

The 8051 family has four 8-bit ports. They are named Port 0, Port 1, Port 2 and Port 3. Each of these ports is a general purpose I/O port. Port 0, Port 2 and Port 3 have multiple functions so that they can support the internal peripherals and the expansion mode for external memory. Port 0 and Port 2 generate the AD0 to AD7 and A8 to A15 signals, respectively. That is, these two ports generate the address and data buses for the purpose of external expansion of memory or I/O. Port 3 generates the multiple functions supporting the external interrupts, timer gating, counter inputs, serial I/O and also the /WR and /RD as the control bus signals for external expansion.

2.3.1 Port 0

This is an 8-bit port which is assigned 8 pins (Fig. 2.3), Pin 39 to Pin 32, which are then relabelled P0.0 to P0.7, sequentially. This port's output is an open drain output, which implies that if the output is switched on, by making the output field effect transistor (FET) conduct, its corresponding pin will be at logic 0, or near to 0 volts. This is because the FET conducts and thus connects its pin to near 0 V. When the FET is made nonconducting, or switched off, the associated pin will have no voltage on it as there is no load resistor for the drain of the FET (as it is open drain). This produces the tri-state condition which is useful for connecting buses. Port 0 also functions as the multiplexed address and data bus (AD0 to AD7) for accessing external memory or peripherals.

The other function of Port 0 is as a general-purpose port. It can be used to sink a current of 1 (one) TTL load and in case it is to output or input voltages, a pull-up resistor is to be added using a resistor array of eight 4.7 kilo ohms.

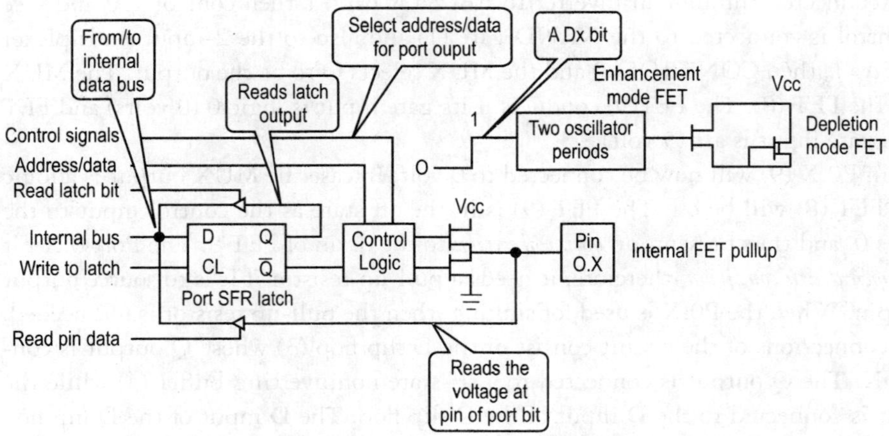

Fig. 2.6(a) *Pin configuration of Port 0*

Figure 2.6(a) shows the Port 0. The internal bus is where the data is input/output. Data input is indicated by the signal on Read Latch Bit for Latch status and Read Pin Data is used for inputting the pin logic condition. If the pin outputs a logic 1 then the Read Latch bit will read a logic 1, whereas the read pin data may or may not read a logic 1. This is because the pin may be loaded and thus result in a logic 0 being read at pin by read pin data. Loading occurs if the device being driven by the pin is drawing currents greater than what a single TTL input does.

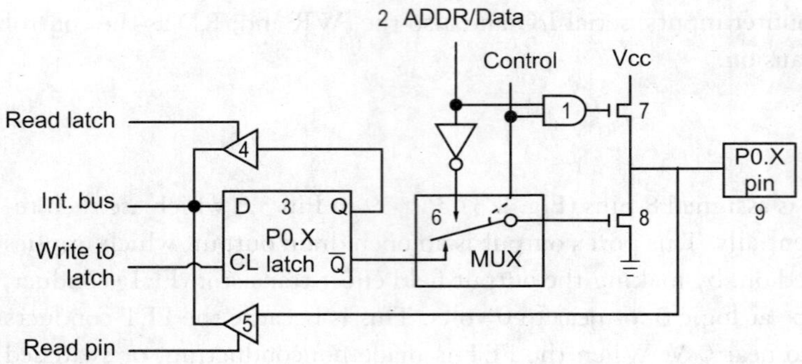

Fig. 2.6(b) *Circuit diagram of one bit of Port 0*

Figure 2.6(b) shows the circuit diagram of one bit of Port 0. The numbers in the figure are used to refer to the operators in the text which follows. The description of this circuit is given, starting from the control and the output part.

The *external access (EA) pin* (pin number 31 of 8051) is used to choose whether the memory and I/O are internal only or external also; this is done by making EA=1 or 0, respectively. The control *line* is connected through an inverter to EA. So if EA =1 then control = 0 and vice versa. The control is connected to the NAND gate (1) and also to the 2-input multiplexer MUX (6). If EA=1, then CONTROL=0 and the MUX selects Q to be the output. The MUX output drives the FET (8). The FET(9) conducts if its gate input is logic 0 (0 volts) and FET (8) opens if its gate input is a 1 (5 volt).

The Port pin P0.X (9) will now be connected to 0 volt. In case the MUX output is a logic 1 (5 V), then FET (8) will be off. The FET (9) is in the off state as the control input to the NAND gate is 0, and thus presents an *open connection* to the drain of FET 8. The Port 0.X bit will be in an *open drain condition*; therefore, it needs a pull-up resistor if it is to source output voltage at its pin. When the P0.X is used for sinking, then the pull-up resistor is not needed.

The input connections of the circuit consist of the D flip flop (3) whose Q output is connected to MUX. The Q output is connected to a tri-state noninverting buffer (4) while the buffer's output is connected to the D input of the D flip flop. The D input of the D flip flop is connected to the *internal data bus* of 8051. The *tri-state buffer* (4) has a control line which is connected to a signal *read latch*. This signal enables the buffer (4) whenever it is asserted and the latch output Q is read by the 8051 through the buffer (4). That is the reason why this signal is called a read latch.

The other tri-state buffer (5) has its input connected directly to Pin 0.X and its control line is called the *read pin*. Certain MOV instructions perform the *read latch* and some the *read pin*. They are called 'read–modify–write' instructions. When the destination operand is a port, or a port bit, these instructions read the latch rather than the pin. Some instructions which read the latch and not the pin are given here:

ANL P1, A ORL P2, A XRL P3, A JBC P1.1, LABEL CPL P3.0 INC P2 DEC P2 DJNZ P3, LABEL MOV, PX.Y, C CLR PX.Y SETB PX.Y

Read–modify–write instructions are directed to the latch and not the pin because of the voltage level at the pin. Sometimes, in order to drive relays and medium power devices, the port pin is interfaced to a transistor driver. The transistor driver base is driven by the port pin and so the voltage at the pin will be reduced due to loading. This may result in the pin being at a different voltage level from the latch corresponding to that pin, thus causing a difference in logic levels. In order to read the actual status of the port bit, the latch is read and not the pin.

Port 0 loading and interfacing

The output buffers of Port 1, Port 2 and Port 3 can each sink 1.6 mA at 0.45 V (see Fig. 2.7 and Fig. 2.8 for the circuit diagram). These port pins can be driven by open-collector and open-drain outputs although 0-to-1 transitions will not be fast, since there is little current pulling the pin up. In the external bus mode, Port 0 output buffers can each sink 3.2 mA at 0.45 V; however, being port pins, they require external pull-ups to drive any inputs.

2.3.2 Port 1, Port 2 and Port 3

The remaining three ports are similar and a clear understanding of Port 0 will lead to an understanding of the other three. In this section, the changes in the circuit when the other ports are used are explained.

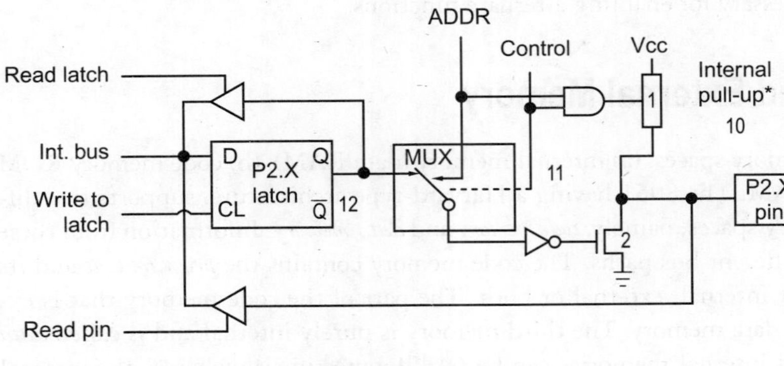

Fig. 2.7 *Circuit diagram of one bit of Port 2*

Port 2

This differs from Port 0 in two ways. The first is that an active pull-up resistor is used which is a FET (10). The gate is under control from the NAND gate(1). The second point is that the inverted Q output of the D flip flop is used as the input of the MUX followed by an inverter at the MUX output. The inverter is needed because Port 0 had the Q output connected to the MUX input.

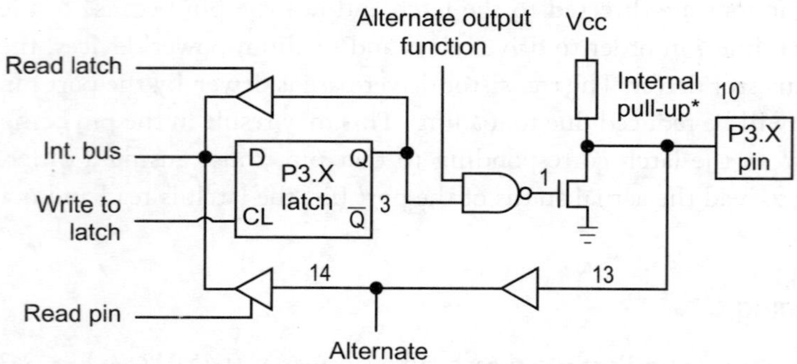

Fig. 2.8 *Circuit diagram for Port 1 and Port 3*

Port 1 and Port 3

These do not have the MUX multiplexer as the choice is of alternate functions only. They have instead two additional buffers, one having a tri-state and the other without. Alternate functions such as RXD, INT0, INT1 are taken directly from the Pin P3.X or P1.X through the buffer (13) with the buffer (14) in tri-state. The four alternate functions are enabled if the ports are written with a one, as is clear from the connection of Q from NAND gate (3) to the AND gate (1) input.

Whenever an I/O port of 8051 is to be used as a general purpose I/O, then it has to be set to logic 1. It is also necessary for enabling alternate functions.

2.4 Internal and External Memory

The 8051 has three memory spaces: (a) internal memory (data RAM); (b) code memory ROM and (c) internal data RAM. The 8051 having a Harvard-type architecture, supports two differently accessed memory spaces, namely, *code memory* and *data memory*. Information from these memory spaces takes different bus paths. The code memory contains the *program code* and its location could be either internal, external or both. The part of the code memory that is external is called external data memory. The third memory is purely internal and is called *data RAM*. The external and internal memories can be 64 kilobytes in size whereas the internal data RAM is at least 128 bytes. The distribution of memory in the 8051 is illustrated in Fig. 2.9.

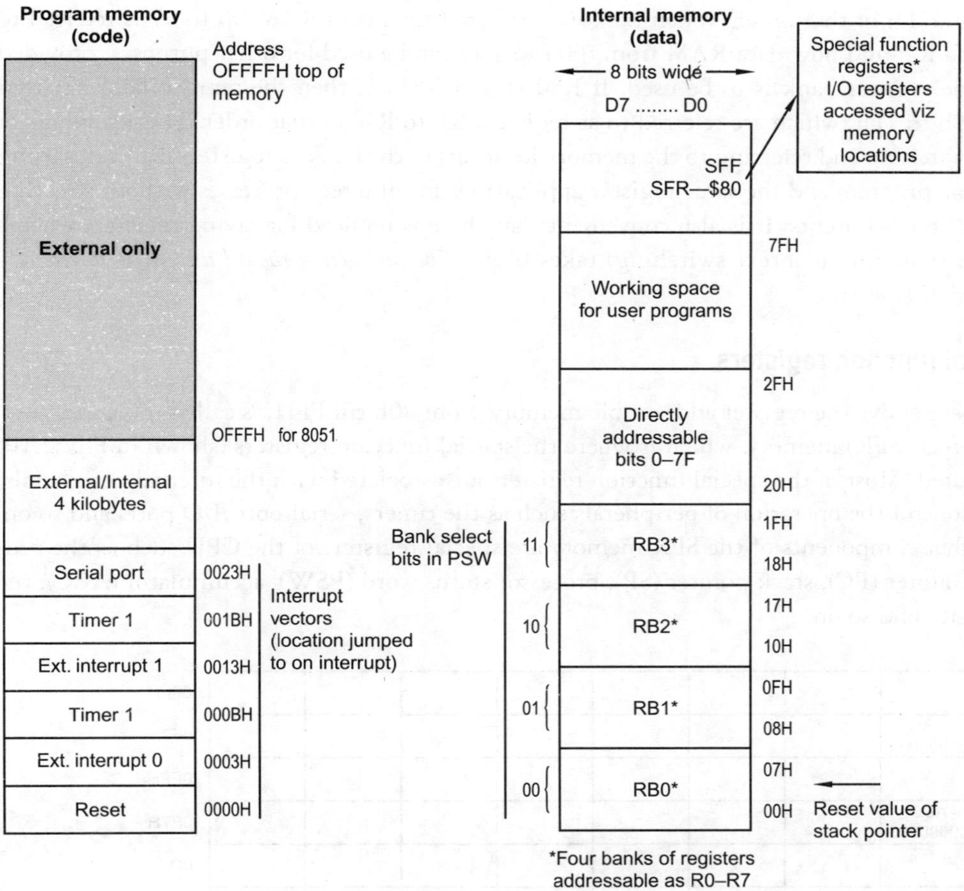

Fig. 2.9 *The memory map of the 8051*

2.4.1 Internal Data RAM

The internal data RAM in the 8051 is 128 bytes. It is further divided into three portions: (1) register addressable bank; (2) directly addressable bit; and (3) work space for user data.

Register addressable bank

This consists of 32 bytes treated as four separate banks. The banks are referred to as Bank 0, Bank 1, Bank 2 and Bank 3 (labelled RB0–RB3 in Fig. 2.9), each of which is equal in size, that is, 8 bytes. There are eight registers, namely R0, R1,R2, R3, R4, R5, R6 and R7 which are supposed to represent the 8 bytes of these banks. The register banks are switched by using the RS0 and RS1 bits of the processor status word (PSW). If RS0=0 and RS1=0, then Bank 0 is selected and any reference to R0 to R7 will be like referring internal data RAM location

00H to 07H, in that order. When Bank 0 is referred then data RAM 00 to 07 is referred to as R0 to R7, and now data RAM from 08H to 1fH can be used for other purposes, provided only one register bank is to be used. If RS0 = 1 and RS1 = 1, then the register bank referred to is 18h to 1Fh, which are referred to as registers R0 to R7, in that order. The advantage of bank switching and referring to the memory locations in the bank as registers facilitates using the same program and the same register applications for different processes without affecting the registers' contents. It is also convenient that there is no need for saving registers when a process switching (context switching) takes place. *The instruction should use MOV to refer the data RAM memory.*

Special function registers

The space above the register addressable memory, from 80h till FFH, is called the *special function register* (SFR) memory, which is where the special function registers (shown in Fig. 2.10) are located. Most of the special function registers are associated with the internal peripherals. They control the operation of peripherals such as the timers, serial port, I/O ports and so on. The other components of the SFR memory are special registers of the CPU such as the program counter (PC), stack pointer (SP), processor status word (PSW), accumulator (ACC), the B register and so on.

OF8H									OFFH
OF0H	B 00000000								OF7H
OE8H									OEFH
OE0H	ACC 00000000								OE7H
OD8H									ODFH
OD0H	PSW 00000000								OD7H
OC8H									OCFH
OC0H									OC7H
OB8H	IP XX000000								OBFH
OB0H	3P 11111111								OB7H
OA8H	IE 0X000000								OAFH
OA0H	P2 11111111								OA7H
98H	SCON 00000000	SBUF XXXXXXXX							9FH
90H	P1 11111111								97H
88H	TCON 00000000	TMOD 00000000	TLO 00000000	TL1 00000000	THO 00000000	TH1 00000000			8FH
80H	PO 11111111	SP 00000111	DPL 00000000	DPH 00000000				PCON 00000000	87H

Fig. 2.10 *Special function registers at internal address 80H to FFH*

2.4.2 Code ROM

Internally, the code ROM is a minimal 4 kilobytes in the 8051. Other variants have larger ROM size. The total code memory accessible is 64 kilobytes. Any access to the code memory in the range of 000 to 0FFFH, when the external access pin (EA) is equal to 1 is to the internal code memory. With EA=1, an attempt to access memory beyond 0FFFH will make the 8051 access the external ROM using the *program store enable* (PSEN) signal informing the external circuitry that the address and data buses are now to access *ROM (code) memory*.

If EA=0, any access to code memory will be referred to the external ROM only. *The instruction should use MOVC to refer the code memory.*

External data RAM

This data RAM is purely external and 64 kilobytes is supported by the 8051. If the EA pin is at Logic 0 (0 volts) then the external RAM is selected. The external data RAM is referred as *XDATA RAM* in order to distinguish it from the internal memory (which is called the *DATA RAM*). When EA=0, the Port 0 pins emit multiplexed address and data, Port 2 emits the upper part of the address and Port 3 bits P3.6 and P3.7 emit RD and WR as part of the control bus.

Internal code ROM

This starts at 0000H and ends at 0FFFH, which amounts to 4 kilobytes. The location 0000H is the reset vector, which is the value forced into the program counter after a *reset pulse* is given to the *reset pin* of the 8051. Usually, at this location, a 3-byte *jump instruction* is put so that the 8051 jumps to the location where the application program begins. The next available location is 0003H, which is the vector address of *Interrupt 0*, INT0 (the external interrupt). From location 0003H, eight bytes are free for INT0 service routine. Eight bytes are usually not sufficient, a 3-byte *jump instruction* is also put here, which transfers control to the INT0 service routine. Location 000BH is the timer 0 interrupt vector and eight bytes are available for any code for timer 0 interrupt. In this case also, eight bytes may not be sufficient, so location 000BH contains a 3-byte *jump instruction* to the timer 0 service routine, and similarly for *INT1 interrupt vector* at 0013H, *Timer 1 interrupt* at 001BH and the *serial communication vector* at 0023H. The serial communication vector is common for both received data and the transmitted data. A look at Fig. 2.9 will give a clear picture.

The locations 0030H to 003FH are used for the signature of the device when the ROM inside the 8051 is a *flash ROM*. The startup code therefore begins from the location 0040H. The *reset vector* at 0000H usually has a *jump instruction* to this location, namely, LJMP 0030H.

2.5 Counter and Timers

There are two timers/counters in the 8051 microcontroller. These two can be used as timers or counters. For timers, a clock of crystal frequency 12 (which for a crystal frequency of 12

MHz will give a clock of 1 MHz to the timers) is given. The counter does not need a clock as it gets its count input from the pins T0 and T1 for counter 0 and counter 1, respectively, on a 1-to-0 transition at the respective pin. Sampling of the inputs T0 and T1 is done at 1/24 of the crystal frequency. There is a register common to both the timers/counters called TMOD. The timers/counters are controlled by another register called TCON.

TMOD: Timer/counter mode control register (Not bit addressable)

Gate	C/T	M1	M0	Gate	C/T	M1	M0
Timer 1				Timer 0			

GATE When TRx (in TCON) is set and GATE = 1, TIMER/COUNTERx will run only while INTx pin is high (hardware control). When GATE = 0, TIMER/COUNTERx will run only while TRx = 1 (software control).

C/T Timer or counter selecter. Cleared for timer operation (input from internal system clock). Set for counter operation (input from Tx input pin).

M1 Mode selector bit (NOTE).

M0 Mode selector bit (NOTE).

Note:

M1	M0	Operating mode	
0	0	0	13-bit timer
0	1	1	16-bit timer/counter
1	0	2	8-bit auto-reload timer/counter
1	1	3	(Timer 0) TL 0 is an 8-bit timer/counter controlled by the standard timer 0 control bits.
1	1	3	(Timer 1) timer/counter 1 stopped.

TCON: Timer/counter control register (bit addressable)

TF1	TR1	TF0	TR0	IE1	IT1	IE0	IT0

TF1	TCON. 7	Timer 1 overflow flag. Set by hardware when the timer/counter 1 overflows. Cleared by hardware as processor vectors to the interrupt service routine.
TR1	TCON. 6	Timer 1 run control bit. Set/cleared by software to turn timer/counter ON/OFF.
TF0	TCON.5	Timer 0 overflow flag. Set by hardware when the timer/counter 0 overflows. Cleared by hardware as processor vectors to the service routine.
TR0	TCON. 4	Timer 0 run control bit. Set/cleared by software to turn timer/counter 0 ON/OFF.
IE1	TCON. 3	External interrupt 1 edge flag. Set by hardware when external interrupt edge is detected. Cleared by hardware when interrupt is processed.
IT1	TCON. 2	Interrupt 1 type control bit. Set/cleared by software to specify falling edge/flow level triggered external interrupt.
IE0	TCON. 1	External interrupt 0 edge flag. Set by hardware when external interrupt edge detected. Cleared by hardware when interrupt is processed.
IT0	TCON. 0	Interrupt 0 type control bit. Set/cleared by software to specify falling edge/low level triggered external interrupt.

Fig. 2.11 *The TMOD and the TCON registers and their bit assignments and operation*

The bit assignments for TMOD and TCON are shown in Fig. 2.11. The first four bits of TMOD are for timer 0 and the next bits are for timer 1. As shown in Fig. 2.11, M0 and M1 select the mode. The selector C/T is used for selecting the counter or timer depending on whether it is at 1 or 0, respectively. The bits TR0 and TR1 in the TCON register enable the timer 0 or timer 1 to run. The bit called Gate allows the timer to start by hardware control if TR0 or TR1 are set, and by setting INT0 and INT1 equal to high for timer 0 and timer 1, respectively. If Gate is cleared to 0, then the TR0 and TR1 bit enable the timer to start as long as they are set. This is how the timer is controlled.

The TCON register is also shown in Fig. 2.11. Here, as mentioned earlier, the TR0 and TR1 bits are called *run control bits*, and when set to 1, they allow the timer to count up on every clock pulse. The timers will overflow, and this is indicated by the TF0 and TF1 bit for timer 0 and timer 1, respectively. This bit causes an interrupt after its corresponding timer overflows, provided the respective interrupts are enabled in the *Interrupt enable register*. Apart from the TFx and TRx bits, there are other bits—IE1, IT1, IE0 and IT0. These bits are assigned for rising-edge input at INTx triggering (IEx) and for falling-edge or low-level triggering at INTx causing interrupt operations (ITx). Fig. 2.11 gives the details.

2.6 Serial Data Input/Output

The universal asynchronous receiver transmitter (UART) built in the 8051 allows serial communications with external devices which also have UARTs. The assignments and the definition of the bits in the serial control register SCON are shown in Fig. 2.12.

The PCON.7 bit in the *power control register* (PCON), doubles the baud rate if it is set. The baud rate is decided by the setting of timer 1 registers TH1 and TL1. Timer 1 is used in mode 3, which is the auto-reload mode. This use of timer 1 for baud rate is applicable for serial modes 1 and 3 only because the other modes directly use the crystal frequency after dividing with 12, 64 or 32. The auto-reload mode uses TL1 and TH1 as two 8-bit registers loaded with the same value, not like the other modes of a timer where they are clubbed together and treated as one register. This value in TL1 is counted up to 0FFH and causes an overflow indicated by the flag TF1. The UART now transmits the current bit. The TH1 register has the original value in it, and on receiving TF1, reloads timer 1. Timer 1 is auto-restarted by the setting of the TR1 bit by the hardware. This process is repeated until all the bits in the transmit register are sent out through the TXD pin of the 8051. The same process is done whenever a bit is received at the RXD pin of the 8051. Transmitting and receiving can be done at the same time as timer 1 will always be running, and there are separate registers to transmit and receive known as *transmit register* and *receive register*, respectively.

There is one more register associated with serial communications which is a buffer register called SBUF. The received character or the transmit character is loaded into the buffer register. In reality, this register is made up of two registers having one common control signal for reading or writing issued by the 8051's CPU. One of these registers is connected to the read signal and the other to the write signal.

SCON: Serial port control resister (bit addressable)

SM0	SM1	SM2	REN	TN8	RB8	TI	RI

SM0	SCON.7	Serial port mode specifier (NOTE).
SM1	SCON.6	Serial port mode specifier (NOTE).
SM2	SCON.5	Enables the multiprocessor communication feature in mode 2 and 3. In mode 2 or 3, if SM2 is set to 1 then RI will not be activated if the received 9th data (RB8) is 0. In mode 1, if SM2 = 1 then RI will not be activated if a valid stop bit was not received. In mode 0, SM2 should be 0.
REN	SCON.4	Set/cleared by software to enable/disable reception.
TB8	SCON.3	The 9th bit that will be transmitted in modes 2 and 3. Set/cleared by software.
RB8	SCON.2	In modes 2 and 3, it is the 9th data bit that was received. In mode 1, if SM2= 0, RB8 is the stop bit that was received. In mode 0, RB8 is not used.
TI	SCON.1	Transmit interrupt flag. Set by hardware at the end of the 8th bit time in mode 0, or at the beginning of the stop bit in the other modes. Must be cleared by software.
RI	SCON.0	Receive interrupt flag. Set by hardware at the end of the 8th bit time in mode 0, or half way through the stop bit time in the other modes (except see SM2). Must be cleared by software.

Note:

SM0	SM1	Mode	Description	Baud rate
0	0	0	Shift register	Fosc./12
0	1	1	8 bit UART	Variable
1	0	2	8 bit UART	Fosc/64 OR Fosc./32
1	1	3	8 bit UART	Variable

Fig. 2.12 *Serial control register (SCON)*

When data have to be transmitted, the SBUF register is loaded with the character to be transmitted. This character is automatically transferred to the transmit register after adding the appropriate start and stop bits. The *transmit interrupt bit* (TI) is cleared and the bits in the transmit register are sent out to the TXD pin. After all the bits are transmitted, the TI bit is set by the UART. The TI bit could be read by the program, and after it is set, the next character can be loaded into the SBUF register and then the TI bit is cleared by the program. In case the interrupt bit for serial interrupts is enabled, then an interrupt occurs which could startup an *interrupt service routine* (ISR).

The receive pin is always sensed and when a serial reception is detected, the received bits are stored in the receive register. The RI bit is set after all the bits as per the serial settings are received. The receive register data are transferred to the SBUF. The program can test for RI bit being set and then read the SBUF. After reading the SBUF, the RI bit is to be cleared by the program and the next character received tested. The RI bit can also cause an interrupt if serial interrupts are enabled.

The algorithm for setting the serial port is as follows:

1. Set timer 1 for mode 2 (auto-reload).
2. Set serial mode to usually 1 or 3.
3. Load TH1 and TL1 with the computed value of the count to overflow based on the desired baud rate. TH1 = TL1 = 256 – ((Crystal/384) / Baud). The 12 MHz crystal gives some deviation from the standard set of baud rates. The crystal which gives values close to the standard baud rate is 11.059 MHz.
4. Set PCON.7 as desired for multiplier 1 or 2.
5. Start Timer 1 by setting TR1.

Now the serial port is set.

For transmission: Clear the TI bit `CLR TI`

`MOV A,# char`

Copy character to SBUF register `MOV SBUF,A`

Wait till TI is set `JNB TI,$`

Character sent

For Receiving: Wait till 8051 sets RI `JNB RI, $`

Read the character from SBUF `MOV A,SBUF`

Clear the RI bit `CLR RI`

2.7 Interrupts

In systems using 8051, programs are executed sequentially. All expected events, which are periodic or sequential, are dealt with in the program. On the other hand, events that are neither periodic and recur with a specific time period, nor sequential to any another event are dealt with by a method called polling. Polling is a test to determine whether the event has occurred or not. Event polling is kept in the loop of execution of the main program. If the program being executed is one that exhibits neither a time period nor event reference, the 8051 will waste time while testing for such an event. It is at this point that a mechanism is needed which will change the flow of the main program and run an associated program which will service the event that has taken place. On completing the service, the 8051 should return to the main program to continue execution from the point where it left to execute the special routine. The above occurrence interrupts the flow of the main program and transfers execution to a service routine. This procedure is referred to by the term *interrupt*.

The routine which services the interrupting event is called an *interrupt service routine*. At the end of the interrupt service, an *interrupt return instruction* is put so that the execution returns to the main program from where it deviated. Interrupts can be caused externally in the 8051 by events which generate the signal to apply to the *external interrupt pins* of the 8051. They can also be caused internally in the 8051 by bits which are set.

The 8051 provides five levels of interrupts, three of which are internally triggered and two are external. The internally triggered interrupts are those caused by the timers and the UART (serial communication interface). The *timer overflow flags* TF0 and TF1 of the two timers individually cause the internal interrupts, while the RI and TI flags of the UART together (they work logically through OR algebra) cause the third internal interrupt. The external interrupts are accepted from the 8051 pins 12 and 13, which are named INT0 and INT1. These are inputs which are to be given either an edge-triggered or level-triggered signal. Edge-triggered means that the signal causing the interrupt should be rising from 0 volts to 5 volts (rising edge) for the interrupt to be accepted. After this happens, only the next rising edge will cause an interrupt. Level-sensitive means that as long as the signal is at 0 volts (Logic 0), the interrupt will be continuously accepted till the level changes to 5 volts (Logic 1). Level-sensitive signals are used only in special cases.

Whenever an interrupt occurs, an *interrupt service program* is executed after completing the current instruction. On completion of the service, the control goes back to the main routine's next instruction. Each of these five interrupt levels has its own vector address where there will be a jump instruction to the service routine specific to that interrupt. After the completion of the service routine, which is when the *interrupt return* instruction is encountered, the execution continues from the main. Nested interrupts occur when the main execution is interrupted by interrupt 1. While the service routine of interrupt 1 is executed, another interrupt occurs, say Interrupt 2. Interrupt 2 will be executed now, provided its priority is higher than interrupt 1. While the operation of the interrupts is one part of the story, the other part is how they are applied.

The two registers and their bit assignments are shown in Fig. 2.13. These registers are the *interrupt enable* and the *interrupt priority register*. Reading the figure, it is clear that the *interrupt enable register* is for masking those interrupts which are not required. A bit value of '0' in the *enable all* will mask all the interrupts. If interrupts are to be enabled, a '1' in the *enable all* position would do so based on another condition. Even if EA=1, only those interrupts will be available whose bit position has a value '1'. While the individual interrupts have been enabled with a '1' in the respective positions, they all can be disabled by a Logic 0 in the enable all bit. This is also called a global interrupt *enable/disable*. Next is the priority of execution of interrupts. The default value of the priority is (from the highest to the lowest) INT0, TIMER0, INT1, TIMER1, SERIAL (common to both RXD and TXD). In case the priority is to be changed by the programmer then the *interrupt priority register* is used which is also shown in Fig. 2.13. The bit positions for priority change are to be set. For example, if the TIMER1 priority is to be raised, then IP.3 is set to '1'. How this works is shown at the top portion of Fig. 2.14. The IE and IP register are depicted here as switches and the switch position in the interrupt enable register is shown as closed corresponding to a bit value of '1'. The enable all is shown as an 8-ganged switch in closed condition for EA=1.

IE: Interrupt enable register (bit addressable)

If the bit is 0, the corresponding interrupt is disabled.
If the bit is 1, the corresponding interrupt is enabled.

EA	–	–	ES	ET1	EX1	ET0	EX0

EA	IE.7	Disables all interrupts. If EA=0, no interrupt will be acknowledged. If EA=1, enables all interrupt flags
–	IE.6	Not implemented, reserved for future use*
–	IE.5	Not implemented, reserved for future use*
ES	IE.4	Enable or disable the serial port interrupt
ET1	IE.3	Enable or disable the timer 1 overflow interrupt
EX1	IE.2	Enable or disable external interrupt 1
ET0	IE.1	Enable or disable the timer 0 overflow interrupt
EX0	IE.0	Enable or disable external interrupt 0

IE: Interrupt enable register (bit addressable)

If the bit is 0, the corresponding interrupt has a lower priority and if the bit is the corresponding interrupt has a higher priority.

–	–	–	PS	PT1	PX1	PT0	PX0

–	IP.7	Not implemented, reserved for future use*
–	IP.6	Not implemented, reserved for future use*
–	IP.5	Not implemented, reserved for future use*
PS	IP.4	Defines the serial port interrupt priority level
PT1	IP.3	Defines the timer 1 interrupt priority level
PX1	IP.2	Defines external interrupt priority level
PT0	IP.1	Defines the timer 0 interrupt priority level
PX0	IP.0	Defines the external interrupt 0 priority level

Fig. 2.13 *Interrupt registers and bit assignments*

The interrupt priority register is also shown as switches which are off corresponding to a bit value of '0'. The order of priority is shown on the right and underneath it is the priority ordering. The IP register switches are connecting to the *interrupt polling sequence*, which is the order in which the individual interrupts are tested. If the bits in the IP register are set to '1' , then the switch connects to the *high-priority interrupt*. The bits that have been set will be tested first before going to the default operation. For example, as mentioned before, if TIMER 1 is to be given higher priority, the bit IP3 should be set to '1', IP.3=1. The priority sequence will now be TIMER 1, INT0, TIMER 0, INT1, SERIAL. If the priority of the serial interrupt and the TIMER 0 interrupt is to be raised, then IP.1=1 and IP.4=1, rest are '0'. For this, the sequence is TIMER 0, SERIAL, INT0, INT1, TIMER 1. When priorities of multiple interrupts are raised, the priority-raised interrupts will follow the same priority as default. If INT1, TIMER 1, SERIAL are priority-raised, then the interrupt polling order would be **INT1, TIMER 1, SERIAL**, INT0, TIMER 0.

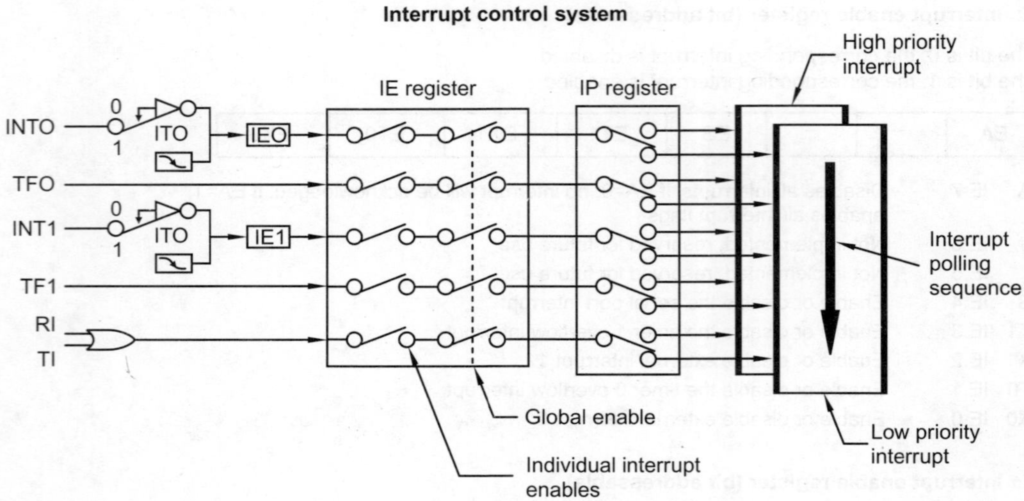

Interrupt	Source	Vector address
System reset	RST	0000H
External 0	IE0	0003H
Timer 0	TF0	000BH
External 1	IE1	0013H
Timer 1	TF1	001BH
Serial port	RI or TI	0023H

Interrupt flag bits

Interrupt	Flag	SFR registration and bit position
External 0	IE0	TCON.1
External 1	IE1	TCON.3
Timer 1	TF1	TCON.7
Timer 0	TF0	TCON.5
Serial port	TI	SCON.1
Serial port	RI	SCON.0

Fig. 2.14 *Interrupt circuitry, vector addresses and flag bits register*

The top circuitry, shown in Fig. 2.14, has on its left side gates and edge sensors. The INT0 and INT1 are low true as shown by the bar on their legend. The switches are shown for IT0 and IT1 in TCON register set, indicating level-triggered inputs. The output of the inverter is given to an interrupt-enabling circuit, as shown. If ITx is not set, then the switch is changed to the edge-sensor circuit for detecting the falling edge and giving input to IEx bit of the interrupt enable register. The TF0 and TF1 are given directly to the interrupt enable circuitry. The RI and SI interrupt bits of SCON are logically made to work as OR by means of an OR gate and given to the SERIAL interrupt input of the interrupt enable circuitry. In the interrupt enable circuitry, the outputs of the enable switches are connected to enable all 5-ganged switches individually. The term ganged means that they are all operated by one signal and that is the ENABLE ALL signal. If bit EA=1 in the IE register then the 5-ganged switches will be closed and will connect the individual interrupt switches to the priority circuitry. This circuitry has switches to connect to the regular-priority or higher-priority section depending on whether the switch is OFF or ON, respectively.

Fig. 2.14, bottom left, shows a table which gives the vector address of each interrupt. This address is in the ROM address area. If serial interrupt is received, its service routine starts from address 0023H. Similarly for the remaining interrupts. In this table, there are six addresses. The first one is for the SYSTEM REST vector. This occurs when the external pin RESET (Pin Number 9) of the 8051 is taken low for a short duration. This input causes the interruption of the program and forces the program counter with this value 0000H. This is also included here, as it is also a differing interrupt. That is, the PC value just before the RESET occurred is not saved on the stack as is done in the remaining five interrupts.

Fig. 2.14, bottom right, shows the interrupt flag bits, their legend and also indicates in which register they are available. For example, the TIMER1 interrupt is caused when its counter overflows, causing the TF1 bit to be set. This bit is in TCON register and is referred as bit TCON.7.

Summary

The use of microprocessors and microcontrollers plays a vital role in the development of embedded systems. This chapter started with an introduction of microprocessors and showed-how the VLSI development led to the evolution of microcontrollers. There are a wide range of microcontrollers available and in each of them are a wider range of variants. Two types of microcontrollers were briefed in Chapter 1.

In this chapter, the 8051 microcontroller was discussed as an example of a microcontroller. The pin assignment of 8051 was discussed and a typical minimal application was described. The internal general purpose registers were studied. Memory maps of the 8051, both the internal and external memory, were elaborated on.

Internal peripherals were then discussed along with their registers: the I/O ports, their internal circuitry and registers; the timer/counters and their registers; the serial port with its associated registers.

The interrupt structure with masking and priority control was explained with the respective registers. An example of an algorithm for using the serial interface was also shown. Apendices B,C,D,E deal with how to use the timer, counter, serial and interrupt interfaces of 8051.

Self Evaluation Questions

1. How does a microprocessor differ from a microcontroller?
2. What is the type of architecture used for an 8051 and how does it differ from other architectures?
3. How many bytes of ROM and RAM are available on board the 8051?
4. How many I/O ports are available on the 8051?
5. What are the address spaces available on the 8051?
6. Describe all the peripheral devices available in the 8051.

7. Explain all the interrupt levels available in the 8051.
8. How many general purpose registers are available in the 8051?
9. If the registers of all 4 banks are used, how much of data RAM would be available?
10. Explain the I/O operations of the 8051 describing each of the four ports.
11. Using a diagram, explain the internal memory map of the 8051.
12. Explain the special function registers in 8051.
13. Explain the registers of the timer/counter.
14. What are the registers for the UART and their functions?
15. What is the procedure for programming the serial port of 8051?

3 Concepts in Assembly Language Programming

3.1 Introduction

Programming computers is an art. It has to be done carefully and the application must always be kept in mind. Application programs have been dealt with in this book in a separate chapter; the main steps involved in developing application programs are discussed here.

Embedded system development needs both hardware and software skills. Normally when one speaks about a skilled person, what strikes the mind is an artisan, for example, a potter, a carpenter and so on. In this chapter, software tools needed are discussed and in the next chapter, assembly language programming is discussed.

The topics of microprocessor and microcontrollers are usually dealt with in the third chapter so this topic may not be totally new; however one may wonder why assembly language is being dealt with here. Application developers use high level languages like 'C', BASIC, 'C++', Java for developing applications. The applications are usually developed using modular functions. While testing the application, during the debugging phase, the debugger may not to be able proceed beyond a certain function by exiting normally from it. This could happen due to many reasons, for example, like waiting for a hardware or software event. The individual testing the application, if he/she is trained in only high level languages, may not be able to understand the reason for such a behaviour as this involves tracing through the machine code to discover the cause for the bug. It could be just an infinite loop waiting for the closing of a switch. The switch can be forced to close using assembly language to make the code exit. In case it does not do so then the fault is traced to hardware and the steps to rectify it may be initiated. Thus, a refresher session of assembly language is a must for embedded systems development in any branch of engineering.

In this chapter the tools used for development is discussed. The reader may keep track of the order in which the tools are used and understand the development process.

3.1.1 Algorithm

After deciding to develop an application program for a user, creation of an alogrithm is the first step in the developing process. Algorithms must *first* be written in simple human language, after decomposing the application function or operations into smaller, easier steps. *Secondly*, it must be ensured that the termination of the application is possible only from one end. *Thirdly*, it must be checked that the algorithm is finite in nature, that is, the program is not too large. *Lastly*, the efficiency of the algorithm, both in execution time and size, is checked.

The completed algorithm should be such that even a person with no knowledge of computers would be able to understand it. Thus, when application users read the algorithm they should have no doubts about how the application program would perform the tasks. That is, the algorithm assures the user that the application developer has understood the application as it was done before the computerisation.

3.1.2 Flow Chart

The next step is to make a flow chart of the individual modules. When doing this, efficient use is made of connectors and off-page connectors. Care should be taken that these are properly labelled. This is done by referring to the algorithm carefully. The connectors and off-page connectors are drawn as shown in Fig. 3.1.

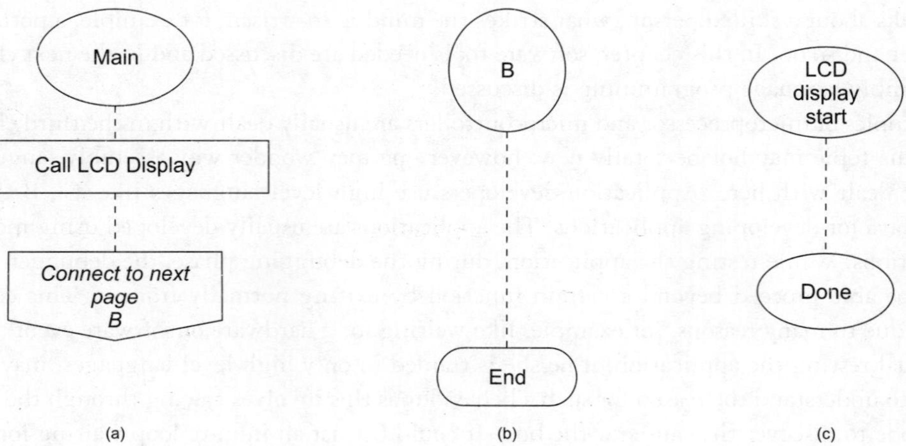

Fig. 3.1 *Flow chart representing (a) an off-page connector; (b) a connection to the next page and (c) termination of function call*

In Fig. 3.1(a) if we had to represent the full program, the flow chart will spill beyond one full page. So an *off-page connector* is used to indicate that the flow chart is continued in the next page. In Fig. 3.1(b) the off-page reference of B is connected by the on-page block marked B. The next part, Fig. 3.1(c), shows the function 'LCD display start'. The dashed line indicates any function which ends with the *terminator*—an oval labelled 'Done'. According to the programmers need, this could be used to indicate a RETURN call, a jump to another connector or just a *self-looping instruction*.

Flow charts can be better understood with illustrations. We give in Fig. 3.2 flow charts for two typical loops. These are the FOR and the DO-WHILE. The WHILE loop is similar to the FOR loop, except that it can be made to use events as an exit.

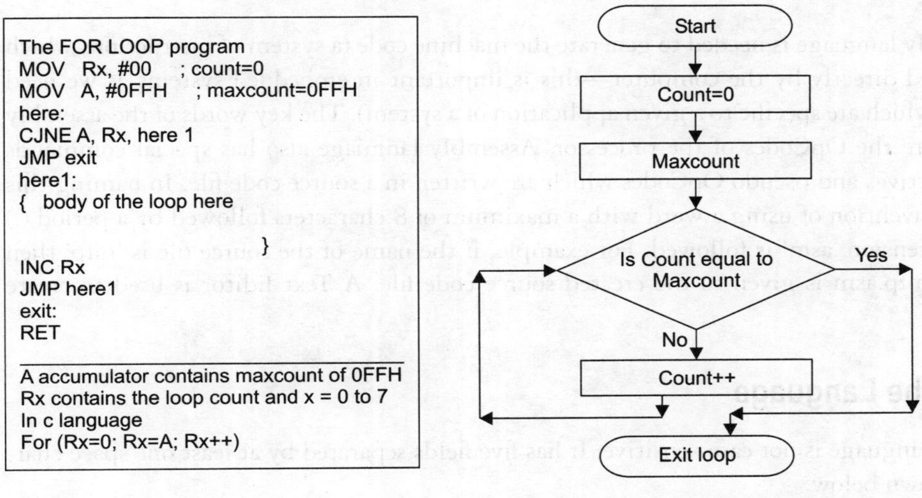

(a) Flow chart and program of a FOR loop

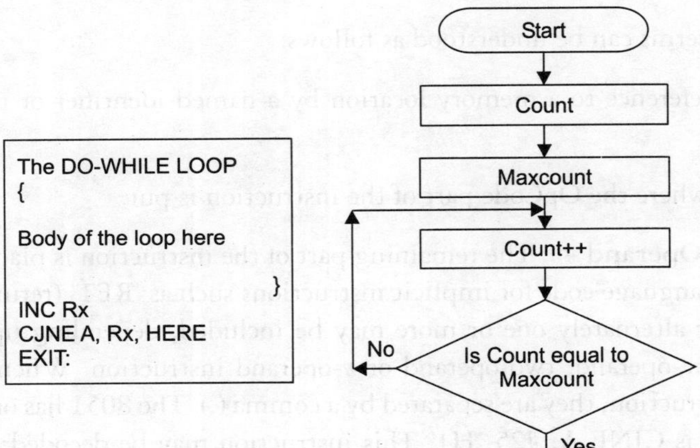

(b) Flow chart and program of a DO-WHILE loop

Fig. 3.2 *Illustrations of flow charts: (a) FOR loop; (b) DO-WHILE loop*

Making a flow chart before actually writing the program goes a long way in helping the programmer build a properly structured code. It is essential to make flow charts in the case of assembly language programming, as they lack the highly structured form of high-level languages.

3.2 Assembly Language Programming: The Process

An assembly language is needed to generate the machine code (a system of instructions which are executed directly by the computer—this is important in embedded systems as we need programs which are specific to a given application of a system). The key words of the assembly language are the OpCodes of the processor. Assembly language also has special commands called directives and pseudo OpCodes which are written in a source code file. In naming this file, the convention of using a word with a maximum of 8 characters followed by a period (.) and the extension 'asm' is followed. For example, if the name of the source file is 'mfp' then the name mfp.asm is given to the created source code file. A Text Editor is used to create this file.

3.2.1 The Language

Assembly language is not case-sensitive. It has five fields separated by at least one space character as shown below:

FIELD1	FIELD2	FIELD3	FIELD4	FIELD5
Label	OpCode	Operand #1	Operand#*n*	comments

In the above, the terms can be understood as follows:

Label: This is a reference to a memory location by a named identifier or that of a variable storage.

OpCode: This is where the OpCode part of the instruction is put.

Operand #1 and Operand #*n*: The remaining part of the instruction is placed here. In writing the assembly language code for implicit instructions such as 'RET' (return), the operands can be left out, or alternately one or more may be included, depending upon whether the instruction is a one-operand, two-operand or *n*-operand instruction. When there are many operands in an instruction, they are separated by a comma (,). The 8051 has one three-operand instruction which is CJNE A, #25, H1. This instruction may be decoded in the following way: CJNE stands for the OpCode; A stands for Operand 1; #25 stands for Operand 2 and H1 stands for Operand 3.

3.2.2 Directives

'Directives' direct the assembler on how to create the machine code. The tool that does this is called the assembler. Some of the most frequently used directives are the following:

ORG: This instructs the assembler to start assembling the machine code from the address specified on its right. Thus the directive ORG 2000H instructs the assembler that the code generated after this directive is to start from 2000H (8192D).

EQU: This is used to instruct the assembler to replace named items with a number. The item to be replaced is given on the left and the new value with which it is to be replaced is given on the right. For example, CR EQU 0DH is a directive to the assembler to replace the named item CR with the number 0DH.

END: This is a directive that indicates the end of the assembler code and is usually the last line of the program.

; : This is used for comments. Any text following this directive until the end of the line is ignored by assembler.

3.2.3 Declaration of Variables

Some directives are used in the declaration of variables. The following are some directives of this type:

db: This declares a byte-sized variable. The label on its left-hand side is the identifier and the value on its right-hand side is the initial value. For example,

```
Number8    db    150
```

This means that `Number8` is the variable name of size byte and initial value of 150 which is in the decimal system.

dw: This declares a double-byte sized (word) variable. The label on its left-hand side is the identifier and the value on its right-hand side is the initial value. For example,

```
Number16    db    1500H
```

This means that `Number16` is the variable name of size 16 bits, and it has an initial value of 1500 which is in the hexadecimal system.

dd: This declares a double-word sized variable. The label on its left-hand side is the identifier and the value on its right-hand side is the initial value. For example,

```
Number32    db    FFE01500H
```

This means that `Number32` is the variable name of size 32 bits and it has an initial value of FFE01500 which is in the hexadecimal system.

Identifiers for the variable should not be more than 40 characters and should begin with a character and not a number. These are placed on the left-hand side of the directives and the initialising values are placed on the right-hand side of the directive. For example, if an 8-bit variable *number1* is to be declared with an initial value of 25H then the code would be

```
Number1    db    25H
```

String variables are declared by enclosing them within single quotes. Some assemblers expect double quotes and others both types of quotes. An example will make it clear.

```
Message1    db    ` This is a message prompt '
```

The above string declaration is of size 26 bytes including the space before 'T' and the space after 't'. So the size of the string identified as `message1` is 26 bytes.. This is also how arrays are declared in assembly language.

3.2.4 Declaring Subroutines and Functions

The directives used in order to declare subroutines or functions and procedures are PROC and ENDP. The syntax usually is as follows:

```
LCDDISPLAY            PROC
{Body of functions code
followed by RETURN}
LCDDISPLAY            ENDP
```

In most assemblers, a simpler method is used

```
LCDDISPLAY:
{Body of functions code
followed by RETURN}
```

The above declaration (`PROC`) uses the name of the function (`LCDDISPLAY`) as a label. There is no harm caused by this short form, barring the fact that the assembler does not know that this is a subroutine.

3.2.5 Segment Declarations

Segment declarations are the next set of directives that are used very often. It is very useful to know these, especially when programming microcontrollers. This is because microcontrollers have memories that fall into different types. These different types are internal data RAM, external data RAM, the code ROM, the EEROM and so on. It does not make a difference whether the code ROM is placed externally or internally, as the code is read by the processor from one source only. Many microcontrollers can generate an external microprocessor bus, which gives a scope for extending memories and also the input and output (I/O). In the case of I/O, peripheral chips can be added, but they have to be treated as memory mapped ones.

Some such segment declarations are the following:

CSEG: This is a declaration that the code segment begins there.

DSEG: This is a declaration that the internal data memory segment begins there.

XDATA: This is a declaration that the external data memory segment begins there.

3.3 Programming Tools and Techniques

The developer is now ready to code the program in assembly language. The developer needs tools for, writing the program, testing modules and the entire application. The tools and techniques that come in useful in this process are discussed here.

3.3.1 The Editor

This is a tool used for creating the assembly language source code and editing it. The file name containing the code is made up of a part which is specific. It is made of eight characters and a part which can be '.ASM'—a general extension. Some conventions allow extensions '.A51' or '.A68' which indicate the processor for which the code is being written. It is advised that such a convention be avoided and the standard extension '.ASM' for assembly files be followed.

If one is working with different processors, different directories could be used for storing the relevant files. Usually an Integrated Development Environment takes care of this and calls it the project workspace. More about this can be read in Appendix F.

For example, if the program being developed is named as mfp (standing for My First Program) then it is to be created using the editor and the name 'mfp.asm' is given to the program.

3.3.2 The Assembler

The assembly language source code created and modified using the editor is now to be processed by the assembler. The assembler converts the '.ASM' file into an object file which contains the translated '.ASM' file. The contents of this file are the machine code produced from the assembly language source code. The assembly language source code is a plain ASCII text file, whereas the object file contains machine code in binary form. When creating the object file, the rule of giving the extension '.OBJ' is followed by the assembler. For example, let the assembler program have the name 'assemble.exe', then the command line statement would be

```
Assemble mfp.asm
```

The assembler would convert the source code 'mfp.asm' into an object file. When a list of files with the name "mfp" is produced by the following command line:

```
dir mfp.*
```

it would result in the following list:

```
mfp.asm
mfp.obj
mfp.lst (provided the list file is requested)
```

The mfp.lst contains the machine code in ASCII Hex along with the ASCII source code. This file helps the developer to see whether the assembler has produced the expected machine code.

3.3.3 Linker

This tool converts the object file (mfp.obj) to 'mfp.exe' an executable file. This tool also creates an 'mfp.map'—a file which contains the memory map of the various segments used in the code like the code, data, stack, heap and a table called the *symbol table*. The symbol table gives a record of all the symbols used such as labels, identifiers for variables, constants, function names, their sizes and locations.

An additional function of this tool is what its name specifies, that is, linking multiple files which have been passed on to it through the command line. When multiple code modules are being developed for an application, then one of these modules will be designated the main module and this would call the other modules. The variables in one or more modules could be used by another module. These variables are declared as 'PUBLIC' in the module containing them, and modules not containing these variables use 'EXTERNAL' as a reference to them. Now, it is the function of the *linker* to make one unified file by stitching together all the memory references to 'PUBLIC' and 'EXTERNAL' components by referring to the contents of all the modules.

For example, look at the instruction:

```
link.exe mfpmain.obj+mfpmodle1+mfpmodle
```

This makes the linker stitch all the files together to produce a file which it names:

```
mfp.exe
```

The '.exe' file is the end result of this tool's operation. The DOS command 'dir' given below:

```
Dir mfp.*
```

will now produce the following list of files:

```
mfp.asm
mfp.obj
mfp.lst
```

and if specified in the command line, the following will also be listed:

```
Mfp.map
Mfp.exe
```

3.3.4 Creating Bin: EXE2BIN

The file 'BIN' is an image file of the entire machine code as it is to be put in the ROM. A tool called exe2bin.exe is usually used to produce this. For example:

```
exe2bin.exe mfp.exe
mfp.bin
```

The files carrying the extension .bin are not readable by human viewers. They have to be made readable and reviewable by those desiring to see them. For this reason the '.bin' files are the first to be converted to ASCII hex files.

3.3.5 Viewing Bin: BIN2EXE

The tool 'BIN2EXE' converts the '.bin' file to a screen-viewable version. The extension '.hex' is given to the screen-viewable version. The '.hex' file can be viewed using an editor. The format used by this is Intel hex 8-bit/16-bit or Motorola hex. These formats are discussed in Chapter 7. The '.hex' files are used for transferring the code to the embedded system under development.

To summarise, the tools needed for development of assembly language programs are:

The Assembler
The Linker
The EXE2BIN
The BIN2HEX
and
The Downloader

In case the language used is 'C' then a *C compiler* in which the source code is a '.C' file is used. The C compiler generates the '.asm' file and the rest of the files come into production after the appropriate tools are used.

It is possible that after the source code file is used, the compiler may forget to use the rest of the tools. In this case, the final '**.hex**' would not be the result of the latest modification of the source file. For this reason, the '**MAKEFILE**' tool is used in the command line operations. This takes care of the dependency of the output of the Assembler on the Linker; the Linker's output on the Exe2bin and the Exe2bin's output on the Hex2bin converter.

In order to develop a program without forgetting the appropriate tools to be used, an Integrated Development Environment is used. It is generally called as an IDE. The currently popular IDE and how it is used in developing the program is discussed in Appendix F.

3.4 Programming the 8051: Data Transfer and Logical Instructions

An important thing to know when writing a program in assembly language is how to move data from one part to another and how to perform arithmetic and logic operations on data. The first part—moving data—involves knowing how to identify the locations or *'addressing'* data and then how to instruct the compiler to move it. This is dealt with before the problem of performing arithmetic and logic operations is tackled.

3.4.1 Modes of Addressing

There are several ways in which a memory location can be addressed. These are listed and described below. To understand how exactly the instructions differ, the reader is encouraged to actually use them in a program and run them. The instructions used here, such as MOV, will each be explained in detail in Section 3.4.2.

Broadly speaking, the choice of which mode to follow depends on the source and destination of the data to be accessed. Accordingly, the programmer may choose one of the following types of instruction.

Immediate addressing

This is the mode to be used when the data are given in the instruction itself and therefore no memory referencing is needed. For instance,

```
[MOV A,#20h],[MOV Rx,#nn],[MOV P0,#mm].
```

Such an instruction has as the first part, the OpCode, followed by zero, one or more operands.

Direct addressing

This is a mode in which the instruction contains the address where the data is to be found. For instance,

```
[MOV A,30h].
```

Indirect addressing

In this mode, the instruction does not directly indicate the address where the data are located. Instead it contains an address or register which, in turn, contains the address where the data are to be found. This mode (indirect addressing) is not supported by 8051, so the direction is done through a register and only R0, R1 or DPTR are to be used. The symbol '@' indicates that the instruction is indirect. The example below shows how this is done:

```
[MOV A,@R0]
```

In this example, it is implied that the register R0 contains a value which is the address of the location where the data will be found.

External indirect

This is the mode used when the external memory has to be accessed. All access to external memory is done indirectly through the DPTR. A separate OpCode (that is, MOVX) is used for these references.

An example of the format using external indirect addressing mode is the following:

```
[MOVX A,@DPTR]
```

Code indirect

In this mode of addressing, all references to code memory (the ROM), regardless of whether it is internal or external, is done indirectly through a combination of DPTR and the accumulator. There is also a separate OpCode for these addressing modes, namely MOVC. The format is as given below:

```
[MOVC A,@A+DPTR]
```

PC relative

This uses the PC instead of the DPTR in combination to access data relative to the PC position. Here also a separate OpCode(MOVC) is used. The format used is:

```
[MOVC A,@A+PC]
```

3.4.2 Instruction Set

The instruction set consists of a set of codes that are used as commands in the assembly language. Mastering the use of all these instructions will come only with extensive practice, but this section aims to basically introduce the words and define how they can be applied in programs. Some easy-to-understand instructions, such as MOV, have been introduced and used already, in Section 3.4.1, to explain addressing modes. Given here are more complete, tabulated lists.

Data transfer instructions

The common data transfer instructions are listed in the first column of Table 3.1 which follows. The instruction is given in the format with the OpCode first, followed by the destination (*dest*) and source (*src*). Of these, *src* could refer to any among the registers R0 to R7 or it could be a direct memory location. There will be an exception when *src* and *dest* are both registers. In this case, care must be taken while programming. The symbol '@' indicates indirect addressing.

The second column of Table 3.1 is an Register Transfer Language (RTL) format depicting the action performed by the instruction.

The addressing mode is given in the third column of Table 3.1 and it is made into sub-columns showing the addressing modes accepted by the instruction. An X mark in the column or row indicates that the addressing mode is valid. The addressing modes shown are Dir, which stands for direct; Ind which means indirect; Reg, which stands for register and Imm, which means immediate.

The fourth column of Table 3.1 shows the time taken to complete execution of the instruction in column one. A single machine cycle of 8051 takes a time of 12 clock pulses for its completion. Assuming that a crystal with a frequency of 12 Mhz is connected to the clock generator (XTAL1, XTAL2 pins), each machine cycle would take 1 microsecond.

Table 3.1 *Data transfer instructions*

Mnemonic		Operation	Addressing modes				Execution time (μS)
			Dir	Ind	Reg	Imm	
MOV	A, <src>	A = <src>	×	×	×	×	1
MOV	<dest>, A	<dest> = A	×	×	×		1
MOV	<dest>, <src>	<dest> = <src>	×	×	×	×	2
MOV	DPTR, #data16	DPTR = 16-bit immediate constant				×	2
PUSH	<src>	INC SP : MOV '@SP', <src>	×				2
POP	<dest>	MOV <dest>, '@SP'; DEC SP	×				2
XCH	A, <byte>	ACC and <byte> exchange data	×	×	×		1
XCHD	A, @Ri	ACC and @Ri exchange low nibbles		×			1

Row 1: MOV A, *src* instructs that the contents of 'src' are copied to 'A' which is a register. In this instruction, the source '*src*' could be the internal data RAM, R0 or R1 could contain the address where the data can be accessed from. The value of 'src' is constant and can be anything from R0 to R7.

Row 2: MOV *dest*, A This is an instruction for the contents of location 'A' to be copied to '*dest*' the destination. Here, '*dest*' could be the internal data RAM; R0 or R1 could contain the address where the data are available; R0 to R7 can be *dest* and immediate addressing is invalid here.

Row 3: MOV *dest*, *src* This means the contents of 'src' are copied to '*dest*' the destination. Both '*src*' and '*dest*' could be the internal data RAM. R0 or R1 only could contain the address where the data are available or to be stored. In this case, any of R0 to R7 may be used as either '*src*' or '*dest*' and not as both. If it is *dest* then "*src*" is a constant value. For example,

```
MOV    R0,#55H ;
```

R0 is *dest* and the *src* is 55H, a constant value indicated by # which implies immediate mode of addressing.

```
MOV    55H,    R0 ;
```

R0 is now *src* and the destination is 55H which is an eight-bit data RAM location whose address is 55 H(H is for hexadecimal). It is obvious that this is a direct addressing mode and the 55H is not a constant (the absence of # sign shows that it is not an immediate addressing mode.

Row 4: MOV DPTR, #*data16* Only the immediate mode is valid here, and the data transferred to DPTR is a 16-bit number.

Row 5: PUSH <src> Only the direct mode is valid in this case. The 'Push' instruction is to be carried out by using the memory address of the registers and SFRs (Special Purpose Registers). For instance, the instruction 'PUSH 0E0H' will push the accumulator contents to the stack using the SP (Stack Pointer) contents as the pointer. The entry '0E0H' gives the address of the accumulator register. It is an important point that in 8051, the SP is first incremented and then the contents transferred. This is just the opposite of the way in which other processors do stack pushes.

Row 6: POP <src> In this case, only the direct mode is valid. The 'Pop' instruction is to be carried out by using the memory address of the registers and the SFRs. For example, the instruction, 'POP 0F0H' will pop the stack contents pointed by SP to the Register B. Here, '0F0H' is the address of the Register B. Note that in 8051, the contents are first transferred and then the SP is decremented. As before, it must be mentioned that this is the opposite of the way other processors do stack pops.

Row 7: XCH A, <byte> The contents of the Register A and a byte in the direct RAM are exchanged. The byte refers to the address in data RAM whose contents will be exchanged with the Accumulator. Indirect addressing of data RAM is done using either R0 or R1 and the register should contain the 8-bit data RAM address only. For register direct operation, the contents of registers R0 to R7 are exchanged with that of Register A. The <byte> is to be the *src* operand.

Row 8: XCHD A,@Ri The lower nibble of the contents of the direct RAM pointed by R0 or R1 only are exchanged with the lower nibble of the accumulator.

External memory data transfer instructions

The instructions used for external memory data transfer are shown in Table 3.2. These were explained briefly earlier when addressing modes were discussed in Section 3.4.1. There are two varieties of transfer: one as a 8-bit address reference and the other, a 16-bit address reference. This is shown in the first column of Table 3.2. Both cases refer to indirect addressing only. The 8-bit address references use Register R0 or Register R1 as shown in the second column of Table 3.2. The third and fourth columns of Table 3.2 show the operation performed and the time taken for execution, respectively.

MOVX is the OpCode used for external RAM access. This is pronounced as 'Move external Memory'. Notice that Table 3.1 shows OpCode MOV which is for internal data RAM addressing. Table 3.2 is clear by itself, and there is no need for detailed explanation of each row as was done earlier. It is a useful exercise to write down an explanation as was done in the case of Table 3.1 because embedded system developers should learn how to look up instruction set tables and understand their operation.

Table 3.2 *External memory data transfer instructions*

Address width	Mnemonic	Operation	Execution time (μs)
8 bits	MOVX A, @Ri	Read external RAM @ Ri	2
8 bits	MOVX @Ri,A	Write external RAM @ Ri	2
16 bits	MOVX A, @DPTR	Read external RAM @ DPTR	2
16 bits	MOVX @DPTR,A	Write external RAM @ DPTR	2

Program memory data transfer instructions

Now we look at instructions specific to PC relative or DPTR data transfer. Here, the Program Counter (PC) or DPTR are used, unlike the external RAM transfer which used R0 and R1 also. The address width is fixed at 16-bit, as the PC and the DPTR are themselves 16-bit in size. The OpCode has to be different from that for other types of data transfer as shown in Table 3.3. Here it is 'MOVC'. This is pronounced as 'Move DPTR/PC relative'. The accumulator is added to the PC/DPTR and so gives a displacement relative to the PC. Note that this is used only with the program memory.

Table 3.3 *PC relative data transfer instructions*

Mnemonic	Operation	Execution time (μs)
MOVC A, @A + DPTR	Read Pgm Memory at (A + DPTR)	2
MOVC A, @A + PC	Read Pgm Memory at (A + PC)	2.

These instructions are different from the earlier ones, as explained below.

Row 1: MOVC A, @ A + DPTR The accumulator value is added to the DPTR giving the effective address. The contents of this effective address are transferred back to the accumulator, that is, A {A+DPTR}. The effective address EA=DPTR+A is where the data are fetched from and copied into the accumulator.

Row 2: MOVC A, @ A + PC The accumulator value is added to the PC, giving the effective address. The contents of this effective address are transferred back to the accumulator, that is, A {A+PC}. The effective address EA=A + PC is where the data are fetched from and copied to accumulator. This instruction is used to access data that are appended at the end of a function. A preliminary approach to member functions used for accessing encapsulated data is object oriented programming at high level. The reverse transfers are not valid for these instructions as the ROM cannot be written into.

Summary

This chapter would have steered the reader through the development tools used. The algorithm is the starting step which the developer and user get to understand that they have understood each other. The user knows that the developer has understood the requirement. The flow chart helps in the structure and the module requirements for the application. The compilers and assemblers are used for writing the code. In this chapter, the assembler syntax, format, directives would have been clear. Further, declaring variables, the data types, functions and segments would be clear. The tools used and their order for development of the applications and the use of MAKEFILE and the IDE were explained.

The programming of a typical workhorse microcontroller, the 8051 and its data transfer and logical instructions are discussed. Rest of the instructions are discussed in Chapter 4.

Self Evaluation Questions

1. Explain the use of algorithms and flowchart in application development.
2. What are assembly language directives? Explain two of them.
3. How are string variables declared?
4. What are the various segments in the memory space of microcontrollers and how are they declared?
5. Explain the various fields in a line of assembly language.
6. Explain clearly the tools used for developing applications, maintaining the order in which they are used.

7. What is Makefile and why is it needed?
8. What are the files which are created and when are the tools used? Put them in order from the .asm file (included) onwards.
9. What are the addressing modes of 8051?. Explain clearly.
10. What are the data transfer instructions of 8051?
11. There are different instructions used for the different memory spaces o0f 8051. What are they and explain them?
12. What are the exchange instructions of 8051? Explain them clearly.
13. What are the data transfer instructions for which no address is needed to be specified and why?
14. What are the external data transfer instructions and how are they used?
15. Differentiate between the use of PC and DPTR in the external data move instructions.

4 Arithmetic Transfer Control Instructions

This chapter deals with the rest of the instruction set and also some typical programming examples. The concepts of logical, arithmetic and control transfer are much needed even though they can be performed using high level languages (HLL). The machine code generated in high level languages is usually longer in size than what can be written using assembly language. However writing code entirely in machine language takes a long time and is difficult to debug. At the same time, any changes needed in the application take longer to implement and test. There are many techniques which allow a mixture of assembly and high language coding. One of the most popular mixed language programming is 'in line assembly language' programming. This helps in getting the best of both worlds—high level language and assembly language i.e., ease of coding and understanding in high level language plus the small size and greater speed of assembly language. This type of a mix takes care of applications where certain intricate interactions between hardware and software need to be optimised for smaller size and speedier operations. Thus a knowledge of assembly language instructions and techniques comes in handy.

In this chapter starts with arithmetic instructions and their functions. These arithmetic instructions could help in creating transcendental functions for an application if speed is required.The reader is advised to use an IDE like the KEIL µvision whose evaluation version would be available at the KEIL.COM web site and would be good practice. Again Appendix F can be of help in using this IDE. The reader could possibly find time to test the functioning of the instructions by writing tiny three to four line programs, loading the registers used, executing the instruction then verifying the results in the registers. A senior or an associate with prior experience could be requested to lend a helping hand.

The logic and bit manipulation instructions are dealt with next. The atomic operation of the assembly instructions can be of great help in developing hardware interactive application where the hardware device has multiple bits for evaluating its status. The commonly used Moving Message Displays in airports and other terminals for information dissemination, for example, has software which is required to do a lot of bit shifting and logical operation. This makes it necessary to understand these operations.

Appendix A has the instruction set presented in a tabular manner which could add to clarity of the text read here. Further, this appendix also deals with the memory access methods (addressing) differently.

The chapter concludes with some examples of arithmetic operations which can be studied instruction by instruction keeping a record of the input, temporary and output register/memory location values and verifying the execution stage by stage. This is generally called code walking. Many consider that understanding programs written by others is a waste of time and it is better to rewrite the program by one self. Understanding codes written by others for a common application develops the style of the code walker. Do remember to keep a paper and pencil by the side while code walking. The author does the same using a notepad.

4.1 Arithmetic Operations

Now we come to arithmetic instructions. These instructions are shown in Table 4.1. One word of caution here is that the words 'instruction' and 'OpCodes' are used as if they mean the same thing. This is not so, as an OpCode is a part of an instruction specifying the operation to be performed. The other part of the instruction are the operands on which the operations are to be performed. There could be 0,1,2,3 or more operands in an instruction. However as the OpCodes are explained along with the operand types, they are referred to here as instructions. The first column of Table 4.1 contains the mnemonic of the instruction (or the short form that is used in the program). The second column contains the operation performed by the instruction. The third column is further sub-divided into four, namely, the addressing modes—'×' in this column indicates that this mode is supported by the instruction. The fifth column contains the time taken for execution, which is measured in microseconds, assuming a crystal frequency of 12 MHz.

The various mnemonics in the first column represent specific locations as given below:

1. **ADD A, <byte>**: The byte could be an internal data memory location; the address contained in R0 or R1 registers as an indirect value, Register R0 to R7, or an immediate value, when preceded by a #, as for example, ADD A, #40H.
2. **ADDC A, <byte>**: In the previous instruction, the addition of a byte to A does not take into account any carry from previous executions. *ADDC is ADD with Carry*, and this adds 'byte' to A plus the carry. This is used in multi-byte addition, where the carry is first cleared. The ADD instruction is used for the first byte and the subsequent bytes are added using ADDC. The *byte* can be an internal data memory location: it can be referred indirectly through R0 or R1 registers; it could be a value in the registers R0 to R7 or a constant to be added indicated by the # symbol. For example, suppose ABCD and PQRS

are two 4-digit BCD numbers and A,B,C,D,P,Q,R,S,V,W,X,Y,Z are 4-bit BCD digits. Then from the right-most, the addition goes about as shown below:

i. clear carry.

ii. use ADD instruction and do D + S and store in Z. If Z exceed 9, Carry will be set

iii. use ADC and do C+R. The Carry is now automatically added whether it is a 0 or 1.

iv. use ADC and do B+Q. The Carry is now automatically added whether it is a 0 or 1.

v. use ADC and do A+P. The Carry is now automatically added whether it is a 0 or 1.

vi. the Carry will be the 5th BCD value in the left-most side of the result

```
  ABCD
 +PQRS
 VWXYZ
```

3. **SUBB A,<byte>:** This instruction subtracts from the 'accumulator' using the borrow. The borrow if valid is the carry flag set. There is no subtract without a borrow instruction. Here, the *byte* could be all the four addressing modes as explained in earlier instructions.

Table 4.1 *The arithmetic instruction set*

Mnemonic		Operation	Addressing modes				Execution time (μS)
			Dir	Ind	Reg	Imm	
ADD	A, <byte>	A = A + <byte>	×	×	×	×	1
ADDC	A, <byte>	A = A + <byte> + C	×	×	×	×	1
SUBB	A, <byte>	A = A– <byte> – C	×	×	×	×	1
INC	A	A = A + 1	Accumulator only				1
INC	<byte>	<byte> = <byte> + 1	×	×	×		1
INC	DPTR	DPTR = DPTR + 1	Data pointer only				2
DEC	A	A = A – 1	Accumulator only				1
DEC	<byte>	<byte> = <byte> – 1	×	×	×		1
MUL	AB	B:A = B × A	ACC and B only				4
DIV	AB	A = int [A/B] B = Mod [A/B]	ACC and B only				4
DA	A	Decimal adjust	Accumulator only				1

4. **INC A:** Increments only the value contained in the accumulator. Further, if the value reaches 0FFH then the next increment will make it 00H and the carry is not affected.

5. **INC byte:** Increments *byte*. This could be addressed through direct, indirect and register modes. This is like INC memloc, INC @Ri and INC Rx, where i=0 or 1 and x=0 to 7.

6. **INC DPTR:** Increments DPTR. DPTR is a 16-bit register. If it has a value 0FFFFH, then an increment will make it 0000H; the carry is not affected. *There is no instruction to decrement DPTR*.

7. **DEC A:** The accumulator is decremented, and if its value contains a 00h, the next decrement will make it contain 0ffh.

8. **DEC byte:** Decrements *byte*. This could be addressed through direct, indirect and register modes. This is like DEC memloc, DEC @Ri and DEC Rx, where i=0 or 1 and x=0 to 7.

9. **MUL AB:** The contents of the accumulator are multiplied by the contents of B register and the result is placed in the register combination B:A. The upper byte of the product is in B register and the lower byte of the product is in A register. In the MUL AB instruction, there is no comma separating AB.

10. **DIV AB:** The contents of the accumulator are divided by the contents of the B register. The quotient is placed in the accumulator and the remainder is in the B register. In the DIV AB instruction, there is no comma separating AB.

11. **DA A:** This is the decimal adjust accumulator instruction which checks the lower nibble in the accumulator. If this is greater than nine, then it adds a six. If there is a carry out of this nibble addition, it is stored in the AC (auxiliary carry) flag. The upper nibble is checked and if along with the AC it is greater than nine, then a six is added to it. In case the upper nibble of the accumulator along with the auxiliary carry is not greater than nine, then it is left alone.

As an example, observe this sequence of steps:

1.1 Accumulator contains 99H.

1.2 It is incremented.

1.3 It now contains 9AH.

1.4 DA A instruction executed.

1.5 Lower nibble contains AH which is greater than nine.

1.6 Accumulator now contains 90H with the auxiliary carry set.

1.7 The upper nibble along with auxiliary carry is greater than nine, that is, 0AH. A six is added to it and it results in a 0H, and a carry CY is generated.

1.8 The accumulator contains a 00h and the CY (carry flag is set).

The above sequence indicates how the decimal adjust accumulator works. The accumulator contains 99H, and when a one is added to it followed by a 'DA A' instruction, the result is a CY=1 and A=00H. This is how a binary-coded decimal (BCD) number is incremented and adjusted for decimal operations. It is indicated by the change of the BCD number 99H after incrementing to CY=1 and A=00, that is 99 + 1=1 00. The '1' is in the carry and the '00' in the accumulator. This instruction, therefore, is most useful when a BCD number is being incremented such that the decimal rules are followed and not the binary ones.

4.2 Logic Instructions

The logic instructions are tabulated in Table 4.2 which clearly explains their operations, addressing modes and execution times

1. **ANL A, <byte>:** *byte* can be a data memory location. This could be referred indirectly by R0 or R1; it could be in one of the registers R0 to R7; *byte* could also be a constant. The contents of accumulator are AND-ed and the result is updated in the accumulator.
2. **ANL <byte>, A:** *byte* is only in the internal data memory.

Table 4.2 *The logic instructions*

Mnemonic		Operation	Addressing modes				Execution time (µS)
			Dir	Ind	Reg	Imm	
ANL	A, <byte>	A = A .AND. <byte>	×	×	×	×	1
ANL	<byte> ,A	<byte> = <byte> .AND. A	×				1
ANL	<byte> ,#data	<byte> = <byte> .AND. #data	×				2
ORL	A, <byte>	A = A.OR. <byte>	×	×	×	×	1
ORL	<byte> ,A	<byte> = <byte> .OR. A	×				1
ORL	<byte> ,#data	<byte> = <byte> .OR. #data	×				2
XRL	A, <byte>	A = A .XOR. <byte>	×	×	×	×	1
XRL	<byte> ,A	<byte> = <byte> .XOR. A	×				1
XRL	<byte> ,#data	<byte> = <byte> .XOR. #data	×				2
CRL	A	A = 00H	Accumulator only				1
CPL	A	A = .NOT. A	Accumulator only				1
RL	A	Rotate ACC left 1 bit	Accumulator only				1
RLC	A	Rotate left through Carry	Accumulator only				1
RR	A	Rotate ACC right 1 bit	Accumulator only				1
RRC	A	Rotate right through Carry	Accumulator only				1
SWAP	A	Swap nibbles in A	Accumulator only				1

3. **ANL <byte>,# data8:** *byte* is in the data memory only.
4. **ORL A, <byte>:** *byte* could be accessed in all the four addressing modes.
5. **ORL <byte>,A:** *byte* is only in direct memory.
6. **ORL <byte>,# data:** Here also, the *byte* is only in direct memory (the internal data memory).
7. **XRL A, <byte>:** *byte* can be accessed in all the four addressing modes.
8. **XRL <byte>,A:** *byte* is only in direct memory.
9. **XRL <byte>, # data:** Here also, the *byte* is only in the direct memory (the internal data memory).
10. **CLR A:** Clears the accumulator. It puts a 00H in the accumulator.
11. **CPL A:** Complements what is in the accumulator
12. **RL A:** Rotates the accumulator left by one bit. The bit 0 goes to bit 1 position, bit 1 goes to bit 2 and so on, until bit 7 which goes to carry. The contents of bit 0 are forced to a zero. These Rotate instructions do not do a circular rotate. In this case the Carry bit is discarded.
13. **RLC A:** Similar to RL A except that the carry bit goes to bit 0. These Rotate instructions do a circular rotate. In this case the Carry bit is rotated to the LSB bit position.
14. **RR A:** Rotates the accumulator right by one bit. The bit 7 goes to bit 6 position, bit 6 goes to bit 5 and so on till bit 0 which goes to carry. The contents of bit 7 are forced with a 0. These Rotate instructions do not do a circular rotate. In this case the Carry bit is discarded.
15. **RRC A:** Similar to RRC A except that the carry bit goes to bit 7. These Rotate instructions do a circular rotate. In this case the Carry bit is rotated to the MSB bit position.

In all these rotate cases, the original bit values are moved to the next position first, then the preceding bit value is copied. No previous bit values are lost

The RLC and RRC are very useful in I/O applications whereas the RL and RR are useful in mathematical operations to implement the algorithms for arithmetic and mathematical operations. The algorithms can be picked up from any standard book on computer organisation.

4.3 Flags Affected by Instructions

The instructions, whether arithmetic or logical, affect the flag register which is also known as the program status word (PSW). In this section, the way the instructions affect the flags is explained. This is shown, case by case, in Table 4.3. The change is then stored in the flag register or PSW as shown in Table 4.4.

Table 4.3 *The arithmetic instructions affecting the flags in PSW*

Instruction	Flag			Instruction	Flag		
	C	OV	AC		C	OV	AC
ADD	×	×	×	CLR C	0		
ADDC	×	×	×	CPL C	×		
SUBB	×	×	×	ANL C,bit	×		
MUL	0	×		ANL C,/bit	×		
DIV	0	×		ORL C,bit	×		
DA	×			ORL C,/bit	×		
RRC	×			MOV C,bit	×		
RLC	×			CJNE	×		
SETB C	1						

1. ADD affects the carry, overflow and Auxiliary carry
2. ADDC affects the carry, overflow and Auxiliary carry
3. SUBB affects the carry, overflow and Auxiliary carry
4. MUL affects the Overflow and the Carry is always 0
5. DIV affects the Overflow. The Carry is always 0
7. DA affects only the Carry
8. RRC affects only the Carry
9. RLC affects only the Carry
10. SETB only sets the Carry to 1
11. CLRC only clears the Carry to 0
12. CPLC affects only the Carry
13. ANL C,bit affects only the Carry
14. ANL C,/bit affects only the Carry. It ANDs the CY to bit and complements the CY
15. ORL affects only the Carry
16. ORL C,/bit affects only the Carry. It ORs the CY to bit and complements the CY

17. MOV C,bit affects only the Carry
18. CJNE affects only the Carry

Table 4.4 *The Program Status Word bit assignment*

Bit	7	6	5	4	3	2	1	0
flag	CY	AC	F0	RS1	RS0	OV	F1	P
Name	Carry flag	Auxiliary carry flag	User flag 0	Register bank Select 1	Register bank Select 0	Overflow flag	User flag 1	Parity bit

1. The most significant bit in the PSW is the CY bit in bit position 7
2. The AC flag is in bit 6 position—this flag is set when there is a carry from the lower nibble to the upper nibble and is used by the decimal adjust instruction for BCD arithmetic.
3. There are two flags for the user, namely F0 and F1, in bit positions 5 and 1. These can be used by the developer to SETB or CLR PSW.5 or PSW.1 respectively for F0 and F1.
4. Bits 4,3 are used for selecting the four banks of registers. Instructions which specify the registers ie. MOV R1,#0AAH, use the data memory location as per the value in RS1 and RS0. If RS1 and RS0 are 00, then the memory location 01H in data Ram is used for R1. If RS1, RS0 are 01, then R1 is 09H of data Ram and so on till RS1, RS0 being 11, the R1 is placed in 19H memory location in data Ram.
5. The OV flag shows the overflow condition in the accumulator. This flag is in bit position 2.
6. The accumulator bit contents parity is reflected in the P parity bit which is position 0 in the PSW.

The PSW is also referred to as Flag Register and Processor Status Word especially when the CPU is multitasking. This is because the CPU executes many processes and when it switches from one process to another (process switching), the CPU condition flags for that process have to be stored.

Bank switching helps in multitasking as the instructions can use the registers by name and not by their address. In case bank switching is not allowed, then referring R0 to R7 registers by (now four) different processes will not be possible without modifying the other processes register contents.

4.4 Bit Manipulation Instructions

Table 4.5 lists the instructions common in bit manipulation.

Table 4.5 *Bit manipulation instructions*

Mnemonic		Operation	Execution time (μS)
ANL	C.bit	C = C .AND. bit	2
ANL	C./bit	C = C .AND. .NOT. bit	2
ORL	C.bit	C = C .OR. bit	2
ORL	C./bit	C = C .OR. .NOT. bit	2
MOV	C.bit	C = bit	1
MOV	bit,C	bit = C	2
CLR	C	C = 0	1
CLR	bit	bit = 0	1
SETB	C	C = 1	1
SETB	bit	bit = 1	1
CPL	C	C = .NOT. C	1
CPL	bit	bit = .NOT. bit	1
JC	rel	Jump if C = 1	2
JNC	rel	Jump if C = 0	2
JB	bit,rel	Jump if bit = 1	2
JNB	bit,rel	Jump if bit = 0	2
JBC	bit,rel	Jump if bit = 1; CLR bit	2

1. **ANL C, *bit***: Current value of Carry is AND-ed with bit and the Carry is updated. The bit does not change its value.
2. **ANL C, */bit***: Current value of Carry is AND-ed with the complement of bit and the carry is updated.
3. **ORL C, *bit***: Current value of Carry is OR-ed with bit and the carry is updated. The bit does not change its value.
4. **ORL C, */bit***: Current value of Carry is OR-ed with bit and the carry is updated. The bit does not change its value.
5. **MOV C, *bit***: Bit value is copied to C.
6. **MOV *bit*, C**: C value is copied to bit.
7. **CLR C**: The value 0 is copied 0 to C.
8. **CLR *bit***: Value 0 is copied 0 to bit.

9. **SETB C:** Value 1 is copied to C.
10. **SETB *bit*:** Value 1 is copied to bit.
11. **CPL C:** Whatever the bit value in C is complemented and copied to C.
12. **CPL *bit*:** Whatever the value in bit is complemented and copied to bit. The next bit manipulated instructions do Transfer control.
13. **JC addr:** *addr* is an 8-bit address to which the program will jump to execute if the C bit is set. The location to jump to is calculated by twos complementing *addr* with the Program Counter lower 8-bit contents, ignoring any resulting carry. This means that only the lower 8 bits of the PC are used for transfer. The operation is called relative jump and results in shorter instruction size (in embedded systems each byte counts—it could be the last straw on the camel's back). Such 8-bit address jumps are called short jumps. 12-bit address jumps are called absolute jumps and consequently the 16-bit address jumps are called long jumps. Many assemblers optimise and so one need not search for the right type of Jump, a simple JMP would do.
14. **JNC addr:** Jumps to *addr* if carry is clear
15. **JB *bit*, addr:** The *bit* is tested and if it is set (=1), the control is transferred to the relative address *addr*, else the next instruction is executed. The relative address is calculated as discussed in (13) for JC addr.
16. **JNB *bit*, addr:** The *bit* is tested and if it is not set (=0), the control is transferred to the relative address *addr*, else the next instruction is executed. The relative address is calculated as discussed in (13) for JC addr.
17. **JBC *bit*, addr:** The *bit* is tested and if it is set (=1), the control is transferred to the relative address *addr* plus the *bit* is complemented, else the next instruction is executed. The relative address is calculated as discussed in (13) for JC addr.

4.5 Jump and Call Instructions

Instructions used for transferring control are listed in Table 4.6 and 4.7.

Table 4.6 *Transfer control instructions (unconditional)*

Mnemonic		Operation	Execution time (μS)
JMP	addr	Jump to addr	2
JMP	@A+DPTR	Jump to A + DPTR	2
CALL	addr	Call subroutine at addr	2
RET		Return from subroutine	2
RETI		Return from interurpt	2

1. **JMP addr:** The execution of the program is continued from the location specified as *addr*.
2. **JMP @ A +DPTR:** This address to jump to is calculated by adding the A(accumulator) contents to DPTR. A is 8-bit and DPTR is 16-bit. This is a long jump using a 8-bit displacement in the A register. Such jumps are used for look-up tables.
3. **CALL addr:** This is a subroutine call to a program which is located at the value specified in *addr*. The current PC content is saved so that on returning from the subroutine, the Program Counter is loaded with the return value. Storing and retrieving is done using the stack. The subroutine must have a RET instruction at the end of the subroutine for fruitful operation of the CALL instruction.
4. **RET:** It is used as the last instruction in a functional complete subroutine. On executing this instruction, the CPU will read the stack and up date the Program Counter. Thus it helps in the execution to return to the instruction after the CALL instruction.
5. **RETI:** This is also a Return instruction but is different from the RET as indicated by the 'I'. This is used for returning from an interrupt. It returns to the instruction after the instruction when the interrupt occurred. Interrupts are asynchronous, meaning thereby that there is no known time when they will occur as they are external events for the CPU. When interrupts occur, the instruction currently being executed is completed. After that, the Program Counter and the PSW contents are saved on stack and the Interrupt Service Routine is forced into the Program Counter. The Interrupt Service routine is executed and whenever the RETI instruction is encountered by the CPU, the PSW and the Program Counter contents are restored and the execution continues as if no interrupt occurred.

Table 4.7 *The transfer control instructions (conditional)*

Mnemonic	Operation	Addressing modes				Execution time (μS)
		Dir	Ind	Reg	Imm	
JZ rel	Jump if A = 0	Accumulator only				2
JNZ rel	Jump if A ≠ 0	Accumulator only				2
DJNZ <byte>,rel	Decrement and jump if not zero	×		×		2
CJNE A,<byte>,rel	Jump if A ≠ <byte>	×			×	2
CJNE <byte>,#data,rel	Jump if <byte> ≠ #data		×	×		2

1. **JZ rel:** This is a conditional transfer instruction which tests the Accumulator for a zero value and jumps to the relative address *rel*. The *rel* is twos complemented with the lower 8 bits of the PC ignoring the Carry and the result is the lower 8-bit value in the PC. The control is transferred to the address in the lower 8-bit value in the PC. In case the condition is not met, execution continues as usual.
2. **JNZ rel:** This is a conditional transfer instruction which tests the Accumulator for a non-zero value and jumps to the relative address *rel*. The *rel* is twos complemented with the lower 8 bits of the PC ignoring the Carry and the result is the lower 8-bit value in the PC. The control is transferred to the address in the lower 8-bit value in the PC. In case the condition is not met, the execution continues as usual.
3. **DJNZ <byte>, *rel*:** This instruction decrements the value in *<byte>* and loops to address given in *rel*. If the value in *<byte>* is zero, it executes the next sequential instruction. *<byte>* could be a register or a memory location but it should not be a constant. The *rel* is twos complemented with the lower 8-bits of the PC ignoring the Carry. The control is transferred to the address in the lower 8-bit value in the PC. In case the condition is not met, the execution continues as usual.
4. **CJNE A, <byte>, *rel*:** This is like the if-then-else statement in high level languages. The CJNE stands for Compare and Jump if Not Equal. It compares A with *<byte>* and if they are not equal, it jumps to *rel,* else it continues to the next instruction. The *<byte>* could be a register, data memory location or if preceded by a #, it could be a constant while *rel* is the relative 8-bit address to jump to as explained earlier.

Appendix A has details of the instruction set and the reader is advised to go through the same. At first glance it may look overpowering. But such topics are understood only after browsing through them a couple of times without being overwhelmed. Appendix A has the instruction set followed by memory access techniques. This shows the different ways of accessing the different memory areas of 8051. A memory area block is shown and in the block a table number is given to lookup along with the access technique number. Access #1 refers to registers as memory and vice versa (register banks), Access # 2 is for Bit Addressed Memory, Access #3 is for internal user data RAM, Access #4 is for Special Function Registers (SFRs), Access # 5 is for indirect addressable RAM access which is parallel to the SFRs. The SFRs are addressed directly from 80H to 0FFh and this access #5 is for the indirectly accessible memory from 80H to 0FFh located in parallel with SFRs—they are distinguishable only in the way they are addressed. This is available in the upward compatible 8051s like 8052. Access #6 is for AUX RAM using DPTR, Accesses #7 & 8 are for external memory access, both ROM and RAM. The tables for internal and external accesses give the associated instructions with the accesses. The Hex to OpCode table follows. This table is useful to those who are programming their microcontroller using Hex opcodes and not assembly language. It is also useful for those who have a hex source code of the program and no assembly source code—they can look up the hex–OpCode table and build the assembly code.

4.6 Examples of Binary and Decimal Arithmetic Operations

In this section we will look at some examples of how arithmetic operations, both binary and decimal are carried out using the instructions studied in the previous sections.

Example 1: Add the contents at memory locations 34h and 35h and store the results in R5 and R6.

PROGRAM:

```
org 0000h
jmp start
org 40h
start:
mov 34h,#9dh
mov 35h,#0feh
mov a,34h
add a,35h
mov r6,a
mov a,#00h
mov b,#00h
addc a,b
mov r5,a
jmp $
end
```

Example 2: Subtract the contents of R2 from number 0f3h and put the result in external RAM 028bh.

PROGRAM:

```
org 0000h
jmp start
org 40h
start:
mov a,#0f3h
mov r2,#0ffh
subb a,r2
mov dptr,#028bh
movx @dptr,a
jmp $
end
```

Example 3: Multiply the data of RAM 22h with the data in RAM 15h and store the result in 19h and in 1Ah

PROGRAM:

```
org 0000h
jmp start
org 40h
start:
mov 22h,#0feh
mov 15h,#0efh
mov a,22h
mov b,15h
mul ab
mov 19h,a
mov 1ah,b
jmp $
end
```

Example 4: Divide the data at RAM 3Eh by the data in RAM 12h and store the quotient in R4 and the remainder in R5.

PROGRAM:

```
org 0000h
jmp start
org 40h
start:
mov 3eh,#05h
mov 12h,#00h
mov a,3eh
mov b,12h
div ab
mov r4,a
mov r5,b
jmp $
end
```

Example 5: Multiply two 16-bit numbers using the classical method. The 16-bit numbers are located at 31H, 30H and 41H, 40H (higher byte first, lower byte next.) The result is to be stored in 53H, 52H, 51H.

The classical method of multiplying two 16-bit numbers, ABCD and JKLM, is as follows. A,B,C,D,J,K,L,M,S,T,U,V,W,X,Y are four bits representing a hexadecimal digit. The ZYX-WVUTS is the 32-bit result of this multiplication.

```
          ABCD
        × JKLM
   ------------
        M(ABCD)
      +L(ABCD)
     +K(ABCD)
    +J(ABCD)
   ------------
    ZYXWVUTS
```

The ZYXWVUTS gives the product of ABCD × JKLM

The program given below can be analysed keeping the above procedure in mind. Code walk through this program—it could be a good exercise in concentration. Use a paper and pencil for the first attempt.

PROGRAM:

```
org 0000h
jmp start
org 40h
start:
mov a,30h
mov 0f0h,a
mov a,40h
mul ab
mov 50h,a
mov r0,0f0h
mov a,30h
mov 0f0h,a
mov a,41h
mul ab
add a,r0
mov r0,a
mov a,#00h
addc a,0f0h
mov r1,a
mov a,31h
mov 0f0h,a
mov a,40h
mul ab
add a,r0
mov r0,a
mov a,r1
addc a,0f0h
```

```
mov r1,a
mov a,#00h
addc a,#00h
mov r2,a
mov a,31h
mov 0f0h,a
mov a,41h
mul ab
add a,r1
mov r1,a
mov a,r2
addc a,0f0h
mov r2,a
mov 51h,r0
mov 52h,r1
mov 53h,r2
```

Summary

This chapter would have made the arithmetic and transfer control instructions clear. Using these instructions and the instructions from Chapter 3, one would be ready to write simple programs using the instruction set of 8051. The examples given here would have shown how programs are to be developed and how to use instructions in writing programs. Code walking was explained in the introduction to this chapter and here the author wishes to lay more emphasis on code walking and suggests that the reader makes variations in the code and tries it out. There are more assembly language programs in the next chapter. A word of advise to the reader is that writing code by one self will become easy only when an independent attempt is made starting from a simple application like adding two numbers located in memory processing and then returning the result in a register or a memory location. This gradually develops the competence of the programmer, which will grow exponentially. The author can be contacted for any guidance in this regard.

Self Evaluation Questions

1. What are the instruction grouped as arithmetic instructions?
2. Are there any instructions in 8051 for taking products and for division? If so, what are they and how are they to be used. If not, then how would such a feature be performed using the available instructions?
3. What is the need for DA A and how is it used?
4. Distinguish between SWAP and XCHG? In which groups are they present? How many types of XCHG are there?

5. Write a program based on the description of multi-byte arithmetic using ADDC A,<byte>. Assume that the numbers are 4-digit BCD numbers. [**Hint:** Initially there is no need to use a loop. The loop can be worked out later]. Take the numbers as 1234 and 4321. Do the multibyte addition and verify the answer.
6. Do MOV instructions affect the flags? There is one 8051 MOV instruction which affects the flag. Which one is it?
7. What is the function of F0, F1, RS0, RS1 bits in the flag register?
8. Given the following, compute the address from where execution will take place for contents of Accumulator being zero and, non-zero respectively.

```
1000   JZ   50h      ; PC=1002 because the instruction at 1000 is two
                     ; bytes long
```

   Where will the transfer take place if Accumulator=0 and if Accumulator? 0?
9. What jump instruction is used for Look up Table and why?
10. What are the different uses for Rotate and Rotate through carry instructions?
11. What are the other ways the PSW is called?
12. Differentiate between JB and JBC OpCodes?
13. Write a program using Rotate instructions to do simple eight multiplication without using the MUL or DIV instructions? [**Hint:** Refer to a standard computer organisation book].
14. Write a program to transfer 16 bytes of data from the ROM 1000H-100FH location to the internal data RAM 50H-5FH?
15. Differentiate between the three types of jumps—the Short, the absolute and the Long.

5 Application Programming

This chapter explains the interfaces commonly used in embedded systems. It is not exhaustive but will certainly start the reader on their way into making the necessary interfaces for embedded systems applications. The first embedded systems application for the beginner is lighting up a Light Emitting Diode (LED). This application blinks an LED at an ON–OFF rate controlled by software and is called by most embedded systems trainers as Blinky. The beginner then learns to put together a group of LEDs and make them ON and OFF sequentially or per a stored pattern. The next step is to take inputs. Simple inputs like switch closures to the input from keyboards like those on digital telephones.

The next step in developing embedded application is the display of messages as numbers, using seven segment LED digits or characters using the liquid crystal display modules.

The fourth stage for the evolving embedded systems professional is data conversion from digital to analog/analog to digital.

This chapter discusses all these issues. The reader is advised to use their capability of code walking acquired from the previous chapter. Read the interface operation and then code walk the given application while relating the software to the expected hardware action. This chapter could probably be called the trysting point of hardware and software. Refer to the author's web site regularly for embedded application news, techniques, interfaces, devices and applications.

5.1 Developing Applications

Developing a system, an application which is to be part of another system, needs much more expertise than that required for developing software. The reason is that these systems usually do not have standard I/O devices that are available in personal computers, for instance, like PC keyboards, video display units, mouse interfaces and a host of other devices. Application development in embedded systems requires that one should know how to interface the I/O devices needed by the application. Skill in optimising space and reducing costs and power plays a major role in the development of embedded systems. This chapter deals with some typical interfaces that will be needed. It is not a complete document on all the devices to be interfaced; however, about 70 per cent of such interfaces will be discussed.

5.2 Display

The display is the first thing which has to be interfaced, because a displayed output is the quickest way to find out whether the hardware is functioning at all. It has many types of which the simplest is the prompt lamp.

5.2.1 Prompt Lamps

These are simply lamps indicating what sort of an action is expected by the applications. The lamps are usually built using light emitting diodes (LEDs) or incandescent filament lamps. Of these two, incandescent filament lamps are brighter and usually are the preferred solutions in automotive applications. Their drawback is that they have short lifetimes and are not power efficient. The opposite is true of LEDs, which are now available in various sizes and shapes, offering a range of output intensity levels from normal to very bright. The advantage is that LEDs are both power- and cost-efficient and also stay much cooler during operation than incandescent filament lamps.

5.2.2 LED Displays

5.2.2.1 LED lamps

Interfacing LED lamps is very straightforward as all that is to be ensured is that the port bit to which it is connected can provide the current required by the LED. For instance, the ports of microcontrollers have a lower capability for current sourcing as compared to that for current sinking. "Sourcing current" means that the port bit would provide the voltage to drive the LED. Sinking current means that the port bit will provide the path for current flow, and the driving voltage will be from the power supply. Care must be taken to ensure that the quantity of current sourced or sunk should not exceed the maximum that the LED or port bit can carry. A good design is one where this current is kept around 50 per cent of the maximum value, which is specified in the data sheets. For ports, the sourcing value is less than one-half of the TTL load, and the value corresponding to sinking is about 1 TTL load (equal to the TTL load). A numerical estimate of the maximum current is 20 mA for 5-mm-thick LEDs. The forward voltage drop of these LEDs depends on their colour output. For example, a red LED has a voltage drop of 1.6 V, and a green LED has a drop of 1.9 V. The design parameters for sourcing and sinking a LED prompt lamp can be calculated from the circuit, as shown in Fig. 5.1.

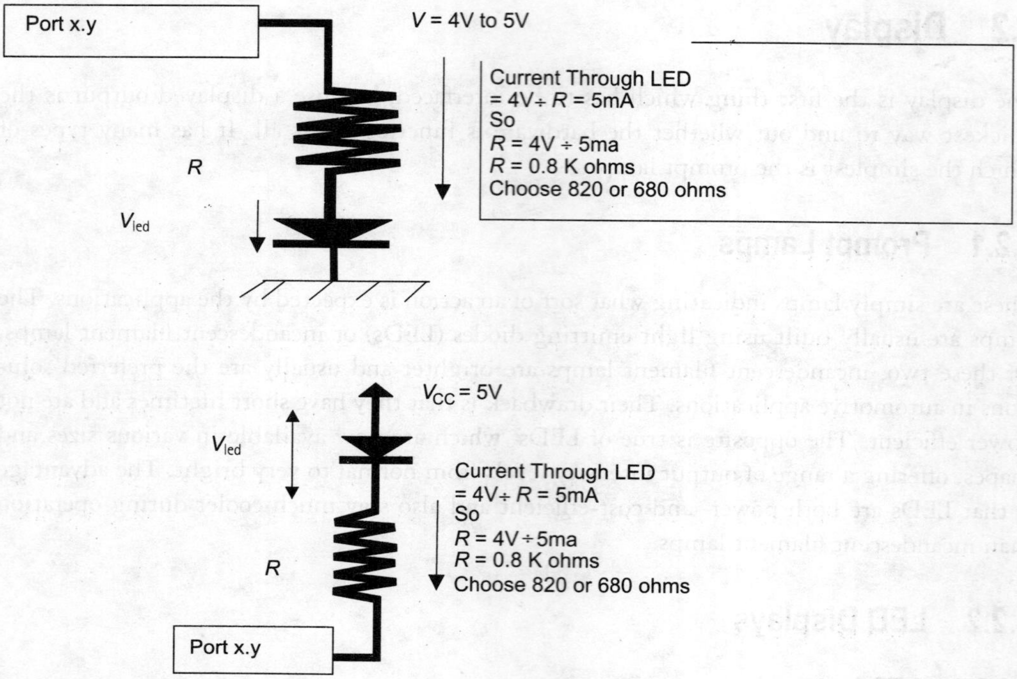

Fig. 5.1 *LED prompt lamps interfacing*

These lamps may be placed by the side of a printed legend which prompts the user to take the required action, and therefore, these are called prompt lamps. They are useful when it is not required to provide elaborate displays.

5.2.2.2 Seven-segment LED displays

This name is given to an assembly of seven LED lamps in a module, such that each one represents one segments of a seven-segment display. There are two types of seven-segment display—the common anode (CA) and the common cathode (CC) types. . Figure 5.2 shows the (a) pin assignments and (b) segment assignments of a CC seven-segment LED display

In the CA display, as one can guess, the anode is the common point, and the segment leads form the cathodes. The common point is connected to the positive of the power supply, and the segments are connected to the port bits through a resistor. The resistor value is calculated as shown in Section 5.2.2.1 on prompt LEDs. In the CC display, all the LEDs share a common cathode and this is usually taken to the negative of the power supply (0 V). The anodes are the segments which must be taken to the respective port bits through a resistor. Figure 5.3 shows how this is done.

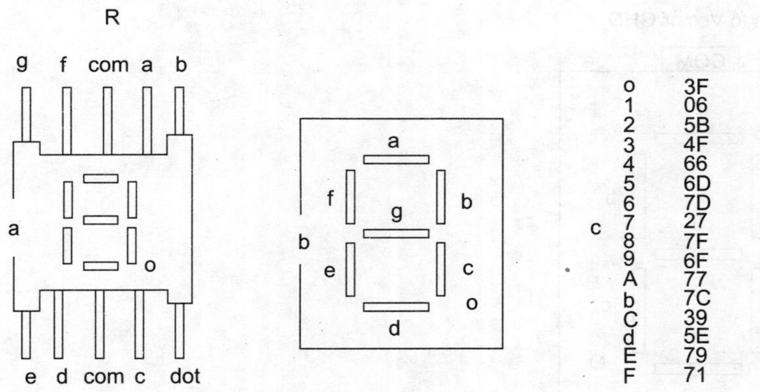

Fig. 5.2 *(a) Pin connections; (b) segment assignments and (c) display code for CC LEDs*

Figure 5.3 shows how the segments a, b, c, d, e, f, g and the decimal point (DP) are connected to bits 0, 1, 2, 3, 4, 5, 6, 7 of any of the four ports of 8051. They are connected to the port through resistors having resistance values of 330 ohm or 470 ohm. In a CA circuit, the common point is taken to the supply, Vcc; on the other hand if it is a CC circuit, it is taken to the ground point (0 V). The CA configuration of LEDs would be preferred if the connection is to Port 0 as the Port 0 is the open collector. In reality, it does not make much difference from the functioning of the LED and the choice is left to the interface designer. The interface designer can choose the ports according to the application's requirements. Such connections are made if not many I/Os are needed. This is because each digit will take eight bits. Thereby, a three-digit display will need 24 of the 32 bits. This is applicable to digital clocks, tachometers, quiz and token displays.

Whether it is common anode or cathode, the seven-segment display must show not only numbers from 0–9 but also the hexadecimal base numbers A to E. There is a code for each of the 16 numbers. Figure 5.2 (c) displays these codes for a CC seven-segment display. A logic 1 on the port will light up the segment. For a display of number nine (9), the segments a, b, c, f and g are lighted; d and e are off. That is, a, b, c, f, g are one and d, e and DP are zero, so the code is 00111111 with the ms-bit being DP (decimal point) and ls-bit being the "a" segment. The hex code is 3FH. For the CA display, ON and OFF are opposite logic so this code could be complimented to give the CA code. The value for CA would be Compliment (3FH), that is, 0C0H.

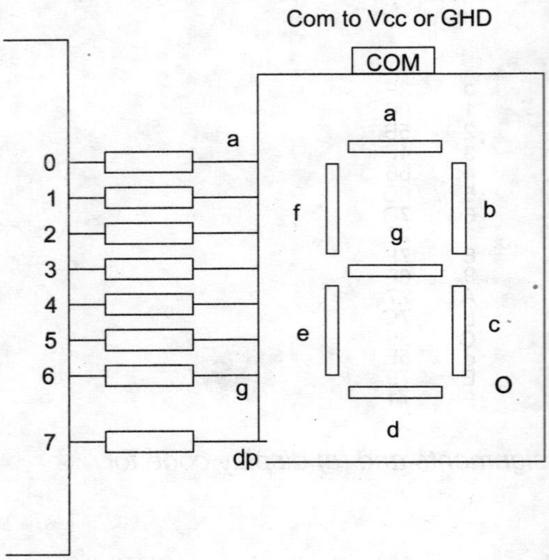

Fig. 5.3 *Connecting a seven-segment LED to port bits and the common connection to Vcc or GND*

5.2.2.3 Multidigit multiplexed display

This is a multidigit display which saves on power and I/O bits of the microcontroller. The principle is to first switch on one digit at a time for a short period, showing the value it has to show. Next, it is switched off and the next digit powered for a short period. The process is repeated until all the digits have been sequentially switched on, displayed and then switched off. The full set of digits is again refreshed in a continuous manner. Take a look at Fig. 5.4 where there are three digits—DS1, DS2 and DS3. The idea is to sequentially display the digits: first the one on DS3, followed by DS2 and then DS1. They will be on for equal periods of, say, 5 ms. The three digits would be updated in 3 × 5 (15) ms. This is done repeatedly, resulting in the display being updated every 15 ms. Therefore, the rate at which it is refreshed is 66 times per second. This makes it possible to perceive it as a continuous display.

As only one digit is on at any single time, the power drawn will be as if only one digit is powered. This results in reduced power consumption. The transistors Q3, Q2 and Q1 control the power to the displays DS3, DS2 and DS1, coming on when their input connections are taken to 0 V and switching off when these are taken to 5 V. This is done by port bits P3.5, P3.6 and P3.7 respectively. The digit to be displayed is presented through Port 3, that is, P3.0, P3.1, P3.2 and P3.3 as BCD digits ABCD, respectively. The BCD data are applied to a decoder IC called "BCD to seven-segment decoder driver" namely SN7447.

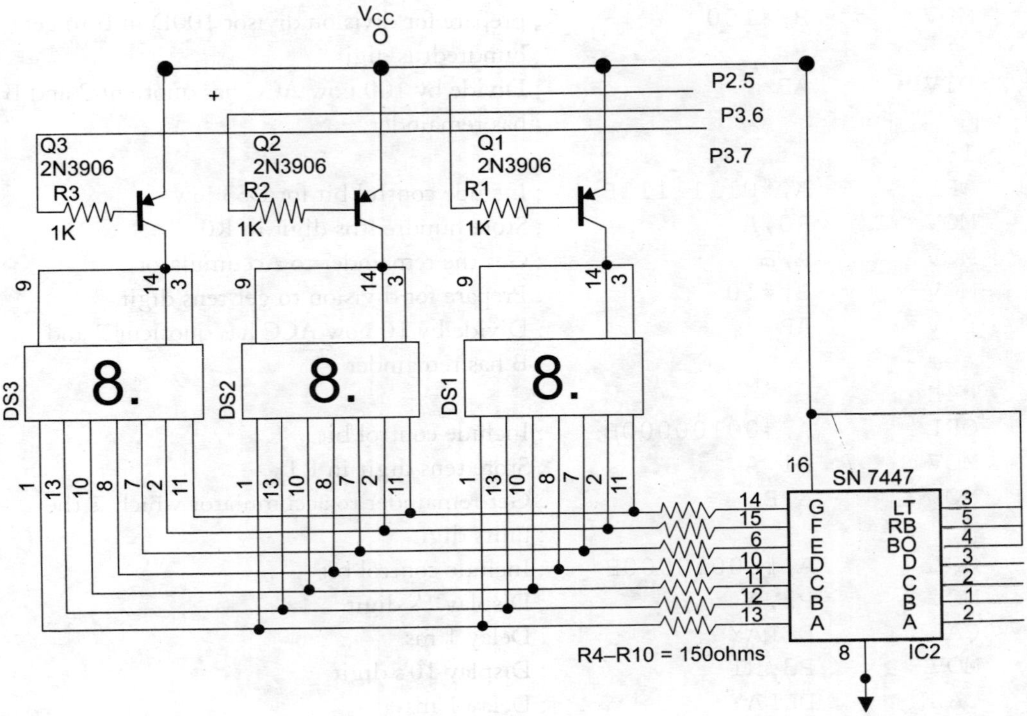

Fig. 5.4 *The multidigit multiplexed display*

The output of the SN7447 is the logic for the segments a, b, c, d, e, f and g. These segment outputs are connected in parallel to all respective segments of the displays DS1, DS2 and DS3. These devices are of the common anode type, and the power is given through the common terminal by the transistors Q1, Q2 and Q3, respectively. If the DS1 is to display the units' digits, the BCD value is applied to SN7447, and the Q1 is made to conduct it by taking its base resistor to logic 0 V (as these transistors are PNP); similarly for tens, it should be Q2; and for hundreds it should be Q3. The program given below will complete the understanding of how the operations are performed

In this application, there is a binary number presented at the Port 1 input whose value would range from 0 to 255 decimal. This binary value is read from Port1 and the three digits are shown on the displays DS3, DS2 and DS1. This binary value is converted to three unpacked BCD and applied to the respective digit. For example, if the input to P1 is 0E0H then the DS3, DS2 and DS1 will show 2, 2, 4, respectively.

```
MOV     P1,#0FFH        ; Set port 1 as input
LOOP
MOV     A,P1            ; Get binary data (0E0H) by reading P1 into
                        ; accumulator
```

```
MOV     B,#100           ; prepare for division divisor 100D in B to get
                         ; hundredths digit
DIV     AB               ; Divide by 100 now ACC has quotient 2 and B
                         ; has remainder
18H
ORL     A,#01111111B     ; Include control bit for DS3 low
MOV     R0,A             ; Store hundredths digit in R0
MOV     A,B              ; Get the remainder to Accumulator
MOV     B,#10            ; Prepare for division to get tens digit
DIV     AB               ; Divide by 10 now ACC has quotient 2 and
                         ; B has remainder
04H
ORL     A,#00100000B     ; Include control bit
MOV     R1,A             ; Store tens digit in R1
MOV     A,B              ; Get remainder to accumulator which is the
                         ; units digit
ORL     A,#00010000B     ; Include control bit
MOV     P3,A             ; Display 1's digit
CALL    DELAY            ; Delay 1 ms
MOV     P3,R1            ; Display 10's digit
CALL    DELAY            ; Delay 1 ms
MOV     P3,R0            ; Display 100's digit
CALL    DELAY            ; Delay 1 1m
SJMP    LOOP             ; Done updating now keep repeating from loop
DELAY:                   ; 1 millisecond delay routine
MOV     R4,#2
REPEAT:
MOV     R5,#230
REPEAT:
DJNZ    R5,repeat
DJNZ    R4,repeat
RET
```

5.2.2.4 Multidigit non-multiplexed display

The multiplexed display works fine as long as the rate of refreshing is not disturbed. In the above example, the data are taken and displayed so there is no cause for a disturbance. If a keyboard has to be scanned and the result displayed, then also there will be no problem if the keyboard is always ready with the output. But this is not always the case. So the program will wait for the keyboard and will not update or refresh the display during this time. This will make the display go blank during that period.

There are keyboard display controller ICs available which remove the burden of multiplexing and refreshing from the software and perform the function without an interruption; however, they occupy space and are not economical for displays that have only a small number of digits.

This section presents a multidigit display where multiplexing is not used and the concept of bussing is exploited. At the heart of this scheme is a BCD LATCH seven-segment decoder driver, the Integrated Circuit (IC). There are three sub-sections in this IC. The latch, which is the first section, takes the input presented to its BCD inputs and stores it in a register whenever its latch-disable pin goes from high to low. The latched BCD input is given to the second section, BCD to seven-segment decoder, which gives a seven-segment code presented to the drivers. The drivers drive the LED segments of the the display connected to it and are the third and last section of the IC. This IC (integrated circuit) is identified by the number CD 4543 and is a CMOS device consuming very less power, and at the same time being less expensive.

The circuit is shown in Fig. 5.5. Here, there are four CD 4543 devices which are connected to drive their displays directly. Their BCD inputs are parallelled and connected to Port 0, bits 0, 1, 2 and 3. The latch-disable pins of each of these four devices are connected to Port 3, pins P3.4, P3.5, P3.6 and P3.7, respectively. This is how it works. Assume that the display is being updated from right to left. The data for the right-most digit is put on the lower nibble of Port 0 (P0.0, P0.1, P0.2 and P0.3). Next, its latch-disable pin, P3.4, is pulsed High-Low-High for a very short period. This latches the data on the P0 nibble to be latched by the rightmost CD 4543 device, and the rightmost display is updated. The BCD data of the next digit is put on the lower nibble of P0 and the corresponding CD 4543 latch is pulsed High and Low. This latches the data and the LED that is second from the right is updated. The steps are repeated for the next CD 4543 device until at last, the LED to the left extreme is done.

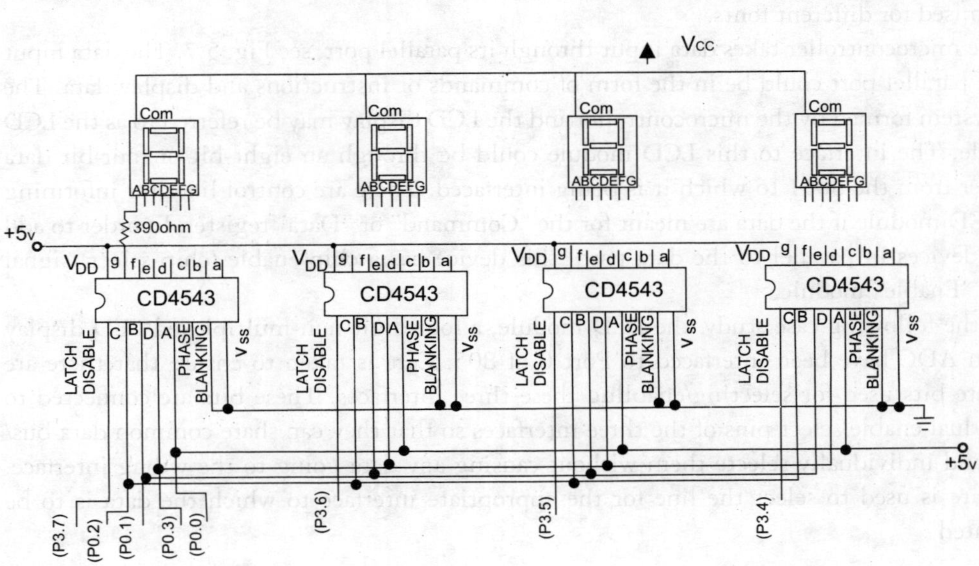

Fig. 5.5 *Four-digit non-multiplexed LED display*

There is a point to note here. In this configuration, all the displays are switched on, so the power-saving advantage of the non-multiplexed display is not available. The port bit saving advantage is still present as the data bus concept has the given advantage, although even in the non-multiplexed case too seven bits are needed to display three digit display.. The greatest advantage is that the duty of updating the display is reduced from the software, and in case the software is stuck in a routine, the display will not blank out.

5.2.3 Liquid Crystal Display Modules

The liquid crystal display modules by themselves form a sub-system. Earlier, LCD displays were available as seven-segment or 5 × 7 dot-matrix independent units, just like LED displays. These were difficult to drive as their segments cannot be operated at a constant logic voltage level. The drive signals had to be pulsed uniformly with equal time-periods for on and off states. So an AC-type signal is used to drive it, since a constant DC-type voltage would damage the display by permanently lighting up the segments. Also, these LCD displays are of either reflective or transparent type. Usually, the active segment becomes transparent whereas the inactive ones are opaque. To view these transparent segments, a mirror is kept behind the display.

Unlike LED displays which are self-luminescent, the LCD displays need external light for visibility. The extra circuitry needed to make up the drive for the LCD displays was the reason why these LCD modules were introduced. The LCD modules, shown in Fig 5.6, function with a microcontroller at the heart. The function of this microcontroller is to drive the LCD display it is interfacing. The LCD display used here is a 5 × 7 dot-matrix display and may be customised for different fonts.

The microcontroller takes data input through its parallel port, see Fig. 5.7. The data input to the parallel port could be in the form of commands or instructions and display data. The sub-system formed by the microcontroller and the LCD display may be referred to as the LCD module. The interface to this LCD module could be through an eight-bit or four-bit data transfer from the 8051 to which it is being interfaced. There are control lines for informing the LCD module if the data are meant for the "Command" or "Data" register. In order to add more devices in parallel to the data path, this device has a chip-enable (chip-select) signal called "Enable" module.

In the following case study, the LCD module, a four-digit non-multiplexed LED display and an ADC have been interfaced to Port 0 of 805. Care is taken to ensure that there are separate bits used for selecting/enabling these three interfaces. These bits are connected to individual enable/select pins of the three interfaces so that they can share common data bus/lines and individually selecte them without causing any data going to the wrong interface. Software is used to select the line for the appropriate interface to which the data is to be presented.

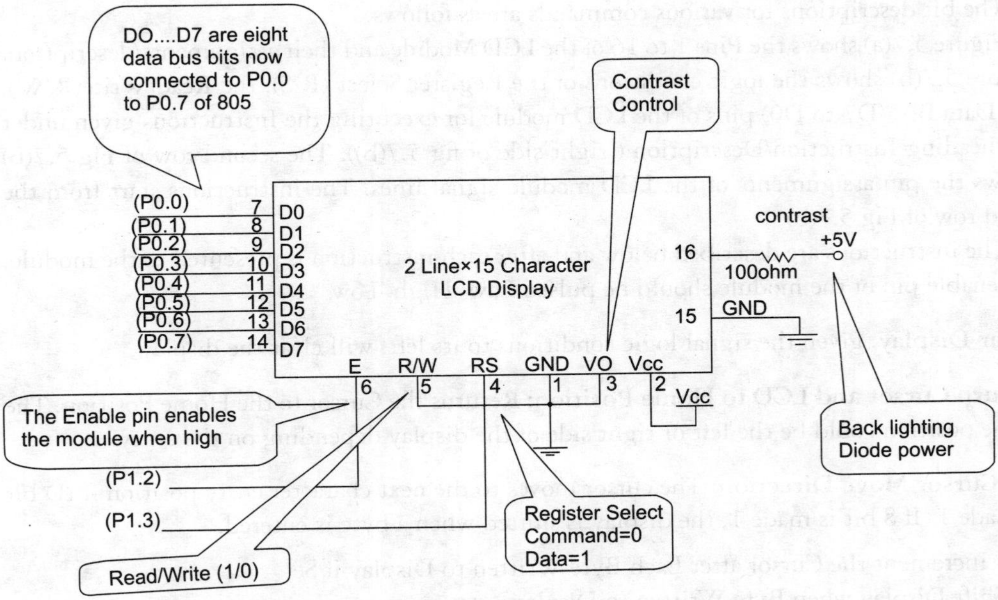

Fig. 5.6 *LCD module of 16 characters X 2 Lines*

Pin	Description	
1	**GND** (Ground)	
2	**Vcc** (Supply Voltage)	
3	**Vee** (Contrast Voltage)	
4	**R/S** (Instruction/Register Select)	
5	**R/W** (Read/Write)	
6	**E** (Clock)	
7	**D0** (Data0)	
8	**D1** (Data1)	
9	**D2** (Data2)	
10	**D3** (Data3)	
11	**D4** (Data4)	
12	**D5** (Data5)	
13	**D6** (Data6)	
14	**D7** (Data7)	
15	Backlighting	Cathode
16	Backlighting	Anode

(a)

R/S	R/W	D7	D6	D5	D4	D3	D2	D1	D0	Instruction/Description
4	5	14	13	12	11	10	9	8	7	Pins
0	0	0	0	0	0	0	0	0	1	Clear Display
0	0	0	0	0	0	0	0	1	*	Return Cursor and LCD to Home Position
0	0	0	0	0	0	0	1	ID	S	Set Cursor Move Direction
0	0	0	0	0	0	1	D	C	B	Enable Display/Cursor
0	0	0	0	0	1	SC	RL	*	*	Move Cursor/Shift Display
0	0	0	0	1	DL	N	F	*	*	Set Interface Length
0	0	0	1	A	A	A	A	A	A	Move Cursor into CGRAM
0	0	1	A	A	A	A	A	A	A	Move Cursor to Display
0	1	BF	*	*	*	*	*	*	*	Poll the "Busy Flag"
1	0	D	D	D	D	D	D	D	D	Write a Character to the Display at the Current Cursor Position
1	1	D	D	D	D	D	D	D	D	Read the Character on the Display at the Current Cursor Position

(b)

Fig. 5.7 *LCD module— (a) Pin assignments and (b) Commands table (*- Not Used/Ignored.)*

The bit descriptions for various commands are as follows.

Figure 5.7(a) shows the Pins 1 to 16 of the LCD Module and their assignments/description. Figure 5.7(b) shows the logic conditions of the Register Select (R/S), the Read/Write(R/W), the Data Bus (D7 to D0) pins of the LCD module for executing the Instructions given under the heading Instruction/Description (right side of fig 5.7(b)). The second row of Fig 5.7(b) shows the pin assignments of the LCD module signal lines. The instructions start from the third row of Fig 5.7(b).

The instructions are described below and after each instruction is presented to the module, the enable pin of the module should be pulsed Low–High–Low.

Clear Display: given the signal logic conditions to its left, will clear the display

Return Cursor and LCD to Home Position: Returns the Cursor to the Home Position. The home position could be the left or right side of the display depending on the entry.

Set Cursor Move Direction: The cursor moves to the next character entry position if ID bit is made 1. If S bit is made 1, the display is shifted when a byte is entered.

ID - Increment the Cursor after Each Byte Written to Display if Set
S - Shift Display when Byte Written to Display

Enable Display/Cursor: Cursor to be displayed or not is controlled by 'C'. If cursor is to be a blinking cursor then 'E' is a logic 1. If display is to be turned on, the 'D' bit should be logic 1.

D - Turn Display On(1)/Off(0)
C - Turn Cursor On(1)/Off(0)
B - Cursor Blink On(1)/Off(0)

Move Cursor/Shift Display: 'SC' shifts the displayed characters and the direction of shift is controlled by 'RL'

SC - Display Shift On(1)/Off(0)
RL - Direction of Shift Right(1)/Left(0)

Set Interface Length: The data path (bus/lines) for the LCD module is 8 bits in length. In embedded systems, it is very important to optimise on I/O bits. These modules provide an option to use an 8 bit or a 4 bit data path. This is done by setting the Data Length bit 'DL' aslogic 1 or 0 respectively. If there are two lines to be displayed, the choice is made by the 'N' bit. The character fonts may be changed. However in almost all the applications the 5×7 is standard.

DL - Set Data Interface Length 8(1)/4(0)
N - Number of Display Lines 1(0)/2(1)
F - Character Font 5×10(1)/5×7(0)

Move Cursor to CGRAM/Display: The characters being displayed are taken from a RAM called the Data RAM. The user writes to the Data RAM, if the cursor was to be moved to a specific location in data RAM

A – Address

Poll the "Busy Flag": These LCD modules have a microcontroller which controls the LCD display. It reads inputs given to it and updates the LCD display. If data is being written faster than it can be read, there will be a loss of display. For this reason, the LCD module outputs a bit 'BF'. The 'BF' bit is 1 indicating that the LCD module is busy. Testing of this bit is necessary to avoid loss of Display Data.

BF - This bit is set while the LCD is processing

There are certain practical issues about the busy flag which have to be given careful consideration. They are mentioned below

- Data from the Data RAM is read very infrequently. It is necessary when scrolling between lines and can be overlooked in 99 % of the applications.
- If the microcontroller interfaced to the LCD module is super fast then the application must read the busy flag to ensure that the execution of the earlier written instruction is completed by the LCD module before writing the next instruction to it.
- It is not necessary to read the busy flag of the LCD module in almost all cases. However if a variety of LCD modules are used then a certain delay of 100µseconds to 200µseconds may be inserted between instructions being written to the LCD module

Write ASCII to the Display: To write ASCII data to the display, the register select should be used. If fig 5.7(b) is referred it would be noticed that the RS bit has been at logic 0 for all the above instructions. This is because RS=0 selects the instruction register of the LCD module for executing commands. If data is to be written then the data/display RAM should be accessed by setting the RS bit, allowing access to the data RAM. The R/W bit logic is made a 1 or 0 in order to read or write data respectively. The data is written on the data lines D0 to D7 if it is a 8-bit data length or D4 to D7 if it is a 4-bit data length. In case it is a 4-bit data length, then the upper nibble of the data is written followed by the lower nibble.

D: refers Data

Read ASCII to the Display:

D: Data (on D7 to D0)

To read ASCII data from the display, the register select should be used. If Fig 5.7(b) is referred, it would be noticed that the RS bit has been at logic 0 for all the above instructions. This is because RS=0 selects the instruction register of the LCD module for executing commands. If data is to be read then the data/display RAM should be accessed by setting the RS bit which allows access to the data RAM. The R/W bit logic is made a 1 or 0 in order to read or write data respectively. The data is read from the data lines D0 to D7 if it is a 8-bit data length or D4 to D7 if it is a 4-bit data length. In case it is a 4-bit data length, then the upper nibble of the data is read followed by the lower nibble.

D: refers Data

5.2.3.1 Initialising the LCD module

Before sending commands or data to the LCD, the LCD must be initialised. This has to be done using an initialising algorithm. A simple algorithm to initialise the LCD module for the 8-bit and 4-bit modes is described.

The simpler case to study is the initialising algorithm for the 8-bit mode.

1. After power is applied give a minimum delay of 15 ms.
2. Next send 0x030 to LCD - wait 5 ms the instruction to be processed
3. Next send 0x030 to LCD - wait 150 ms the instruction to be processed
4. Next send 0x030 to LCD - wait 150 ms for the instruction to be processed
5. Set the Operating Mode of the LCD
6. "Set Interface Length" of 8 bit or 4 bit data length
7. Send 0x010 to LCD module to turn off the Display
8. Send 0x001 to LCD module to Clear the Display
9. Send "Set Cursor Move Direction" instruction to LCD module Setting Cursor Behavior Bits
10. Send "Enable Display/Cursor" instruction to LCD module to enable Display and Optional Cursor

The next is the initialising algorithm for the 4-bit mode.

First the high nibble is sent before the low nibble and the E pin is toggled each time four bits are sent to the LCD. The process of initialising is as follows:

1. After power is applied give a minimum delay of 15 ms.
2. Send 0x03 to LCD module and wait 5 ms for the instruction execute
3. Send 0x03 to LCD module and wait 150 msecs for the instruction to complete
4. Send 0x03 to LCD module and wait 150 msecs
5. Set the operating Mode of the LCD
6. Send 0x02 to the LCD module to enable 4-bit mode

The following instruction/data writes require two nibble writes.

7. Send "Set Interface Length" to LCD module to set the interface length to 4 bits
8. Send 0x01/0x00 to LCD module - turn off the Display
9. Send 0x00/0x01 to LCD module - Clear the Display
10. Send "Set Cursor Move Direction" - Setting Cursor Behavior Bits
11. Send "Enable Display/Cursor" - Enable Display and Optional Cursor

5.2.3.2 How to write an LCD module program

Here is an example of how to write an LCD module program. First, the way to connect the pins of the processor and those of the LCD module is outlined and then the parts of the program are explained.

The connections of the LCD module with two line X 16 characters are for 8-bit data and are as follows:

P0 is connected to LCD module data pins as given below:

8051 Pin Number	Port	LCD module Pin number	Designation
39	P0.0	7	DB0
38	P0.1	8	DB1
37	P0.2	9	DB2
36	P0.3	10	DB3
35	P0.4	11	DB4
34	P0.5	12	DB5
33	P0.6	13	DB6
32	P0.7	14	DB7
04	P1.3	04	Register Select
03	P1.2	06	Enable
20	GND	05	Read/ Write
20	GND	01	Vss
40	VCC	02	VCC
---	---	03	Contrast -0 to 2V
---	---	16	Back Light Anode
---	---	15	Back Light Cathode

The code consists of separate modules for initialising; writing instructions; writing data; displaying a message and various delays. The initialising module is called at the start of the program and the other modules are called as given in the main program at the end of the subroutines. The program lines are given in boldface and the explanation for them is given just above them in normal type.

In the following program, the instructions in lines 1 and 2 are the macros for value 80H and 90H. These are instructions to the LCD to use that line for the current display. These instructions are written as follows:

```
line1     equ 080h               ; select line 1 for display
line2     equ 0c0h               ; select line 2 for display
```

The following routine is an initialisation routine for the LCD module as per the 8-bit algorithm given above. This is to be called at the very beginning if the LCD module is to be used:

```
INITIALISE:
        CALL DELAY15MS           ; 15mSec POWER ON DELAY
        MOV A,#30H
        CALL WRITE_INSTRN        ; SELECT IN WRITE MODE
        CALL DELAY5MS            ; 5mSec DELAY
        MOV A,#30H
        CALL WRITE_INSTRN        ; SELECT IN WRITE MODE
        CALL DELAY500US          ; 500uS DELAY
        MOV A,#30H
        CALL WRITE_INSTRN        ; SELECT IN WRITE MODE
        MOV A,#38H               ; SELECT NO.OF LINES (2)
        CALL WRITE_INSTRN
        MOV A,#0FH               ; DISPLAY ON,CURSOR BLINK
        CALL WRITE_INSTRN
        MOV A,#01H               ; CLEAR DISPLAY
        CALL WRITE_INSTRN
        MOV A,#06H               ; NO SHIFT MODE,INC MODE
        CALL WRITE_INSTRN
        RET
```

The following routine writes to the instruction register, the byte in the accumulator. In the initialise routine, this is used for writing commands to the LCD module:

```
WRITE_INSTRN:
        ClR P2.3
        CLR P1.3                 ; INSTRUCTION WRITING SUBROUTINE
        CLR P1.2
        MOV P0,A                 ; SEND INSTRUCTION TO PORT
        SETB P1.2
        NOP
        CLR p1.2
        CALL delay15ms
        RET
```

The following routine writes the byte in the accumulator to the data register:

```
WRITE_DATA:
      CLR p2.3
      CLR P1.3                    ; DATA WRITING SUBROUTINE
      CLR p1.2
      SETB P1.3
      SETB p1.2
      MOV P0,A                    ; SEND INSTRUCTION TO PORT
      NOP
      CLR p1.2
      CLR P1.3
      CALL delay15ms
      RET
```

The following routine writes a message to the LCD module on the line specified in register R2 and the message pointed to by the DPTR register:

```
msg_disp:
      MOV     a,r2
      CALL    write_instrn
      MOV     r5,#16
m1:   CLR     a
      MOVC    a,@a+dptr
      CALL    write_data
      INC     dptr
      DJNZ    r5,m1
      RET
```

The delay routines required for initialisation and other routines are as follows:

```
DELAY500MS:
      MOV  R7,#2
H1:   MOV  R6,#200
H2:   MOV  R5,#250
H3:    DJNZ R5,H3
       DJNZ R6,H2
       DJNZ R7,H1
       RET
DELAY15MS:
      MOV  R6,#30
      JMP  DELAY
```

```
DELAY5MS:
       MOV  R6,#10
       JMP  DELAY
DELAY500US:
       MOV  R6,#1
DELAY:
       MOV  R7,#250
       DJNZ R7,$
       DJNZ R6,DELAY
       RET
```

The following program is the start up module, which uses all the above LCD module routines through the use of **initialise** and **msg_disp**. Reading the code along with the comments that follow after the semi-colon will make the whole algorithm very clear to the reader.

```
Org       00000h                 ; this is the reset vector from where
                                 ; the execution starts
          LJMP main              ; the jump to the startup
                                 ; program main
Org       0040h                  ; location of main from the top of the
                                 ; vectors for timer, interrupt & serial
          MOV psw,#00            ; initialise the register bank to bank 0
          MOV sp,#58h            ; relocate stack from 07h to near top
                                 ; of internal data ram leaving enough
                                 ; space for pushes up to top of ram
          CALL initialize        ; initialise the LCD module
          MOV dptr,#message1     ; point to message1 using DPTR
          MOV r2,#line1          ; choose line 1 for message display
          CALL msg_disp          ; display message #1 on line # 1
          MOV r2,#line2          ; choose line 1 for message display
          MOV dptr,#message2     ; point to message1 using DPTR
          CALL msg_disp          ; display message #2 on line # 2
          JMP $                  ; Embedded systems terminate in an
                                 ; infinite loop after their tasks are
                                 ; over preventing execution of
                                 ; unknown combination of
                                 ; instructions. The $ here signifies
                                 ; that the jump address is to
                                 ; memory location of this instruction
Message1: db "this is line 1"    ; message declaration as a string of bytes
Message2: db "this is line 2"    ; message declaration as a string of bytes
```

5.3 The Keyboard

The previous section discussed the way to interface and program an LCD display module with the microcontroller—which basically means programming the microcontroller to display output. This is usually the first step in developing embedded systems because it offers a way of checking if the microcontroller is functioning as it should. If an elaborate display is not needed to perform this check, a simple prompt light could be used to blink in a particular manner. This would demonstrate at the start the proper functioning of the embedded system under development. The program which is usually executed for the blinking lamp application is very fondly called BLINKY.ASM, BLINKY.C or BLINKY.BAS.

5.3.1 Interfacing Keyboards

The issue next in importance to display interfacing is keyboard interfacing.The switches used for the keyboard are called "momentary switches." They close for a moment when they are pressed and open when they are not pressed. For this purpose, the switches are usually small and match the size of human fingers. They are spaced apart, so that pressing one with a finger will not cause the adjacent switches to close.

Keyboards could be made up of a small collection of keys, for example, four or five, as used in digital clocks and domestic appliances. They could be part of a 12- or 16-key keyboard, in which they are arranged as a 3 × 4 or 4 × 4 matrix. Such keyboards are used in telephones and similar instruments. There are also keyboards with larger number of keys, but usually not exceeding 64 which can be placed in an 8 × 8 matrix. In the next sub-section, the very common PC keyboard will be discussed briefly to explain the concept of how a keyboard becomes an embedded system.

5.3.2 The Non-Matrix Keyboard

This type of keyboard is used in small embedded systems that do not need to use it for character entry or such general purposes. The keyboard shown in Fig. 5.8 could be used for a digital multi-alarm clock.

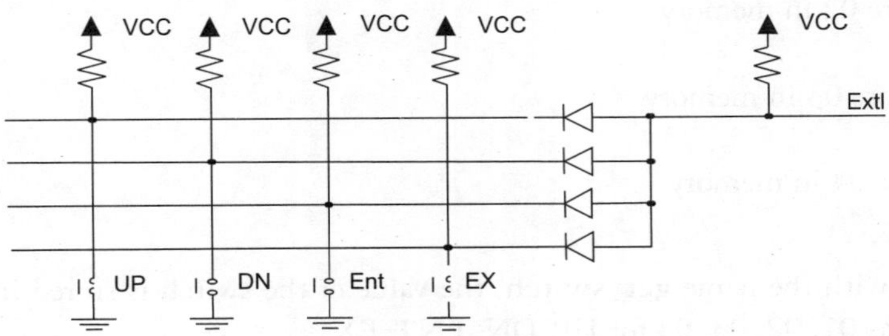

Fig. 5.8 *The non-matrix keyboard*

The legends marked against each switch indicates the response expected from the application program. The switches used here are, from left, "UP" for incrementing; "DN" for decrementing and "ENT" for choosing the displayed value. The switch "EX" is used to exit without ignoring any values entered before "EX" was pressed.

Take Port 2 as the input for this keyboard. Connect P2.0 to UP, P2.1 to DN, P2.2 to ENT and P2.3 to EX. Notice that these switches are pulled up to Vcc by resistors. This ensures that one end of the switches has a potential of Vcc and the other end has a potential equal to 0 V. If the switches are closed, the port bit to which they are connected will go to 0 V, otherwise they will be at Vcc. Notice that the non-grounded end of the switches are connected to the cathode of diodes whose anodes are made common. *This is a diode OR gate.* Whenever the switches are not closed all the diodes will be cut off, as their cathodes and anodes are at the same potential. This makes the signal EXT **high**. If one or more of the switches are closed, the diode connected to the switch that is closed will conduct, as the cathode is at 0 V and anode is at Vcc. The signal EXT will now go **low** for as long as the switches are closed. This signal, if needed, can be used for triggering off an interrupt. However, they are not of importance in a non-interrupt operation, or *polled operation*.

Since the keyboard is connected to Port 2, it may be set to input. Here is the algorithm:

```
1.00 Read port 2
1.10 is it 0ffh
1.20 if yes goto 1.0
1.30 mask port 2 with 00000001B
1.35 if the value is not zero then goto 2.0
1.40 mask port 2 with 00000010B
1.45 if the value is not zero then goto 3.0
1.50 mask port 2 with 00000100B
1.55 if the value is not zero then goto 4.0
1.60 mask port 2 with 00001000B
1.65 if the value is not zero then goto 5.0
1.99 goto 1.00
2.0  UP key pressed store 01 in memory
2.99 goto 1.99
3.0  DN key pressed store 02 in memory
3.99 goto 1.99
4.0  ENT key pressed store 03 in memory
4.99 goto 1.99
5.0  EX key pressed store 04 in memory
5.99 goto 1.99
```

The code is a subroutine with the name **get_switch**, the value of the switch is stored in internal RAM memory 40h as 01, 02, 03, 04 for UP, DN, ENT, EX.

```
Get_switch:
    MOV a,P2                          ; read port 2 and
    MOV b,a                           ; save the value in b registor
    CJNE a,#0ffh,find_switch          ; check if any key pressed
    SJMP get_switch                   ; if not repeat from get_switch
    ANL a,#01H                        ; logically mask Acc to find if the
                                      ; 1st bit ie
    CJNE a, #01H, nxt_switch1         ; least significant bit is zero
    MOV a,#01                         ; if zero then store 01 in memory 40h
    MOV 40h,a                         ; if not then goto nxtswitch1
nxt_switch1:
    Mov a,b                           ; restore a with saved value in b
    ANL a,#02H                        ; check if LSBit +1 switch is closed
    CJNE a, #02H, nxt_switch2         ; if not then goto nxt_switch2
    MOV a,#02                         ; else load memory location 40H
                                      ; with 02H
    MOV 40h,a
nxt_switch2:
    MOV a,b                           ; restore a with saved value in b
    ANL a,#04H                        ; check if LSBit +2 switch is closed
    CJNE a, #04H, nxt_switch3         ; if not then goto nxt_switch3
    MOV a,#04                         ; else load memory location 40H
                                      ; with 04H
    MOV 40h,a
nxt_switch3:
    MOV a,b                           ; restore a with saved value in b
    ANL a,#08H                        ; check if LSB +3 switch is closed
    CJNE a, #08H, nxt_switch4         ; if not the goto nxt_switch4
    MOV a,#08
    MOV 40h,a                         ; else load memory location 40H
                                      ; with 04H
nxt_switch4:
    RET
```

5.3.3 The Matrix Keyboard

In a matrix keyboard, the keys are arranged in a square or rectangle with their contacts connected to a row and a column, as shown in Fig. 5.9. The row connections are called "mPIn" and column connections are called "mPOut".

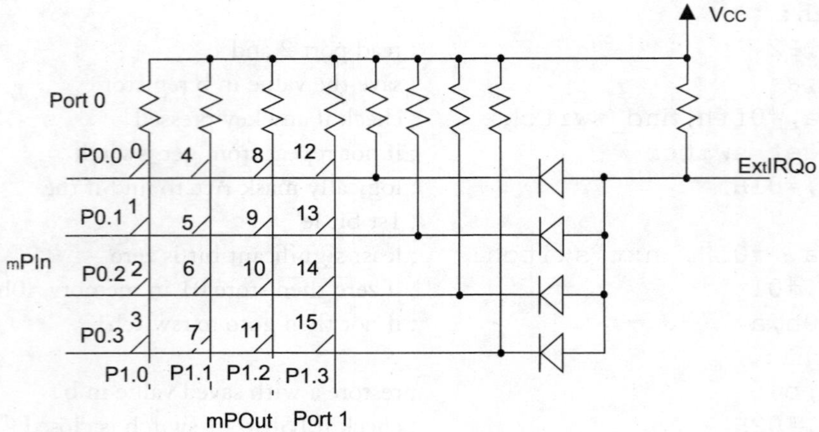

Fig. 5.9 *The 4 × 4 matrix keyboard*

Algorithm to check whether any key is pressed-

1. Set bits of Port P1 as Inputs
2. Make Port P0 outputs Low
3. Read Port P1
   If no key is pressed then the mPin bits are all high. [This is because the mPin pins are not connected to any of mPout pins (which are low) and so the mPin pins will be all at logic 1 or High]. Check if any bit is pressed. If mPin bits of Port 1 are all logic 1s then no key is pressed. Return back to caller routine or step 1 else step 5
4. Start a count position from P1.0 onwards.
5. Make column corresponding to column position Low
6. Read Port 0. Store in a register. Check if no pin is low and goto scan next column in step 11
7. Initialise bitposition counter to 0. Rotate Port 0 value. Read into carry
8. If carry is clear, increment bit position value else goto step 12
9. Goto 8
10. Add 4 column position. Goto 6
11. Add column position to bit position and store in keynum. The keynum value is returned with the numbers specified in Fig. 5.9.

```
start:    MOV a,#ffh
          MOV P1,a                 ; set port p1 as input
          MOV a,#0f0h              ; make 4 bits of mPout low
          MOV P0,a                 ; port P0 outputs P0.0 to P0.3 Low
press:    MOV a,P1                 ; read port 1
          ANL a, #0fh              ; mask those bits not connected to
                                   ; keyboard
          CJNE A, #0fh, press      ; check if any bit of P1.0 to P1.3
                                   ; are zero else
                                   ; keep checking
          MOV a,#01h               ; select column one at a time
                                   ; starting from P1.0
          CPL a                    ; make the corresponding bit low,
                                   ; others high
          MOV r4,a                 ; keep the Port 0 bits values in R4
          MOV r3,#00h              ; start counter keynum in R3
next:     MOV a,r4
          MOV P0,a                 ; make one column low at a time
                                   ; on Port 0 mPout
          MOV a,P1                 ; take input from port P1 mPin
          ANL a, # 0fh             ; mask unwanted bits of port P0—get
                                   ; only mPin
          CJNE a,# 0fh,colscan     ; after getting the row, jump to
                                   ; check column
          MOV a,r4
          CPL a
          RL a                     ; rotate left to check next column
          CPL a
          MOV r4,a
          MOV a,r3
          ADD a,#04h               ; increment counter keynum by 04
                                   ; so the next 4
                                   ; numbers are entered in R4
          MOV r3,a
          SJMP next                ; jump to check next row
colscan:  MOV r5,#00h              ; counter for bit position of input
                                   ; bit low initialised
in:       RRC a                    ; rotate right with carry until get
                                   ; the carry
          JC out                   ; carry tells that bit is out so
                                   ; stop rotate
```

```
          INC r5       ; increment bit position by one count
          JMP in       ; repeat till bit having one enters
                       ; the carry flag
out:      MOV a,r3     ; R3 contains the column weights
                       ; from 0,4,8,12 for
                       ; columns P1.0 to P1.3
          MOV b,r5     ; bit position is in R5 and
          ADD a,b      ; the sum of r3 and r5 gives the
                       ; number of the key
                       ; pressed. The numbers of the keys
                       ; are from 0 to 15
          MOV r3,a
          RET          ; return with key val in R3
```

5.4 Conversion and Interfacing of Different Data Types

Embedded systems need to be interfaced to a variety of sensors and actuators. These could be the ON/OFF type, meaning that they have only two representative states. Like a switch, an input device, which can be either ON or OFF; similarly, the LED lamp which can be lighted or not lighted. There are other situations where there are multiple states for an interface, like the thermistor which is a resistor whose value (resistance) varies with temperature. Such a device could be used for measuring temperature by reading the resistance value. This data is analog in nature and for an embedded system to understand it, it must be converted to digital values. Similarly if a LED lamp is to be lighted giving a varying light output, the digital value produced by a computation on the embedded system should be converted to an analog multistate value. This is called data conversion. Data conversion is very important because real life is not digital; it is analog. The final requirement of any application whose initiator and receptor is an entity of the real world has to relate at both ends to analog data. The digital part is the in-between process which helps in ease of computation and processing. To get the best of both the worlds, the embedded system should handle data conversions wherever necessary. This calls for analog-to-digital/digital-to-analog interconversion. The next section deals with these issues using devices currently available. The adc0808 is a 8-bit analog to digital converter having an 8-channel multiplexer. The digital-to-analog converter MC 1408 is discussed along with a program for generating a dual ramp.

5.4.1 Analog-to-Digital Convertor

We will discuss the ADC0809 as an example of an analog-to-digital converter(ADC). This device has many manufacturers though Analog Devices is the one which is the principal source. It is a 28 pin IC and works off a 5 V power supply. The ADC0809 is an 8-bit converter, meaning that it will take an analog input and convert it to an 8-bit digital value. The range of analog input it can take is set by an input called the reference voltage V_{ref}. The least non-zero analog value which can be converted to a digital value is given by the expression

$$V_{lowest\_value} = (V_{ref} / 256) \times V_{ref}$$

If a V_{ref} of 5 V is applied, then the highest digital value for 8-bit is 11111111b or 0ffh or 255d in binary, hexadecimal and decimal respectively. The lowest value is about 19 mV computed using the expression given above for V_{lowest_value}. This device, if given a 5V reference will digitize inputs from 0V to 5V in 256 steps. The steps are 0V results in 00000000B(0V), 19mV results 00000001B and so on till 4.89 V which gives11111111B(255D).

The ADCs are usually expensive and when they are calibrated they should not be physically disturbed because it causes loss of linearity and calibration. This makes adding more analog channels difficult to make. The device has a multiplexor which permits more than one channel to be used for conversion. There are 8 channels provided here by the multiplexor sharing only one ADC. The 8 channels are selected by three digital inputs. The ADC has to be given a trigger called Start Cconversion. Start conversion starts the process of taking the analog value presented at the ADC input and converting it to digital value. The ADC0809 is an 8-bit successive approximation converter—which means it will take 8 clocks to convert the analog input to a digital 8-bit value. The ADC presents a signal called End of Conversion signal after the conversion is over. A clock signal is provided which is typically 1 Megahertz. If 8 clocks are needed for conversion and each clock time period is 1 microsecond then the conversion time is 8 microseconds. The 8-bit converted output is presented at 8 signal pins called the data pins. These data pins are tri-stateable and they present an output if the Output Enable(OE) pin is asserted. The ADC0809 circuit diagram with the pins is presented in Fig. 5.10. The 8-bit data is available on pins marked D0 to D7. These pins output data if the Output Enable pin is made high. The START is the Start Conversion pin and a short pulse there starts the conversion. The signal that the data is converted is issued as the End Of Conversion signal EOC. The ALE (Address Latch Enable) signal when asserted will make the multiplexor select input from one of 8 inputs marked as IN0,IN1,...IN7 depending on the code present at B0,B1,B2. If B0,B1,B2 had code 111B, then on ALE being asserted, the channel input IN7 is selected as input to the ADC by the multiplexor. The V_{ref} voltage is applied to REF+ and the REF– is connected to the 0 V line. The clock is given at CLK pin.

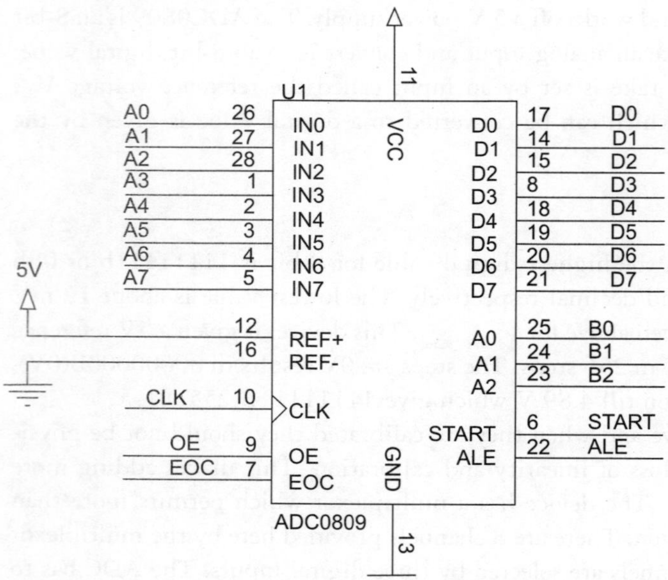

Fig. 5.10 *The analog-to-digital converter ADC0809 which has eight input channels.*

The following program demonstrates how to read data from the analog–digital convertor, shown in Fig. 5.10, to the microcontroller unit. In this the output will be shown in Port 1 as a binary value.

```
; P0.0 = A0 P0.1 = A1 P0.2 = A2
; P3.2 = EOC
; P3.3 = START
; P3.6 = ALE
; P3.7 = OE
DATA = PORT 2
          MOV P0,#00H
          MOV P1,#0FFH
          MOV P2,#00H
          MOV P3,#04H

MAIN:

          SETB P2.0
          SETB P2.1
          LCALL DELAY
          CLR P2.0
          CLR P2.1
```

```
            LCALL DELAY1
            LJMP MAIN
DELAY:
            CLR P3.7 ;OE
            CLR P0.0 ;A2
            CLR P0.1 ;A1
            CLR P0.2 ;A0
            CLR P3.6 ;ALE
            SETB P3.6 ;ALE
            SETB P3.3 ;START
            CLR P3.3;START
HERE:       JB P3.2,HERE                ; wait for end of conversion
            SETB P3.7 ;0E
            MOV r7,P1                   ; read the data
            uB2: mov r6, #3Fh
            uB1: mov r5, #5Fh
            djnz r5, $
            djnz r6, uB1
            djnz r7, uB2
            ret
DELAY1:
            CLR P3.7 ;OE
            SETB P0.0 ;A0
            CLR P0.1 ;A1
            CLR P0.2 ;A2
            CLR P3.6 ;ALE
            SETB P3.6 ;ALE
            SETB P3.3 ;START
            CLR P3.3 ;START
HERE1:      JB P3.2,HERE1               ; wait for end of conversion
            SETB P3.7 ;0E
            mov r7, P1
            uB4: mov r6, #3Fh
            uB3: mov r5, #5Fh
            djnz r5, $
            djnz r6, uB3
            djnz r7, uB4
            ret
            END
```

5.4.2 Digital-to-Analog Convertor

The digital-to-analog convertor is shown in Fig. 5.11. In this figure the parts labelled DAC0808 and MC1408 are 8-bit multiplying D/A converters from Analog Devices and Motorola, respectively. They provide high-speed performance at low cost.

The digital to analog convertor is designed for use where the output current is a linear product of an 8-bit digital word and an analog reference voltage. The output provided by the digital to analog converter is a current.

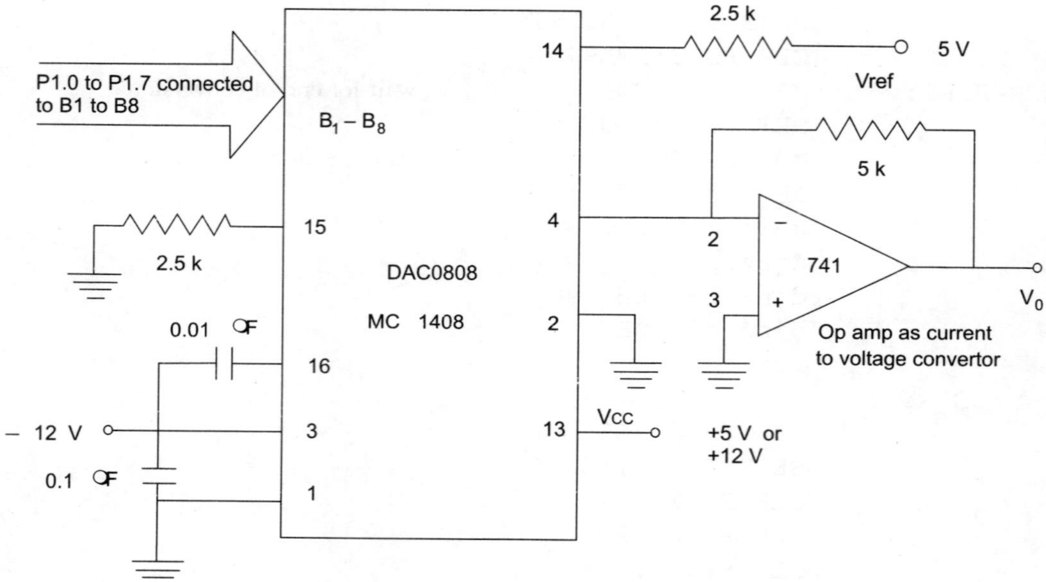

Fig. 5.11 *The digital-to-analog converter DAC0808 /MC1408*

The features of these DA converters are as follows:

- Fast settling time: 70 ns (typically)
- Relatively high accuracy: ±0.19% (maximum error)
- TTL- and CMOS-compatible non-inverting digital inputs
- High-speed multiplying rate: 4.0 mA per second (input slew)
- Output voltage swing: +0.5 V to –5.0 V
- Standard supply voltages: +5.0 V and –5.0 V to –15 V

The output of these converters is current which is proportional to the product of the digital value input to the data pins B1–B8 and the reference voltage applied at Pin 14.

The points of data input for the DAC are pins B1–B8, and they are connected to the Port 1 bits P1.0–P1.7, in that order. The output from Pin 4 is a current, and this is converted to voltage by the current-to-voltage converter using an op-amp IC 741. The reference voltage applied at Pin 14 through 2.5 kilo ohm resistor flows out through the Pin 15 via another 2.5 kilo ohm resistor to the ground. The current which is now flowing is given by 5V/(2.5K+2.5K), which is 1 mA. For a binary input of zero, the output current through Pin 4 is a product of the (reference current/255) and the binary value applied to the inputs. Thus, for a binary input of 0 (0B), the output current through Pin 4 of DAC is 0 and for a binary value of 255 (FFh) it is 1 mA. The 741 op-amp is configured as a current-to-voltage converter. It takes inputs through its Pin 2 and multiplies it with the value of the resistor of value 5 kilo ohms. The output voltage is in the range of 0–5 V.

Given below is a program (DACOUT) which writes a byte passed to it through register ACC to the DAC port. It is a subroutine and is followed by the main program which reads data from a look-up table (LUT) and passes the data to the DACOUT subroutine.

```
DACOUT:                 ; the name of the subroutine
MOV P1, ACC             ; write the contents passed through ACC to P1
PUSH R5                 ; save R5 as it will be used for delay
MOV R5,#0FFH            ; initialize the delay value in R5
DJNZ R5, DACOUT1        ; decrement till the R5 value is 0
RET                     ; this delay may be used to vary the timeperiod
                        ; of the output.

Main:
      ORG 0000H         ; start assembly from reset vector
LJMP START
      ORG 0040H         ; choose ROM location above the reset vector
MOV DPTR, LUT           ; point the data pointer to the Look-Up
                        ; Table base address
MOV R2, # 0 FH          ; initialise counter for 15 values to read
MOV ACC,# 00
Main1:
MOV ACC, @(ACC+DPTR)
CALL DACOUT
INC DPTR
INC R2
DJNZ R2, MAIN1
JMP MAIN
LUT:   DB   00, 10, 20, 30, 40, 50, 60, 70, 80, 70, 60, 50, 40, 30, 20, 10
END
```

The main program will read 16 bytes from the LUT and pass these values to DACOUT using ACC. Here, R2 is used for the size of the look-up table and can be the maximum value which R2 can contain, that is, 255. In this example, R2 has 0FH as its contents, meaning that 16 bytes will be read (R2 varies from 15 to 0 which is 16 times). The output voltage increments in steps of 19.6 mV, as Table 5.1 will clarify:

Table 5.1 *Input–Output table*

Serial Number	Input value	Output Voltage	
0	0	0 V	0 × (5/255)
1	10	0.196 V	10 × (5/255)
2	20	0.392 V	20 × (5/255)
3	30	0.588 V	30 × (5/255)
4	40	0.784 V	40 × (5/255)
5	50	0.980 V	50 × (5/255)
6	60	1.176 V	60 × (5/255)
7	70	1.372 V	70 × (5/255)
8	80	1.764 V	90 × (5/255)
9	70	1.372 V	80 × (5/255)
10	60	1.176 V	60 × (5/255)
11	50	0.980 V	50 × (5/255)
12	40	0.784 V	40 × (5/255)
13	30	0.588 V	30 × (5/255)
14	20	0.392 V	20 × (5/255)
15	10	0.196 V	10 × (5/255)

The values presented are decimal, which is why the 80 decimal input (50H) has produced 1.764 V output. A 128-decimal input (80H) would have produced 2.509 V which is half of the maximum output voltage of 5 V.

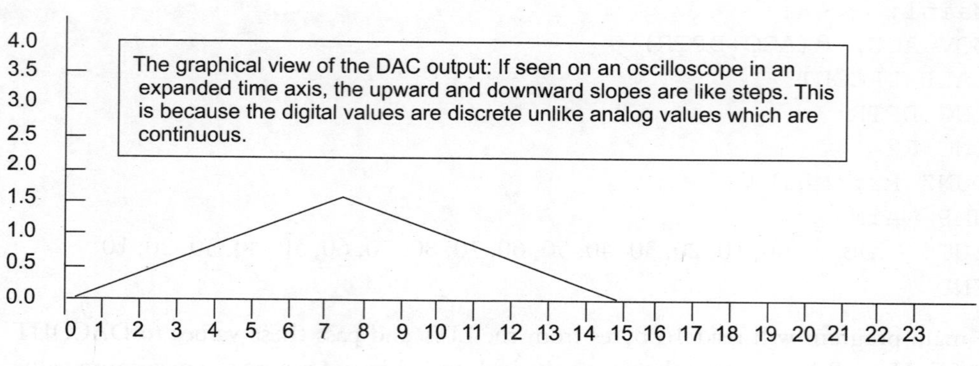

5.5 Multiple Interrupts

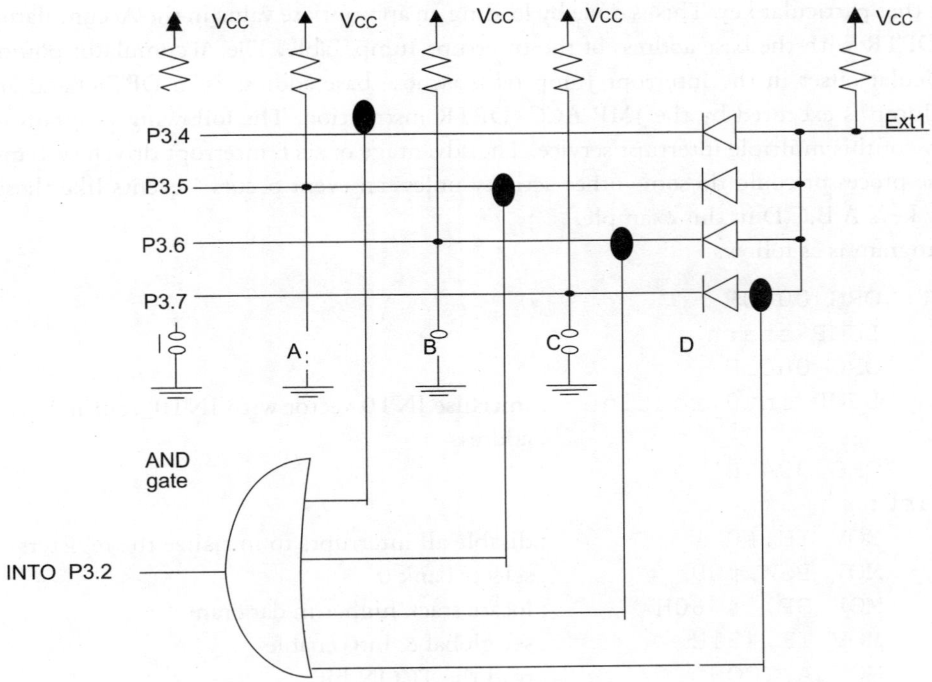

Fig. 5.12 *The multiple interrupts generated by switches*

The similarity between Fig 5.8 and Fig 5.12 is striking. The only difference is that in Fig 5.12 an AND gate is connected to the pulled-up ends of the keys. The keys labelled A, B, C and D are similar to the keys on the keyboard representing UP, DOWN, LEFT and RIGHT keys. These keys when pressed will present a **low** on the line they are connected. If no key is pressed, the lines connected to ports starting from Port 3.4 to Port 3.7 will be at logic **high** (5 V). As these lines are also connected to the 4-input AND gate, these inputs to the AND gate will also be high. Thus the output of the AND gate will be high. The AND gate output is connected to Port 3.2 which is the INT0 pin of the 8051. The INT0 pin is sensitive to a **low** (0 V) level or a negative edge (high-to-low transition) as chosen by the programmer while programming the interrupt registers.

When any key is pressed, the corresponding port pin goes low, and at the same time the AND gate output goes low. If the INT0 and the Enable All are selected in the Interrupt Enable register, then the INT0 interrupt is initiated. The current program execution is paused and the interrupt vector address is loaded into the PC and the interrupt execution starts. The Interrupt Service routine is now responsible for finding out which of these keys have caused the interrupt. This routine now reads the Port 3 and masks off the four lower bits. The four upper bits are tested from P3.4 to P3.7 to see which of them is low. Depending on which of them is low, the Interrupt Service routine executes that particular routine which is supposed to service that particular key. This is done by loading an appropriate value in the Accumulator and the DPTR with the base address of the Interrupt Jump Table. The Accumulator points to a particular offset in the Interrupt Jump table (whose base address is in DPTR) and an Indirect Jump is executed by the JMP ACC+DPTR instruction. The following program is illustrative of this multiple interrupt service. The advantage of such interrupt driven systems is that the processor could do some other activity unless an event occurs—events like those caused by keys A,B,C,D in this example.

The program is as follows:

```
        ORG 0000H
        LJMP start
        ORG 0003H
        LJMP int0_routine      ; initialise INT0 vector with INT0_routines
                               ; address
        ORG 0040H
    Start:
        MOV IE,#0              ; disable all interrupts to initialize the registers
        MOV PSW,#00            ; selectt bank 0
        MOV SP, # 60H          ; locate stack higher in data ram
        MOV IE,#81H            ; set global & int0 enable
        MOV A,TCON             ; read the TCON bit
        ORL A, #01H            ; set the bit corresponding to IT0 in A
        MOV TCON, A            ; The IT0 is now edge triggered
    infinite_loop:
        JMP infinite_loop      ; do nothing else. The main program in an
                               ; embedded system should not terminate and so
                               ; it is to be brought to an infinite loop when the
                               ; main program is over. In this example, the
                               ; program is purely interrupt driven and so the
                               ; main program is meant to initialise the PSW,
                               ; IE, SP, TCON
    Int0_routine:
        MOV DPTR, # int0_jump_table
                               ; DPTR points to the base of the jump table
                               ; where the addresses of the four routines to be
                               ; called are located sequentially
        MOV A,P3               ; read Port 3 to find out which switch caused
                               ; interrupt
        ANL A, 0F0H            ; only interested in upper 4 bits of P3 so mask
                               ; off the lower 4 bits
```

```
        RL A                    ; check if P3.7 is 0 as this bit will now enter the
        JC nxt1                 ; if carry not clear then test the P3.6 bit
        MOV A,#00               ; if P3.7 is clear then load offset of the routine to
                                ; be called in A
        SJMP done               ; go and make the indirect jump
nxt1:
        RL A                    ; check if P3.6 is 0 as this bit will now enter the
        JNC nxt2                ; if carry not clear then test the P3.6 bit
        MOV A,# 02              ; if P3.7 is clear then load offset of the routine to
                                ; be called in A
        JMP done                ; go and make the indirect jump
nxt2:                           ; now do the same for P3.5
        RL A
        JNC nxt3
        MOV A, #04
        SJMP done
nxt3:                           ; now do the same for P3.5
        RL A
        JNC nxt3
        MOV A, #04
done:
        JMP @A+DPTR             ; the indirect jump effective address is
                                ; EA= A+DPTR
int0_jump_table:
        dw  key_A_routine       ; the 16-bit address for A switches routine
        dw  key_B_routine       ; the 16-bit address for B switches routine
        dw  key_C_routine       ; the 16-bit address for C switches routine
        dw  key_D_routine       ; the 16-bit address for D switches routine
                                ; key_D_routine:
                                ; save the register used in this routine put the
                                ; body of the routine the entire job in this
                                ; routine should not take too long
        RETI                    ; return from the interrupt
```

Summary

At this stage, the reader would be familiar with the various interfaces which are used in development of embedded systems. Though the interfaces list is endless those interfaces discussed in this chapter could be used by a creative reader for a large variety of applications. The interfaces discussed were the LED lamp used as a prompt/indicator lamp, the LED seven-segment display for displaying numbers as a single digit or as group of digits. Groups of digit are directly interfaced or multiplexed. The message displays text messages using LCD modules. The LCD module is by itself a dedicated embedded system having its own microcontroller. It has its own command set stating how it could be used for interfacing to a microcontroller and how after interfacing it can be programmed using an 8- bit or 4-bit data interface.

Keyboard interfaces have the keys directly connected to the microcontroller in the form of a matrix of keys. The programming for the keyboard matrix involves giving the key pressed as a number. Such keyboards are used very commonly in embedded systems. The reader would probably be reminded of the telephone keyboard as used in digital telephones or cellphones.

Since the final requirement of any application whose initiator and receptor is an entity of the real world has to relate at both ends to analog data., data conversion is an important task of embedded systems.

The keyboard back is again discussed, this time as an interrupt application. The differences between the earlier keyboard application and the current keyboard application is that the current application gets triggered by an activity on the keyboard and the CPU is not stuck with reading the keyboard even when there is no key pressed.

Self Evaluation Questions

1. List out the type of LEDs used as lamps and displays.?

2a. Design LED prompt lights connected to Port bit P0.0 as sinking and to Port P2.0 as sourcing. The red LED should be connected to P@.0 and green one to P0.0. The current through the LED is to be kept at 5 mA. The LEDs are 5 mm size. The red LED voltage drop is 1.6V and the green LED is 2.0V. Design the interface and the necessary components with their values. Draw a circuit diagram for the LED connection to the port bits.

b. Write a program to light up (ON) the red lamp for a short period of d msecs and OFF for a period 2d msecs. The green LED should be OFF when RED is ON and the red should be OFF when green is ON.

3. Explain how the LCD module is interfaced and discuss the connection signals clearly.

4. Write a program to display a multi-line message on a two-line LCD module?. The top line of the LCD module has to display the title and the second line, line by line messages with a delay of about a second between each message.

5. Make an application where 8 LED lamps are connected to a port and eight switches are connected to another port. Pressing the left-most key lights up one LED. The next key to its right lights up two LEDs and so on till the right-most key on being pressed will light up all eight LED lamps.

6. Describe the various commands used for programming the LCD module. Why are there only two registers available in the LCD module?

7. Interface a 4 × 4 keyboard to ports P2 and P3. Display the keyboard number pressed as a hexadecimal number on 4 LED lamps connected to port 0. Port 0 to be used as sink.

8. Interface a 16 character by 2 line LCD module and a 4 × 4 keyboard to ports of a microcontroller. Write a program to display as a word the key pressed on the keyboard. [Hint: If key number 0 is pressed, the display should be 'ZERO' and so on.]

9. What is the need for data conversion and what are the types of data converters used in embedded systems.How are the bit resolution and voltages related?

10. Explain the the signal pins of the ADC0808.

11. Write a program to read the 8 channels of an ADC0809 and display the same sequential on the LCD module as " Ch. No. XXX"

12. What is the reverse of ADC and how does it work? Explain with the pin functions of this device.

13. Write a program to output a sine wave using the DAC . [Hint: Generate a sine table with radians and the sine of the radians. Use the calculator in MS Windows.]

14. Discuss an application where an embedded system is made which outputs a signal function chosen from the keyboard and the output lights a LED. The ADC checks whether the output is present or not. Draw the block diagram also and the description of the operation. [Hint: No need of a circuit diagram or a program. An algorithmic approach will help a lot.]

15. Discuss why interrupt driven programs are needed. Design a system which calls programs when specific keys are pressed.Write the program and draw the circuit diagram.

6 Real-Time Operating Systems

As will be made clear in this chapter, the term 'real time operating system' (RTOS) is commonly used to refer to a tool which when used for developing an application will create an operating system which has real time response. The application is executed as tasks created for the operating system.

Since the tasks are executed just like the processes in any desktop operating system (UNIX, WINDOWS, LINUX), similar issues like task management, dynamic memory allocation, inter-task communications and synchronisation, timers and device input/output and interrupt routines need to be dealt with. In this context, interrupts are exceptions and gain more importance in RTOS.

Readers familiar with operating systems would find this chapter a quick, readable one. Those who are new to OS will also find it to be a smooth reading—in case they need any further clarifications they could contact the author or refer to a textbook on OS.

6.1 Real-Time Processing

A real-time operating system (RTOS) is one that is not monolithic like other operating systems used in general-purpose or desktop computers such as UNIX, WINDOWS and the like. As a result it is smaller in size with respect to the memory it occupies. This is commonly referred to by the term "small footprint." Further, an RTOS system has to deal with multiple inputs that occur without any correlation in time or where there is no reference time (such inputs are termed asynchronous) and have to be serviced on an "as it happens" basis. That is, on the occurrence of the event, the RTOS has to take immediate action to service it. If the RTOS fails to service this event, a functional failure of the entire system could occur. Such a manner of processing events is called real-time processing.

The RTOS is commonly addressed as aartoss. The developer of the embedded system opts to use the RTOS for several reasons, as was explained in Chapter 1. It is used just like any other integrated development environment (IDE). The development of embedded applications is better managed if the application is divided into many tasks which are executed under the control of an operating system which can respond to real-time events. Therefore the application software is developed using an RTOS development environment. This application when executed will result in an operating system environment which has a real time response capability and runs the hardware by executing individual tasks. The figure given below indicates how the application software is on top of the execution cycle. In the execution process, it creates a single-user multitasking real time response operating system (RTOS). This RTOS then works on the hardware executing the application.

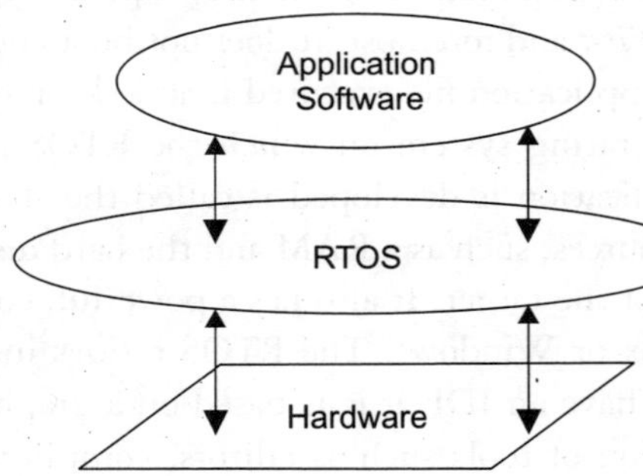

6.2 What is a Real-Time Operating System?

A real-time operating system (or RTOS, as they will be referred to, from now onwards) is a single-user (in embedded systems which are mostly dedicated to specific applications, the 'single user' here means single application) multitasking system. It is generally used for embedded systems, and within this set, most often for real-time applications; however, it may also be used in general-purpose stand-alone applications such as cash registers, automatic teller machines and so on, where the need for a real-time approach is not so pronounced. Typical applications of the RTOS are in mobile telephones; domestic and industrial robots; aero-space applications; supervisory control and data acquisition (SCADA) applications in electricity providers and process control industry; equipment used in scientific and industrial research; household appliances such as washing machines, microwave ovens, automotives; telecommunications; switching equipment; mobile phones; computer networks, in routers, DHCP servers; medical equipment required for computer-aided tomography (CAT), magnetic resonance imaging (MRI) scanners and a host of other applications.

The design of an embedded system is be done considering the tasks which have to be executed concurrently. The concurrency we talk about here is the apparent one experienced by the users. In reality there can be no concurrency as only a single processor is used and it can only execute one task at one time. But if the tasks are executed one after the other in a time-shared manner they will appear to the user as happening concurrently. This happens provided the time-sharing is done quickly and is unnoticeable by the user. Just like the frame in a movie are separate but are presented so quickly that the discreteness is not noticed by the user. This approach speeds up the development time; however, this requires the application to be decomposed into modules that are small, schedulable and form sequential program units. These program units are called tasks.

Software architecture which is more complex than a general-pupose, non-embedded non-real-time operating system is needed. Similarly, greater care is needed to handle multiple tasks; coordination and communication between tasks; and interrupt handling for asynchronous events.

Coming to the RTOS itself, it differs from desktop operating systems like UNIX and WINDOWS in many ways. *First* and foremost, it does not boot and run the application. The RTOS is just a file, like any application file executed in a desktop operating system. One has to choose beforehand the operating system on which the RTOS is to be used. The system on which the embedded application is developed is called the "host." The host system is a computer with abundant resources, such as a RAM and the hard disc; it contains all the tools needed for the development of the target. It also has a powerful, completely featured operating system like UNIX, Linux or Windows. The RTOS resides in such a host system as an application program. It may have an IDE if it is based on a graphical user interface (GUI). The IDE will have a collection of tools such as editors, compilers, assemblers, simulators, debuggers, conversion tools, downloading tools and so on.

The embedded system application is developed using an HLL compiler present in the RTOS. The code written for the application will declare one or more program modules as needed by the application. The RTOS will use the compiler to compile each program module, and then it will create a kernel as process zero (process 0). This kernel will create processes for each of the modules of the source program. The resulting application code is now saved as a file, adding the necessary startup code for its execution from boot up in the target system. This file is called the application boot image.

The *second* difference between an embedded system using the RTOS and the desktop operating system is that in DTOS, the OS runs the applications, whereas in the embedded system developed using RTOS, the application runs the OS. For example, the boot image created by the RTOS is now downloaded into the target system such that whenever the target system boots, it executes the application in the boot image. The boot image then starts execution, loads the kernel and transfers control to the kernel. The kernel will now load the code of the processes and start executing them as developed using the RTOS. These processes will be executed in a specified order (with the default being "round robin") and task (proces) priority.

The *third* point is that the RTOS does not create a fully loaded operating system. The OS created by the RTOS is optimized from the point of memory usage; execution speeds and latencies in response to events. An RTOS does provide as many features as possible but during application development, the choice is made on what features to add to the resultant target OS, as needed by the applications.

Two kinds of RTOS design are common. These differ in the way the system allocates priorities to the tasks that are lined up.

1. One way is to perform a function until a switch has to be made because a task with a higher priority requests a service. This is called pre-emptive prioritising.
2. In the other approach, called round robin, tasks are switched based on a prompt from a clock pulse or the demands of some event. All tasks have the same priority.

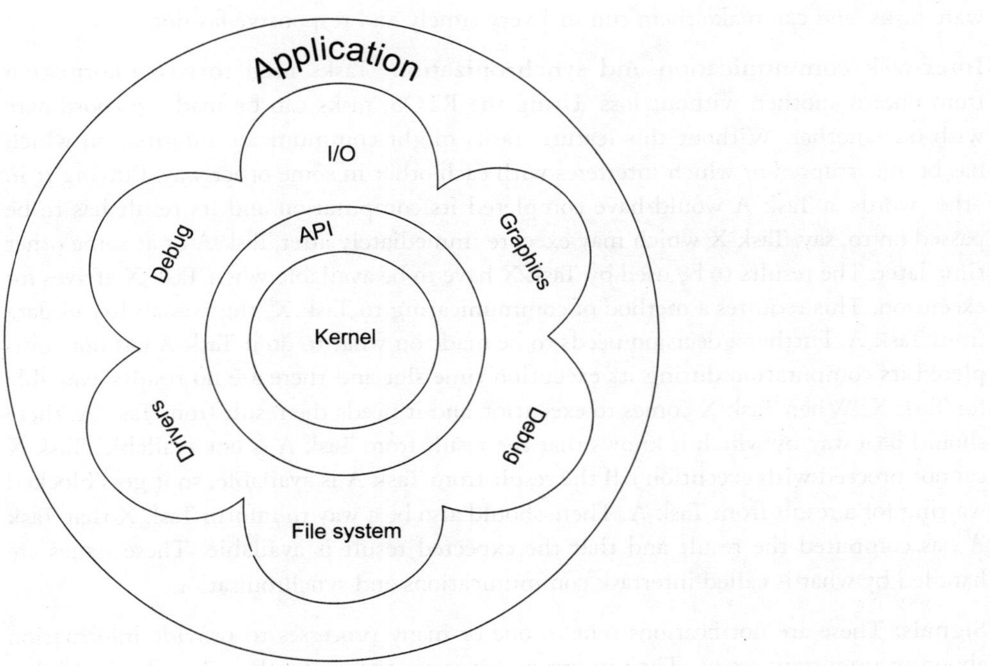

Fig. 6.1 *An embedded real-time operation system working in the "kernel" mode*

The construction of an RTOS in the "kernel" mode can be represented as in Fig. 6.1. Note that this is not a real map or in other words, a photographic replica of an RTOS. It is only a representation of how RTOS works. The "kernel" of an RTOS is so-called because like a masked core, it contains an "abstraction layer" that conceals from the application software the hardware details of the processor (or set of processors) upon which the application software will run.

6.3 The Mode of Operation of an RTOS

The RTOS kernel provides five main categories of basic service to application software. These are shown schematically in Fig. 6.2. To explicitly list them out:

1. **Task management:** It permits the application software developer to design the software as a number of separate modules, each handling a distinct "task," or service, with a real-time deadline. This is aided by its ability to launch tasks and set priorities to them.

   The main RTOS service in this category is the scheduling of tasks when the embedded system is in operation. The task-scheduler controls the execution of the application software tasks, and can make them run in a very timely and responsive fashion.

2. **Inter-task communication and synchronization:** Tasks need to pass information from one to another, without loss. Using the RTOS, tasks can be made to coordinate with one another. Without this feature, tasks might communicate information which has been corrupted or which interferes with each other in some other way. Putting it in other words, a Task A would have completed its computation and its result has to be passed on to, say, Task X which may execute immediately after Task A or at some other time later. The results to be used by Task X have to be available when Task X arrives for execution. This requires a method of communicating to Task X, the availability of data from Task A. Further a decision needs to be made on what to do if Task A has not completed its computation during its execution time slot and there are no results available for Task X. When Task X comes to execution and it needs the result from Task A, there should be a way by which it knows that the result from Task A is not available. Task X cannot proceed with execution till the result from Task A is available, so it gets blocked waiting for a result from Task A. There should also be a way to inform Task X that Task A has computed the result and that the expected result is available. These issues are handled by what is called intertask communications and synchronisation.

3. **Signals:** These are notifications sent to one or many processes to provide information about an important event. They interrupt processes and make them handle the higher priority event. In fact, they are like software interrupts.
   Signals are represented by an integer and a label as well. Each signal usually has a signal handler which is activated as soon as a signal is received—they are in synchronous mode and are usually defined using /usr/include/signal.h. In certain operating systems like Linux, "kill –1" lists the signals available.
   Signals can be sent to processes from the keyboard. Certain key/s are assigned for this purpose:
   `<ctrl><c>`: sends an *INT* signal to immediately terminate the process. This signal function is labelled as "sigint"
   `<ctrl><z>`: sends a *TSTP* signal to suspend execution of the process. This signal function is labelled as "sigtstp"
   `<ctrl><\>`: sends an *ABRT* signal to immediately terminate. This signal function is labelled as "sigabrt"

INT is more flexible than *ABRT*

Signals can be sent to processes from the command line too. The "kill" command accepts 2 parameters:

```
kill <signal> <pid>
```

If process 3421 is to be sent an *INT* signal then

```
kill - INT 3421
```

This has the effect of a <ctrl><c> in the shell that runs this process.

```
kill 3421
```

just kills the process.

Signals can be sent to processes from within other processes. The following shows the function call, its definitions, directories and usage from within a process:

```
# include <unistd.h>
/* std unix functions like getpid() */
# include <sys/types.h>
/* type definitions like pid_t */
# include <signal.h>
/* signal name macros and the kill() prototype*/
pid_t my_pid=getpid();
kill (my_pid,sigstop);
```

There are two types of signals—catchable and non-catchable. Catchability is the ability of a process to receive a signal and take action. Kill() is not catchable—it is usually used if a "not responding process" is to be terminated. System shutdown uses this function only after first sending a *TERM* signal. After a grace period, it *kills* those which did not terminate on their own.

A process which suspended itself will continue after receiving the *CONT* signal. *STOP* and *CONT* are catchable signals whose function call labels are sigstop and sigcont.

Default signal handlers are set up by the run time environment. The default handler for *TERM* is the exit() system call while that for *ABRT* it is the abort() system call which causes a memory image of the process to be dumped in a file called "core"— this is the famous "core dump".

The user can install signal handlers by a signal() system call whose prototype is

```
Int signal(SIGINT , *catchsignal)
```

4. **Timers:** Time-outs and delays are commonly required in any application program, and they also need to be taken care of in embedded systems. This is done through the timer functions provided by the RTOSes. To give a simple example, the RTOS can ensure, because it has a timer-like function, that the LCD display of a cell phone switches off after a user-defined interval.

   Timers also provide checks or alarms after a pre-determined time. They use the `exit.Alarm()` system call to send a signal *ALRM* after a given number of seconds.

`alarm()` along with some signals provides functions like `alarm(0)` which clears previous alarms if any and `sleep(int sec)` which suspends the process for a few seconds.

5. **Memory allocation:** Memory allocation in a single process application is simple. In fact, a large chunk of memory is left in the OS after the single process and therefore such applications do not need an OS. On the other hand, multiple process single/multi user systems do need proper memory allocation. One of the most important issues to keep in mind is that processes should not gobble each other's memory areas or trespass from their allocated locations–this is called protected mode. Further, executing more than one process implies that a proper distribution of available memory has to be done. Much greater care has to be taken to efficiently allocate memory in an RTOS. Embedded systems usually have optimized resources and memory should be judiciously used and more importantly, optimally allocated. If an RTOS has a 16-task capability, it could allocate the available memory equally to the 16 tasks. It may also happen that the application needs only two functional tasks at a particular moment. In such a case, the allotted 14 memory locations would be unused and so the memory is under-managed. When this condition occurs, the memory available should be shared by the currently active tasks, helping the tasks to execute faster. This is *memory management*.

   Memory partitioning is used where the memory is to be partitioned equally between the processes. It features contiguous memory assignments. The disadvantage is that some processes may need more memory than that assigned to it and others may not need that much. Variable memory partitioning is used to overcome the above disadvantage. However, there may be small blocks of unused memory, making it non-contiguous.

   Demand paging is used when processes can be placed in small equal partitions. The process executes the code in the normal fashion till the last instruction on the page copied onto the memory partition. The next page of the executable code is then copied to the allocated memory location and the execution continues.

   There are many more memory management techniques, but most of them are variants of what has been mentioned here.

6. **Handling interrupts:** When one hears of interrupts and their handling, the first thing that we think of is hardware interrupts which are caused by external events. Next is software interrupts which behave like hardware interrupts but to programs. They activate programs by associating with a number. Then there are exceptions which also act as interrupts. They are events occurring inside the computer caused by a runaway process or a badly executed instruction and so on. These are called system exceptions or simply *exceptions*. All these have one thing in common and that is they interrupt the normal flow of execution demanding some sort of service or *handling*.

   Handling interrupts is simple in an RTOS as compared to a general-purpose OS and will be explained further in Section 6.10.

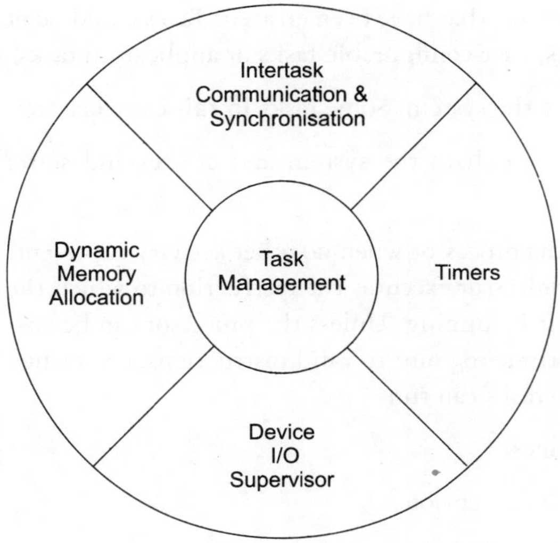

Fig. 6.2 *The services offered by the RTOS – an RTOS architecture*

6.4 Differences Between a Desktop OS and an RTOS

Desktop OS and RTOS differ in the manner that they are isolated from applications. A desktop OS is in control at all times, and it runs other applications. That is, the OS runs in a different address space. Whereas in an RTOS, the OS and its embedded software are integrated. The ES (embedded system) starts and activates the OS, and both run in the same address space. The RTOS is less protected.

It must be noted that the RTOS includes only the service routines needed by the embedded software application and so it is highly optimized.

Some vendors of RTOS are the following: VsWorks; VTRX; Nucleus; LynxOS; uCOS. Most of these conform to IEEE standards for OS interfaces, known as POSIX.

In comparison, RTOS is seen to have significant advantages. It uses less memory, offers an application programming interface and provides debugging tools and support for a variety of microprocessors. It contains network drivers that have been debugged beforehand.

6.5 More about Tasks and Task States

Tasks are simple subroutines that do not have a return statement. These are also the building blocks of an RTOS. An application is developed using one or more tasks. A task object is defined and maintained by its distinct set of parameters and supporting data structures such as an associated name, a unique ID, a priority, a task-control block (TCB), a stack and the task routine. The TCB has the details of all the tasks that have been created. Tasks could be of various types, such as system tasks, kernel tasks, user-configurable tasks or application tasks.

1. **System tasks:** These are tasks that involve the system. Some tasks in this category are:
   - **Initialization or startup** This task initializes the system and creates and starts system tasks.
   - **Idle** This task uses up idle cycles of the processor when no other activity is present. The idle task is necessary because the processor executes the instruction to which the program counter register points while it is running. Unless the processor can be suspended, the program counter must continue to point to valid instructions, even when no tasks exist in the system or when no tasks can run.
   - **Logging** This task logs system messages.
   - **Exception handling** This task handles exceptions.
   - **Debug agent** This is a task that allows debugging with a host debugger.
2. **Kernel tasks:** The priorities of system tasks is assigned by the kernel from reserved priority levels. These priorities are used internally by the RTOS for its system tasks.
3. **User-configured tasks:** Examples of these are user-configured routines to replace the idle task, to be more specific, a routine for power conservation. After a period of idle time, the system is instructed to suspend activity to conserve power.

   Another example is a routine of initiation of application tasks. After the kernel has initialized and created all of the required tasks, it jumps to a predefined entry point (such as a predefined function) that serves, in effect, as the beginning of the application.

At any time, each task (system and application) exists in one of a small number of states. These can be ready, running or blocked. Different designs of RTOS may have different states defined. Generally, the three main states already mentioned are used in typical preemptive-scheduling kernels, and these are:

- The ready state, in which the task is ready to run, but cannot do so because a task having a higher priority is being executed.
- The blocked state, in which the task has requested a resource that is not available, has been requested to wait until some event occurs, or has delayed itself for some duration.
- The running state, in which the task has the highest priority level and is running.

As the real-time embedded system runs, each task moves from one state to another, according to the logic of a simple finite state machine (FSM) (Fig. 6.3).

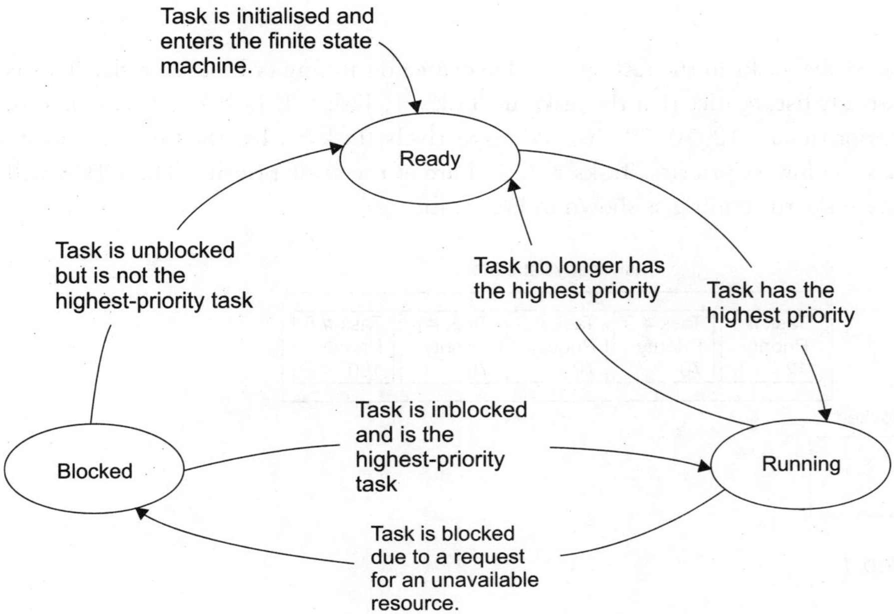

Fig. 6.3 *Tasks and how they change their states*

During this process, the kernel maintains a table with a list of the current states of all tasks running in a system. This is called a task-ready list, and contains all the ready tasks. A scheduler picks up the next task to go for execution from this list.

To understand how these concepts work, let us take an example of how the RTOS deals with the execution of a set of five tasks. How the tasks are prioritized and executed in a smooth sequence is illustrated. The following assumptions are made in the example.

- A priority-based pre-emptive scheduling algorithm is used.
- The lowest priority level is 255 and 0 is the highest.
- For the sake of simplicity, system tasks such as the idle task are not shown.

Figures 6.4a–e show some possible states of the five tasks. These tasks have TID (task identification) as Task # x with a task priority of 0 to 255. 0 is considered the highest priority and the lowest priority is 255. The tasks waiting for execution or running state are arranged as a list in the task queue which is shown as the long rectangular box at the right. The task which is brought into execution or running state is shown in the box on the left side in line with the task queue. The box shown in the line below these two boxes is the one where the blocked tasks are kept till they unblock and go to either the running state or to the task queue.

STEP I

Figure 6.4a shows five tasks in the task queue. There are no running or blocked tasks. This is called the task ready list. Notice that the tasks are Task # 1, Task # 2, Task # 3, Task # 4, Task # 5 and their priorities are 12, 70, 70, 70, 100 respectively. Task # 1 has the highest priority and task #5 has the lowest priority. Tasks # 2, 3, 4 are of the same priority. The RTOS will now bring these tasks to running as shown in Fig. 6.4b.

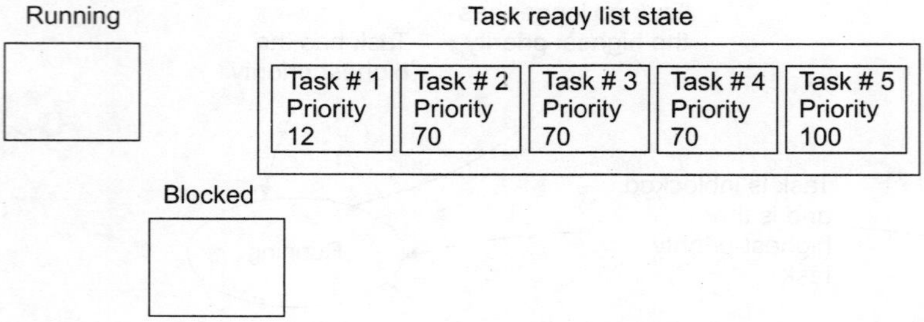

Fig 6.4a *Step 1*

STEP II

The priorities indicated in Fig. 6.4a make it clear that Task 1 has the highest priority level among the tasks in the task queue, that is, 12. Thus, it is ensured that Task 1 will go to execution if no other task of higher than 12 priority is running. There are no tasks running, so Task # 1 is the one which goes to running state.

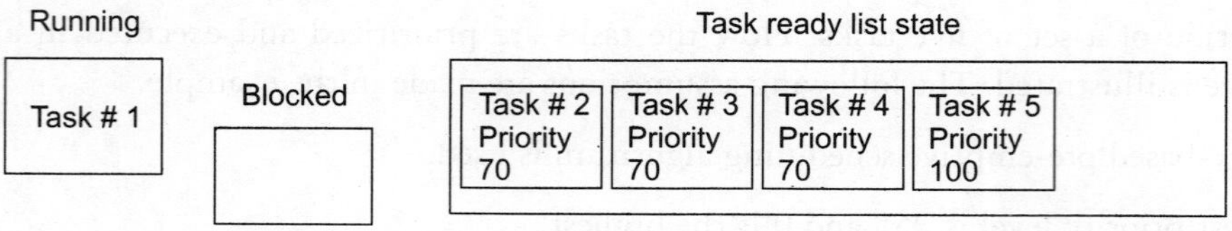

Fig. 6.4b *Step 2*

STEP III

Suppose Task 1, which is currently executing, needs to print out some data. The printer happens to be busy. Task 1 calls the printer routines. As the printer is busy, Task 1 cannot keep running, as it is to wait for the printer to become free. Task # 1 gets blocked and is moved by the kernel to the blocked state (Fig. 6.4c). Next, the kernel puts the next higher or equal-priority task from the task ready list into the running state. Task 2 is the highest priority task in the task ready list and the kernel puts Task 2 into the running state.

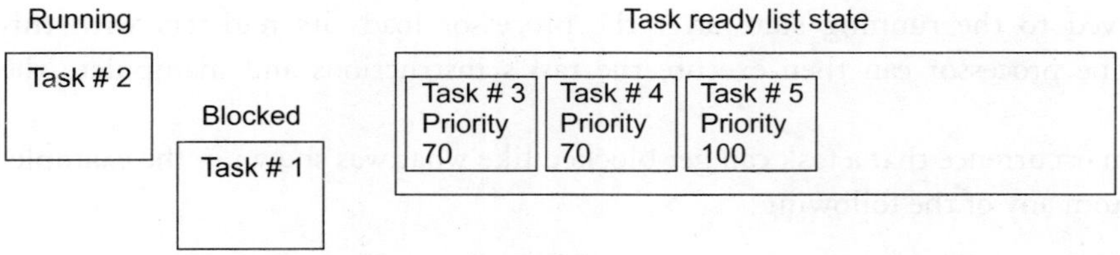

Fig 6.4c *Step 3*

Step IV: Consider a scenario where a blocking call is made by Task # 2, i.e., Task #2 had made a call to check whether an event has occurred and the event has not yet taken place. Task # 2 has to wait for the event and this would make it get into a blocked state. The kernel would then transfer it to the blocked state queue along with Task # 1. This is depicted in Fig. 6.4d where it is shown that the next available task of proper priority, Task # 3, is put in the running condition. Task #1 and Task #2 are now both in the blocked state.

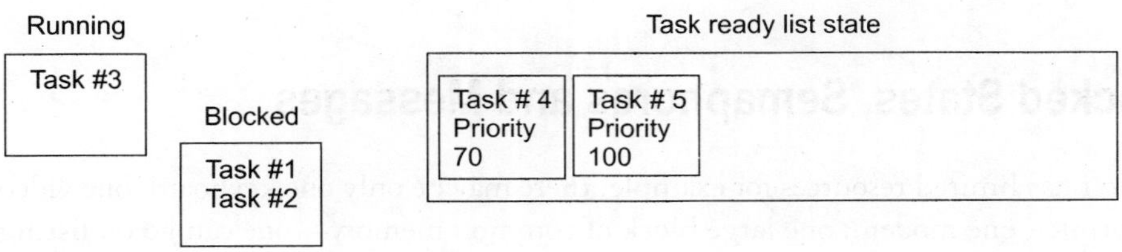

6.4d *Step 4*

Task 3 is now in the running state and causes an event. This is the event that Task 2 was waiting for in the blocked state. Therefore, Task 2 unblocks and is now ready. Task 2 is to be put in the task-ready list. As it is of higher priority than Task 5 and of equal priority with Task 4, it is placed behind Task 4 and ahead of Task 5 (whose priority is lower, that is, 100) (Fig. 6.4e).

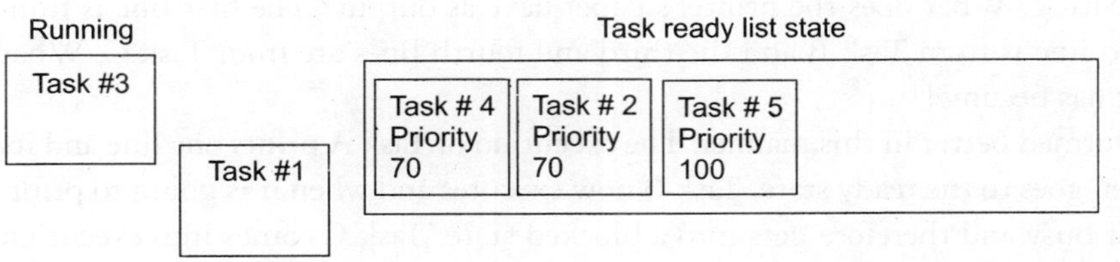

Fig. 6.4e *Step 5*

Task 3 continues as the task running currently.

Tasks are moved to the running state after the processor loads its registers with this task's context. The processor can then execute the task's instructions and manipulate the associated stack.

It is a common occurrence that a task can get blocked like what was shown in the example. This can result from any of the following:

- When it makes a call requesting for an unavailable resource,
- When a call that waits for an event occur
- When a call is made to delay the task for some duration.
- When a higher priority task hogs all the CPU time because of its priority, a situation called CPU-starvation occurs. This situation is characterized by the lower-priority tasks not getting into running states because the higher-priority tasks were dominating. A task which gets blocked remains as such until the **condition for which it got blocked is met**.

6.6 Blocked States, Semaphores and Messages

Every computer has limited resources for example, there may be only one keyboard, one video display, one printer, one modem, one large block of common memory—one can go on listing such resources. The applications running within the computer have to share these. Let us take for example three processes A, B, C. They execute in the order A-B-C-A. When A is executing, it needs to write a 10-line output as the result of its computation. It sends one line of text to the printer and its time is up. Task B is now into running while A goes to a ready state. The printer prints the first line from Task A. Task B is executing when it also has some lines of printout to be made. It outputs one line to the printer and its time is up. Task C comes into running state while Tasks A and B are in the task ready queue. Task C also has few lines of text to be sent to the printer but when it has sent two lines to the printer its time is up and it has to stop executing. What does the printer's paper have as output? The first line is from Task A, the second line is from Task B and the third and fourth lines are from Task C. What a mess the output has become!

It could be performed better in this manner. The execution of Task A prints one line and its time is over. It then goes to the ready state. Task B now executes and when it is going to print, it finds the printer busy and therefore gets into a blocked state. Task C comes into execution and also gets blocked because it has found the printer busy. Task A comes into running and outputs another line. Its time is up and the OS notices that there are no tasks in the ready queue except Task A, so Task A comes into running. This goes on till the printer is not busy (i.e., until all the 10 lines of Task A are printed). After printing the 10th line, Task A gets into ready state and as there is nothing in the printer line buffer, the printer becomes free. This is the time slot for Task B which was blocked till now. The OS notices that Task B was blocked because it needed the printer. As the printer is now not busy, it unblocks Task B and outputs its lines while Task C is still blocked. Task A is in the ready state and continues getting into running condition whenever its time comes. If while Task B has not completed printing, Task A requires the printer, then Task A will get blocked and gives way to Task C. Once Task B finishes printing, Task C will be unblocked when its time slot occurs. Now Tasks A , B , C are in the ready state and will keep executing till they clamour for the same single resource. Blocked states, therefore help in the optimal use of limited resources.

We have seen an example of a blocked state caused by many tasks needing one resource, but it can also be caused by tasks waiting for events.

How does the OS know that a resource is busy and not available? Let us take the example of a railway station with only one platform. There are three trains A, B, C approaching the station. The platform is free and so the railway signal (do not confuse this with the signals in OS, even if they are similar) is "down" at 45 degrees below the horizontal line. Seeing this, Train A enters the platform. As soon as Train A has crossed the railway signal, the railway signal goes "up" to 0 degrees horizontal. Train B is also approaching the station and it sees that the railway signal is "up". So Train B will block … oops! stop before the signal. Train C which is in the earlier section of the track from where Train B is, will stop as it gets no railway signal to proceed. As soon as Train A leaves the station, Train B will get the railway signal to proceed to the station. Train C will get the railway signal to go to the next section. What is the method which ensures that the three trains do not get into the same platform at the same time? It was the railway signals. These give the signals to "go"/ "don't go". The guard of the train uses two sticks with green and red cloth at one end to show whether the train is to go or not. This stick with a cloth attached is called a flag. The two flags and the railway signal give indications to "go"/ "not go".

So, one way of indicating occurrences of events is by using flags. Flags indicate one of two states but when a situation requires the indication of more than two states, semaphores are used. Semaphores were often used in maritime (naval) signaling. The term "semaphore" means a visual signaling apparatus with flags, lights, or mechanically moving arms.

6.7 Semaphores and Shared Data

6.7.1 Semaphores

A semaphore is a variable that can take only whole positive numbers. The binary *semaphore* is one which can take only one of the two values 0 or 1.

Only two operations can be executed on a semaphore variable—wait and signal. Semaphores are used to ensure that when a process is using a resource, it has exclusive access to that resource. Just like addition and subtraction is denoted by "+"and "–", the wait and signal operations also have their own notations:

1. P (semaphore variable), for *acquire*
2. V (semaphore variable), for *release*

the semaphore variable passed as parameter is the variable name assigned to it. Consider a semaphore variable, sv. If P operation is executed on sv,

```
P(sv) :
```

it does the following: if sv is greater than zero, it decrements sv. If sv is zero, it blocks the executing process.

If V operation is executed on sv,

```
V(sv) :
```

it does the following: if some other process has been suspended waiting for sv, it resumes execution, else it increments sv.

6.7.2 Shared Data

Processes do use data generated by each other. This makes it necessary for them to share a common memory. If while a process is using data, another process modifies it, the earlier process would have a coherence problem as far as that particular data being accessed is concerned.

Assume that there are two processes, X and Y, which use a common memory (called a shared memory). When Process X uses the memory, Process Y should be blocked if it needs access to that memory. Once Process X has completed its operations Process Y can be allowed to use the memory. To check this condition, a semaphore could be created. Let it be called check_mem. The values it can take have to be binary as only one process can acquire the semaphore and thus ensure that it is the only process which is using it.

At first, semaphore check_mem has to be initialized to 1.This is done by using the following statement:

```
Init (check_mem,1)
```

After which the following sequence of operations is done.

Process X	**Process Y**
1. P(check_mem); this makes check_mem=0	2. P(check_mem);
3. Reads-Modifies-Writes shared-memory();	4. Blocked
5. V(check_mem);	6. Reads-Modifies- Writes-shared-memory();
7. does_something_else();	8. V(check_mem)
9. does_something_else();	10. does_something_else();

The numbers in the brackets are the sequence of operations.

1. process X does P(check_mem), acquires the semaphore and gets to access the memory
2. process Y does P(check_mem) and blocks access to memory as check_mem=0

3. process X reads, modifies and writes memory
4. Process Y is blocked on check_mem
5. Process X releases check_mem
6. Process Y unblocks and reads, modifies and writes memory
7. Process X does something else
8. Process Y releases the check_mem semaphore
9. Process X keeps doing something else (memory is free for use by any other process)
10. Process Y keeps doing something else (memory is free for use by any other process)

6.8 Message Queues, Mailboxes and Pipes

6.8.1 Message Queues

The kernel provides a message service in the form of message queues. Message services like queues are needed for tasks which share information with other processes. In a queue, new messages are appended "queue-like" to the tail end. Queues have a linked-lists type structure and reside in the memory space of the kernel. These are accessible by multiple tasks. The task which created the message queue assigns it read, write and execute properties. The synchronization is provided by the kernel. The structure of the message queue is

```
struct mymsg {
   long msg_type;
   char mytext[512]; /* rest of message */
   int somethingelse;
   float dollarval;
   };
```

Messages are obtained from the queue in a FIFO manner or by requesting the type of the message. The structure of a message has a message type long as can be seen in the above structure.

Each message queue is limited in terms of both the maximum number of messages and the maximum number of bytes it can contain. New messages cannot be added if *either* limit is crossed and attempts to add new messages will be blocked. The RTOS being used will provide the MSGMAX (total number of messages) and the MSBMNB (max bytes in a queue)

The names of the calling functions like `int msgget(key_t key, int msgflg);` though standard in Unix and Linux, may vary from RTOS to RTOS. It could also be `int vs_msgget (key_t key, int msgflg);` where the vs_ is the prefix the API (application program interface), which will perform as the one in any other OS unless specified in the RTOS manual, uses.

To send a message to the queue the msgsnd() api is used whose prototype is given here.

```
int msgsnd(int msqid, const void * msg_ptr, size_t msg_size,
int msgflags);
```

msgqid is the id returned from the msgget call

msg_ptr is a pointer to the message structure

msg_size is the size of that structure

msgflags defines what happens when no message of the appropriate type is waiting

To recieve a message from the queue, the msgrcv() API is used whose prototype is given here.

```
int msgrcv(int msqid, const void * msg_ptr, size_t msg_
size, long msgtype, int msgflags);
```

msgqid is the id returned from the msgget call

msg_ptr is a pointer to the message structure

msg_size is the size of that structure

msgtype is set to:

= 0 first message available in FIFO stack

> 0 first message on queue whose type equals type

< 0 first message on queue whose type is the lowest value less than or equal to the absolute value of msgtype

msgflags defines what happens when no message of the appropriate type is waiting.

6.8.2 Mail Boxes

This is a high level feature which is used to transfer messages among users. The advantage of the mail box is that its use does not need the developer to write code involving message queues and semaphores—an advantage very much needed in a multi-user environment. Embedded products are single users and so mail boxes are not much needed for these systems—they are mentioned here only for information.

6.8.3 Pipes

Tasks need to communicate. One of the methods it does so is by using message queues. *Pipes* are also used, but they differ from message queues as they have only one way communication between two tasks. Further, the tasks using pipes should have a common parent. To overcome this disadvantage of pipes, FIFOs are used and two way communications is maintained by using two pipes.

The pipe is like a file and so it is treated as such. Its function prototype is given below

```
FILE *popen(char *command, char *type)
```

The above function creates a pipe. It returns a new file stream on success and a NULL if it is unsuccessful. `write()` and `read()` APIs are used passing the file descriptor got from the `popen()` call. A reading of the manual of the RTOS being used will provide clarity in how they can be used in programming.

6.9 Timer Functions and Events

All operating systems have a feature called the *timer tick*. This is a hardware timer that causes an interrupt at precise regular intervals. The function that provides this delay interval counts these ticks and returns when the the required value is reached. For instance, many RTOSes provide functions like task_delay(100), In this, the 100 within parenthesess is the delay in milliseconds after which the function will return. Thus, causing a delay of 0.1 seconds. The timer tick is set up at the startup of the application program. The count depends on the least time interval required. The accuracy of the timer tick depends on the source from which the clock is produced, usually a crystal. The precision of the crystal is a few tens parts per million, typically 10 parts per million (PPM). The IBM PC has a timer tick of 18.2 Hz, which has to be faster in the case of embedded systems. It is usually set to 100 microseconds.

Timers like this are used in many ways. One type is used when it is required to block a function for the duration of a specific time interval. Such a timer is useful in producing delays between events. The second type is used for time-outs. This is useful in the following eventuality: if the application is waiting for an event to occur before it executes the next step, it has to keep checking if that event has occurred. If it has occurred, then the application will proceed further. In case the event has not occurred, the timer should overflow and give a *timed-out event*. Unlike the `time_delay(int)`, which blocks and does not check if an event has occurred, this second function should check for the event and at the same time keep timing the delay for a time-out call.

There is an array of timer services needed for many tasks in an RTOS. One task may be timing out waiting on a message, another for an event like a semaphore and so on. Each of them will have to have an independent timer function which keeps running in parallel. Such timer functions are supported by code for the task to recover from the time-out. Some timers are used for calling each other in a particular sequence after they time out as this is useful for scheduling events in the application.

6.10 Events Management

This is an important service, especially in the case of RTOS and consists of bits assigned to each event expected in the application. It is done at the initial startup after considering each event. These bits which are simply Boolean flags can be set or reset. Events can start-off tasks depending upon the bit's value being set or reset. The call button on a mobile phone is one such event trigger. A bit in the memory of the RTOS is assigned to it. If this button is not pressed, the assigned bit will be reset (0). A task which is supposed to be dialing the number would test this bit whenever it comes up for running. Finding this bit reset, it would do nothing until it is time for the next task to be ready. In case it finds the bit set (1), it starts the dialing process.

Many tasks may get blocked on one event when the event is not ready. As soon as the event is ready, the RTOS will run these tasks in the order of their priority. Events that may be related to each other are grouped together to form a subset, so that assigned tasks could be triggered depending on any event in the group being active. The instant the event occurs, the task gets triggered. After the event service is done, the event bit could be cleared automatically or the task which serviced the event would do so. This is specific to how each individual RTOS is designed.

6.11 Inter-Task Communication

Inter-task communications is a very important issue, especially in embedded systems as there is more than one task in any embedded system application using an RTOS. These tasks work towards the functionality of the embedded system. This means that they may be dependent on each other in many ways.

1. They could be depending on a fixed sequence of events—this is taken care of by the *task scheduling* operation of the RTOS.
2. They could be relying on data from each other—this is through *pipes, message queues, shared memory*.
3. They could also be sharing resources like a common memory and various input/output devices. To take care of coherency and consistency in data input/output *semaphores* are used.
4. The tasks though executed as per a schedule by the RTOS kernel may be dependent on events—this taken care of by *interrupts* and *exception handling*.
5. Some tasks decide what other tasks have to be executed after their execution without depending on the scheduler—this is where *signals* come into the scene. A task may trigger another task by sending it a signal. The dormant task has a signal handler which senses the signal and starts up.

6.12 Interrupt Routines in an RTOS Environment

General-purpose operating systems have a very complicated way of masking interrupts from other threads (threads are lightweight tasks performing a single direct operation). Masking is done in order to ensure that interrupts do not interfere while a task is being done. This is risky because then two tasks are permitted to access a data set simultaneously, which in turn can cause ambiguous or unpredictable results. Masking is made simple in embedded systems using RTOS because of the "kernel" mode of functioning. The kernel itself is protected from the user interface by a mask, so that user-driven interrupts are not allowed to stop the working of the embedded RTOS. The kernel allows interrupt service programming only through the supervisor/super-user mode and not from the user mode. This prevents unauthorised use or modifications of interrupts. Thus, the kernel has full control. Hardware interrupts are allowed on a priority basis. The operating systems report exceptions like memory overflows, instruction faults and tasks running out of control to the kernel. The kernel then activates the appropriate software interrupt to handle such situations called in OS language as exceptions. The OS API (system calls) like signals are also registered in the kernel and are issued and handled on behalf of tasks in the way they have been created and are to be handled. The kernel manages all this even while handling the time slice for tasks and the tasks which are to be brought into running.

Summary

This chapter would have explained the necessity for the use of RTOS even though desktop OSes are available. The RTOS is not an OS but an IDE used for developing an application which consists of an RTOS. The application is made into modules which perform as tasks. They also have priorities just like the processes in desktop OSes.

RTOS have objects used for communication between and synchronising tasks. They also manage memory, task scheduling and events. The objects which are used in communication and synchronisation are schedulers, signals, semaphores, shared memory, message queues, mailboxes and pipes. All these put together in a time-switched execution of tasks is the real time OS within the application. For more information on μCOs-II visit http://www.micrium.com/

Self Evaluation Questions

1. What are RTOSes?
2. What are RTOS used for?
3. How do RTOSes differ from desktop OSes ?
4. Explain the three tier application–RTOS–hardware?
5. Give at least six examples of embedded systems where RTOS can be used?
6. Reason out the meaning of concurrency of task execution.
7. What are the components surrounding the kernel of an RTOS?
8. Explain task management and inter-task communications. Differentiate between them.
9. What are signals in inter-task communication? Give three examples of signals and explain them.

10. What are timers and are they closely associated with any other inter-task communication? Which ones are they associated with and how ?
11. Explain tasks and task states.
12. What are semaphores? Explain how they are used.
13. Explain message queues, mailboxes, and pipes. Differentiate between them.
14. What are shared memories and how are they used by tasks to ensure that there is no coherency problem?
15. Explain events management. How are inter-task communication objects used for communication and synchronisation?

7 Basic Design Using a Real-Time Operating System

Designing a system has been the main topic in many chapters of this book. However in this chapter we will specifically show how RTOSes are used for developing embedded systems applications. We will then discuss various tools and how they process the associated files, general debugging techniques and the way the developed application code is transferred to the target system from the host system.

7.1 Designing with Real Time Operating Systems: Criteria for using RTOS

In the previous chapter we dealt with real time operating systems (RTOS), their features and how they are different from general desktop OS. Before using an RTOS we also need to decide whether the embedded system really requires it. The considerations are as follows:

1. **Obsolescence proof:** Any application which is evolving at a rapid rate needs a faster method of developing it. It helps if the application is in high level language and modular in design, because high level language makes the implementation of changes faster while if it is modular in design, coding, testing, de-bugging is easier. RTOS is the most efficient operating system for dealing with modules which it treats as tasks.
2. **Complex applications:** Applications which are complex need quick turn around time and reliability. RTOSes provide this by the use of time-tested library modules available in its memory.

3. **Modular testing:** Using RTOS, the application can be decomposed to modules. These modules could be extensively tested by separate test groups in tandem. After satisfied testing they can be incorporated as tasks in the RTOS and be kept under further supervisory control. Thus, RTOS helps to further reinforce the reliability factor.

4. **Supervisory control:** The RTOS could incorporate tasks performing supervision on the input/outputs of the embedded systems and provide warnings such as malfunctioning of mechanical actuators, low battery conditions, and other essential activities in the embedded system.

5. **Costs incurred:** Commercial RTOSes are expensive and they also have a licensing fee for each product developed using them and sold. This proves expensive. On the other hand, there are those available from the Open Source which are free of the initial cost and the recurring licensing costs.

6. **Service support:** Although there is a saving of extra costs and time spent on training without an RTOS, when an RTOS is used there is, apart from the above-mentioned benefits, the advantage of a backup support. This support will differ when using a commercial or an Open Source RTOS. The commercial RTOS will have a support team of engineers who are constantly working and solving problems. The Open Source has support in the form of discussion groups and forums which are generally helpful.

7.2 Designing with Real Time Operating Systems: Points to be considered

To start an embedded system application design using RTOS the following are the points to be taken into account. Many of them have already been discussed in previous chapters.

1. Specify the function of the application and the user interaction interfaces.
2. Decompose the application to software modules which perform all the functions required by the application.
3. Evaluate the need for data exchanges between the modules. This is needed to evaluate the requirements for inter-task communication using message queues or other data-passing objects of inter-task communication.
4. Identify the hardware interfaces required.
5. Sort out those interfaces which are used by more than one module. This is needed to provide synchronisation and make available semaphores to ensure that interfaces are used coherently.
6. The software modules are the ones which will be used as tasks keeping the synchronization and data communications in consideration.

7.3 Hard Real-Time Scheduling Considerations

Setting aside all the other points mentioned above, the main issue in an RTOS is that it should guarantee and meet real time considerations. There are two cases we can consider here—one, a situation where a missed event can cause an entire embedded system failure. This is called a hard real time issue and those systems which comply with this are called hard real time systems. The second case is when an event missed does not cause a failure of the system. These are called non-hard real time systems also known as soft real time systems.

If Task n starts processing periodically every n*T units of time (where T is the time taken for completion of one round of the tasks), it must complete its operation before it is time for it to start again. This situation could be analysed further by considering the Task's worst case execution time, the task's priority and the probability of the events occurrence within a period of time n*T. Assumptions can be made that the task switch-time is zero and the tasks do not block.

7.4 Saving Memory and Power

Embedded systems resources are limited, so is its memory. Care should be exercised

- To ensure that two functions are not doing the same thing
- To check that development tools are not sabotaging the application
- To configure the RTOS for only functions that are needed
- To look at the assembly language listing and ensure that there are no c instructions resulting in huge lines of assembly code
- To consider using char variables if an 8 bit processor is used
- To use assembly language programming if all else fails

Embedded systems often use battery power. They have atleast one power saving mode. These modes are SLEEP, LOWPOWER, IDLE, STANDBY.

These modes can be as below:

- LOWPOWER mode: The displays are switched off and on an event they come on.
- STANDBY mode: The display is switched off and if a key is pressed, it comes on.
- SLEEP mode: This is activated by a sleep instruction.
- IDLE mode: All the memory are powered off, the clock is switched off and can be activated into operation by a signal on the interrupt lines.

The above are possible examples and each processor has been designed with its own approach for going into these modes. Some will stop executing instructions, stops clock and peripherals–this is a very efficient power saver. But the disadvantage is that to start it one must give the reset on the system. Another method is to stop instructions but leave the peripherals on, using interrupts to restart the processor.

7.5 An Example of an RTOS: μC-OS (Open Source)

μC/OS-II is a highly portable microcontroller (as its name μC implies). It is a ROMable, very scalable, preemptive real-time, deterministic, multitasking kernel. It can manage up to 64 tasks (56 user tasks available) and has connectivity with μC/GUI and μC/FS (GUI and file systems for μC/OS-II). It is ported to more than 100 microprocessors and microcontrollers. It is simple to use and implement but very effective compared to the price/performance ratio. One major advantage is that it supports all type of processors from 8-bit to 64-bit.

7.5.1 Task Management

μC/OS-II provides the following task management services:

- Task feature
- Task creation
- Task stack and stack checking
- Task deletion
- Change a task's priority
- Suspend and resume a task
- Get information about a task

μC/OS-II can manage up to 64 tasks. The four highest priority tasks and the four lowest priority tasks are reserved for the kernel's use. The lower the value of the priority, the higher the priority of the task.

The process of performing multiple tasks is described in Fig. 7.1.

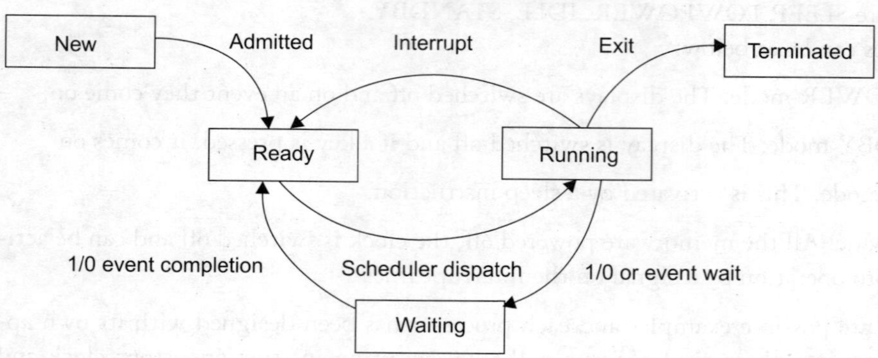

Fig. 7.1 *Task states in an example RTOS*

There are two functions used for creating a task:

- *OSTaskCreate()*
- *OSTaskCreateExt()*

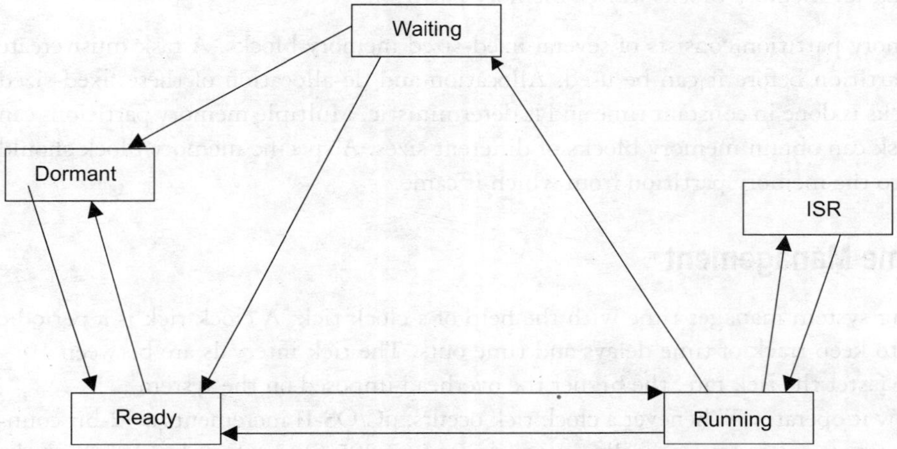

Fig. 7.2 *Creation of tasks and inter changeablity of states*

Figure 7.2 is explained here:

The tasks created are first put in the Dormant state, after which they can move into the ready state and back to the Dormant state if necessary. From the ready state the task can go either to the waiting or running state. The task has to get a stack in which it will store its data. A stack must consist of contiguous memory locations. It is necessary to determine how much stack space a task actually uses.

Deleting a task means the task will be returned to its dormant state and does not mean that the code for the task will be deleted. The calling task can delete itself. If another task tries to delete the current task, the resources are not freed and thus causes irregularity. So the task has to delete itself after it uses its resources.

Priority of the calling task or another task can be changed at run time. A task can suspend itself or another task, a suspended task can resume itself. A task can obtain information about itself or other tasks. This information can be used to know what the task is doing at a particular time.

7.5.2 Memory Management

Memory management includes:

- Initialising the memory manager
- Creating a memory partition

- Obtaining Status of a memory partition
- Obtaining a memory block
- Returning a memory block
- Waiting for memory blocks from a memory partition

Each memory partition consists of several fixed-sized memory blocks. A task must create a memory partition before it can be used. Allocation and de-allocation of these fixed-sized memory blocks is done in constant time and is deterministic. Multiple memory partitions can exist, so a task can obtain memory blocks of different sizes. A specific memory block should be returned to the memory partition from which it came.

7.5.3 Time Management

The operating system manages time with the help of a clock tick. A clock tick is a periodic time source to keep track of time delays and time outs. The tick intervals are between 10 ~ 100 ms. The faster the tick rate, the higher the overhead imposed on the system.

This is how it operates: Whenever a clock tick occurs, μC/OS-II increments a 32-bit counter. The counter starts at zero, and rolls over to 4,294,967,295 (2^32-1) ticks. A task can be delayed and a delayed task can also be resumed.

The μC/OS offers five services:

- OSTimeDLY()
- OSTimeDLYHMSM()
- OSTimeDlyResume()
- OSTimeGet()
- OSTimeSet()

7.5.4 Inter-Task Communication

Inter-task or inter process communication in μC/OS takes place using semaphores, message mailbox and message queues. Tasks and interrupt service routines (ISR) can interact with each other through an ECB (event control block). Different routes are followed for performing a single task and multiple tasks in waiting.

Single task waiting

The interrupt service routine (ISR), after checking the ECB, sends a signal to a task to get into the ready state from the dormant state (Fig. 7.3). This is done in order to make sure that the ISR finishes its action without executing the events requirement by itself. This would cause loss of time and affect the interrupt latency.

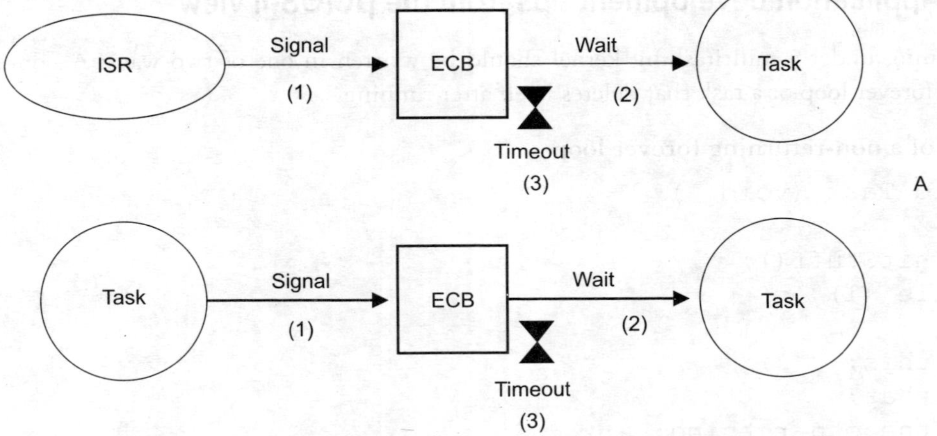

Fig. 7.3 *Single task waiting*

Multiple tasks waiting and signaling

The interrupt service routine (ISR), after checking the ECB, sends a signal to multiple tasks (Fig. 7.4). These tasks would be aware that on this signal a sequence of tasks are to execute. This means that in the sequence, the tasks which are completing will put themselves in a wait state for a signal. The last task of this sequence will give a signal to the other tasks in the wait state enabling them to resume and get into the ready queue.

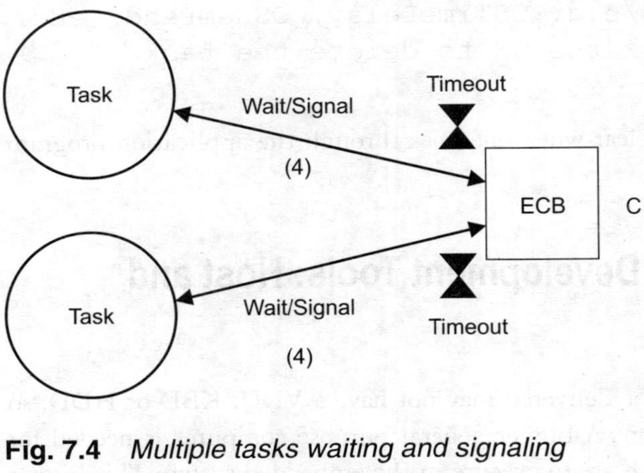

Fig. 7.4 *Multiple tasks waiting and signaling*

Tasks can wait and signal along with an optional time out.

7.5.5 Application development tips from the μC/OS-II view

Tasks running under a multitasking kernel should be written in one of two ways: A non-returning forever loop or a task that deletes itself after running.

Example of a non-returning forever loop

```
void Task (void *)
{
DoInitStuff();
while (1)
{
do this;
do that;
do the other thing;
call OS service (); //e.g. OSTimeDelay, OSSemPend, etc.
}
}
```

Example of a task that deletes itself after running

```
void Task (void *)
{
do this;
do that;
do the other thing;
call OS service (); //e.g. OSTimeDelay, OSSemPend, etc.
OSTaskDelete(); // Ask the OS to delete the task
}
```

These methods will become more clear when one goes through the application program interface provided by the RTOS used.

7.6 Embedded Software Development Tools: Host and Target Machines

Sometimes the embedded systems to be delivered may not have a VDU, KBD or HDD, so it is difficult to modify the application. A bigger general purpose computer is needed for developing and storing programs which are to execute in the embedded system.This bigger machine is the *host* and the embedded system is called the *target*.

The host is a desktop system which comes with compilers, assemblers, and linkers which are called the *native* tools.

Cross compilers are those compilers which develop the machine code of the target system while working on a host, both of who have different CPU's assembler tool chains. A *cross assembler* is one which works on the host but generates binary code for the target machine, just like the cross compiler tools compatible in this way are called tool chains. Linkers used in embedded systems are called *linker/locator* or *cross linker* and does more than the linker in a desktop computer.

Figure 7.5 shows how all the tools are linked.

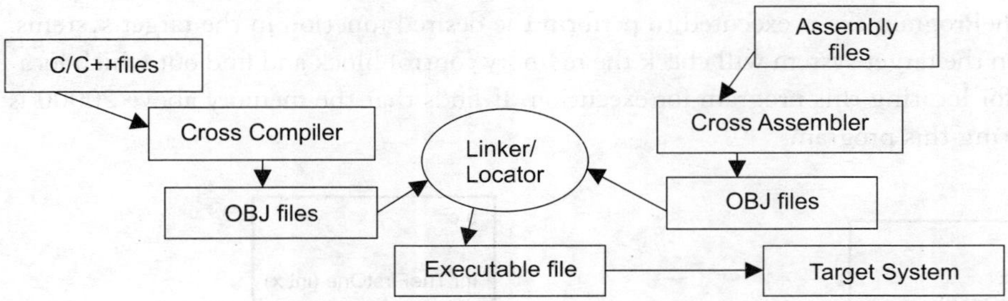

Fig. 7.5 *The process of embedded software development*

Refer to Fig. 7.5 where on the left-side top are the C or C++ files. These files are compiled (a cross compiler is usually there in an RTOS which compiles to the machine language of the target machine and not the host machine) and the products are .obj files. From the left-hand top all assembly language files are cross assembled and .obj files created. The .obj files from the right hand side and the left-hand side are subjected to the linker/locator. These .obj files are linked and relocation information is provided by the linker. The result of this is the executable file which usually has the extension .exe. Now this executable file is transferred to the target machine. In the target system a loader tool is present which loads the .exe file in a free memory location.

7.7 Linker/Locators for Embedded Software

The native linker creates a file on the drive of the host system which is read by the OS's loader to run the program. The loader finds memory to load the program for execution. The locator then glues the application code to the RTOS. This combination is copied to the target system as one. The following example will clarify the process.

In Fig. 7.6, in the top left and the top right position are two files written in 'c' language called a.c and b.c. The a.c file declares a variable of the type, integer and the b.c file declares a function prototype TheFirstOne() returning an integer value. The a.c file is compiled and the I variable is resolved while the call for the function TheFirstOne() is not yet resolved as it is to be the result of the compilers operation on b.c. The a.c file is compiled and results in the a.obj file with variable I resolved. The function TheFirstOne() is yet to be resolved. On the right side, the b.c file is compiled. In this case, the function TheFirstOne() is in its text but the parameter to be passed is not yet known. The compilation of b.c results in the object file b.obj. The linker is invoked to operate on the two object files a.obj and b.obj. This results in the resolution of the relative locations of variable I and the function TheFirstOne. The linker stitches all these and locates the variables and functions along with relocation information and creates a unified file called TheProgram.exe file. In this file the function TheFirstOne() is located at 0789 and the variable i which is a 16 bit value is located at 2097. This file is called the executive file. This executive file is now transferred to the target where a loader locates the program. TheProgram.exe is executed to perform the desired function in the target systems. The loader in the target system will check the memory control block and find out which location is free for locating this program for execution. It finds that the memory above 20000 is free for locating this program.

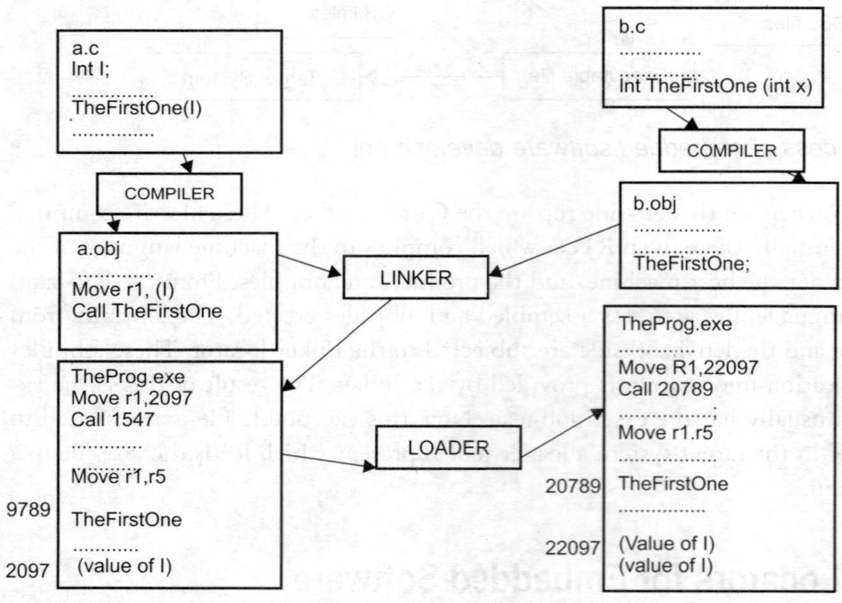

Fig. 7.6 *Compiling, linking, locating and loading*

The program TheProg.exe is relocated [*such that its execution space is above 2000*]. This results in the memory location of function TheFirstOne to become 20789 and the variable i to be at location 22097.

Many a times embedded system applications do not have targets with loaders of the above-mentioned type which can perform relocation. In such cases, the linker should be able to give an image file which is a memory map. This map is copied to the target machine where it is in the same memory locations as in the host machine and executes in the same way as it would have done on the host. Image files are not executive (.exe) files as they do not have relocation information. Such files have an extension .bin meaning that they are binary files. They are very difficult to read and comprehend. For this reason they are converted to ASCII hex format where an 8-bit binary value is represented as a two-byte hex value so that it can be seen on the video display. Consider 0BAH which is a hexadecimal value representing 10111010B binary number or 186D value. If this is to be seen on the screen as it is, it will appear as a graphics character of that value. That is why the hex value 0BAH is converted to two ASCII bytes 42H and 41H which are the hexadecimal codes for ASCII character "A" and "B" respectively. For those more familiar with the decimal system 41H is 65D and 42H is 66D. The tool which converts the binary image file to hex is called an exe2hex converter.

The hex image files have two popular formats—one is the Motorola hex file (Fig. 7.7) and the other is the Intel hex format.

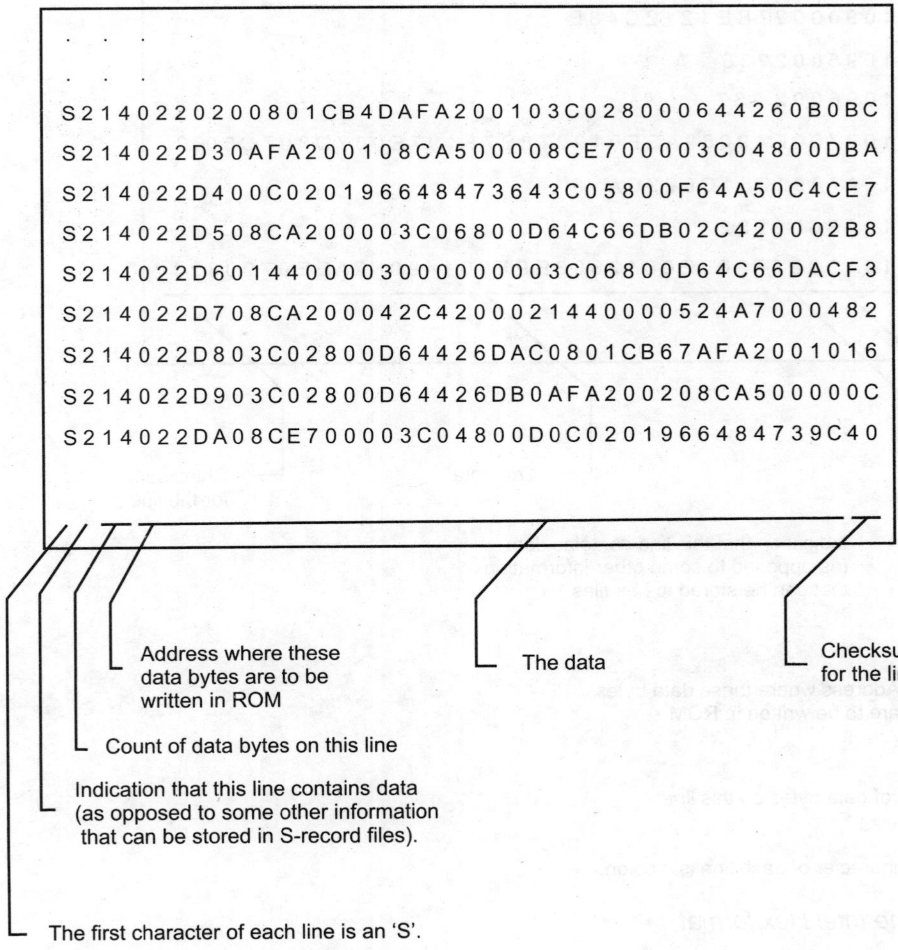

Fig. 7.7 *Motorola hex file format*

Figure 7.7 shows the Motorola format with a 16-bit address capability. The first field on the left starts with a delimiter character–the $ sign. The fields are clearly explained with indicators at the lower part of the figure.

Figure 7.8 shows the Intel format with a 16-bit address capability. The first field on the left starts with a delimiter character–the : sign. The fields are clearly explained with indicators at the lower part of the figure.

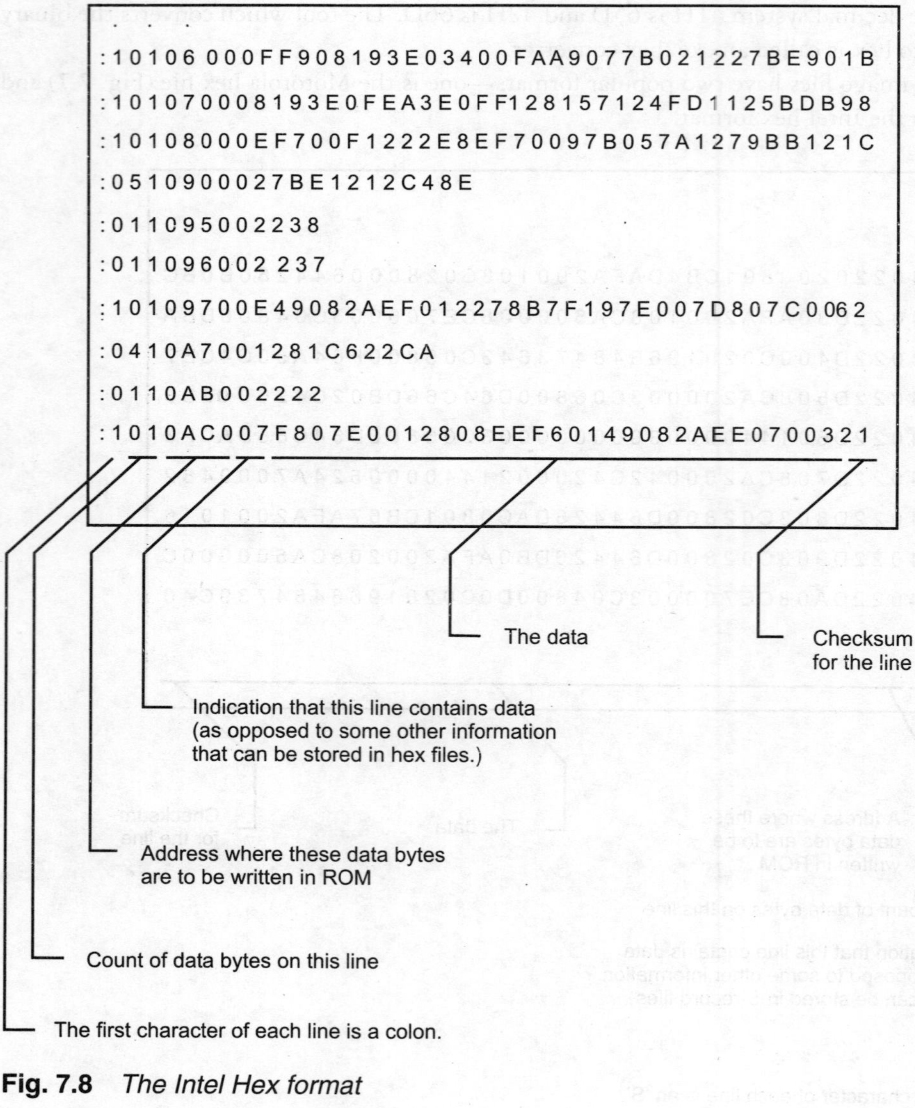

Fig. 7.8 *The Intel Hex format*

7.8 Getting Embedded Software into the Target System

The embedded system has a processor which could be a microprocessor or is usually a micro-controller. Which ever one is present, there has to be memory RAM and ROM. The very first step involves getting the developed program down to the target system. For this sake there is a boot loader program which gets activated soon after the processor resets. The boot loader program does the hardware initialisation, also called the boot image. This program reads the ports like the serial port or the Ethernet port for any data being transferred. The moment the host machine starts up, the boot loader program senses the input from one of the ports mentioned earlier and starts loading the program being downloaded. The program being read from the download port is transferred to memory RAM. The boot loader program is in the ROM of the target machine. After the target has loaded the application program from the host machine, the processor transfers control to the application program from the bootloader.

Figure 7.9 shows the memory map and the functions of each section. The initialisation of the target (Step 1: Target initialisation) and the various hardware components (Steps 2 and 3) is done by the boot image. The boot image varies from processor board to processor board and so the application should gather information about the type of target board from the BSP (the board support package which is usually a part of the purchase deal while buying the RTOS). There a variety of boards available like the PowerPC mother board and the x86 board (the PC board used in our personal computers).

After this the kernel of the OS is executed as a function (Step 4: RTOS initialisation) and this starts of the kernel. The kernel creates tasks with all their priorities and necessities of task management. The functions of the task are initialised (step 5: RTOS components). The RTOS execution is started by the scheduler in the kernel. This starts the tasks running and the application executing in the target machine (Step 7).

Steps 1,2,3 involve hardware initialisation while steps 4,5,6 are software initialization of RTOS. Step 7 does application initialization and execution.

Figure 7.10 shows the host system and the target system connected by a chord called the downloading cable.

7.9 Debugging Techniques: Testing on a Host Machine

Debugging embedded systems can represent more than half of an embedded software project workload. Understanding hardware debugging functions and the issues they tackle is key to selecting the right chips, building debugging systems, and increasing productivity.

Bertrand Déléris, *Freescale Semiconductor* EDN, 12/1/2006

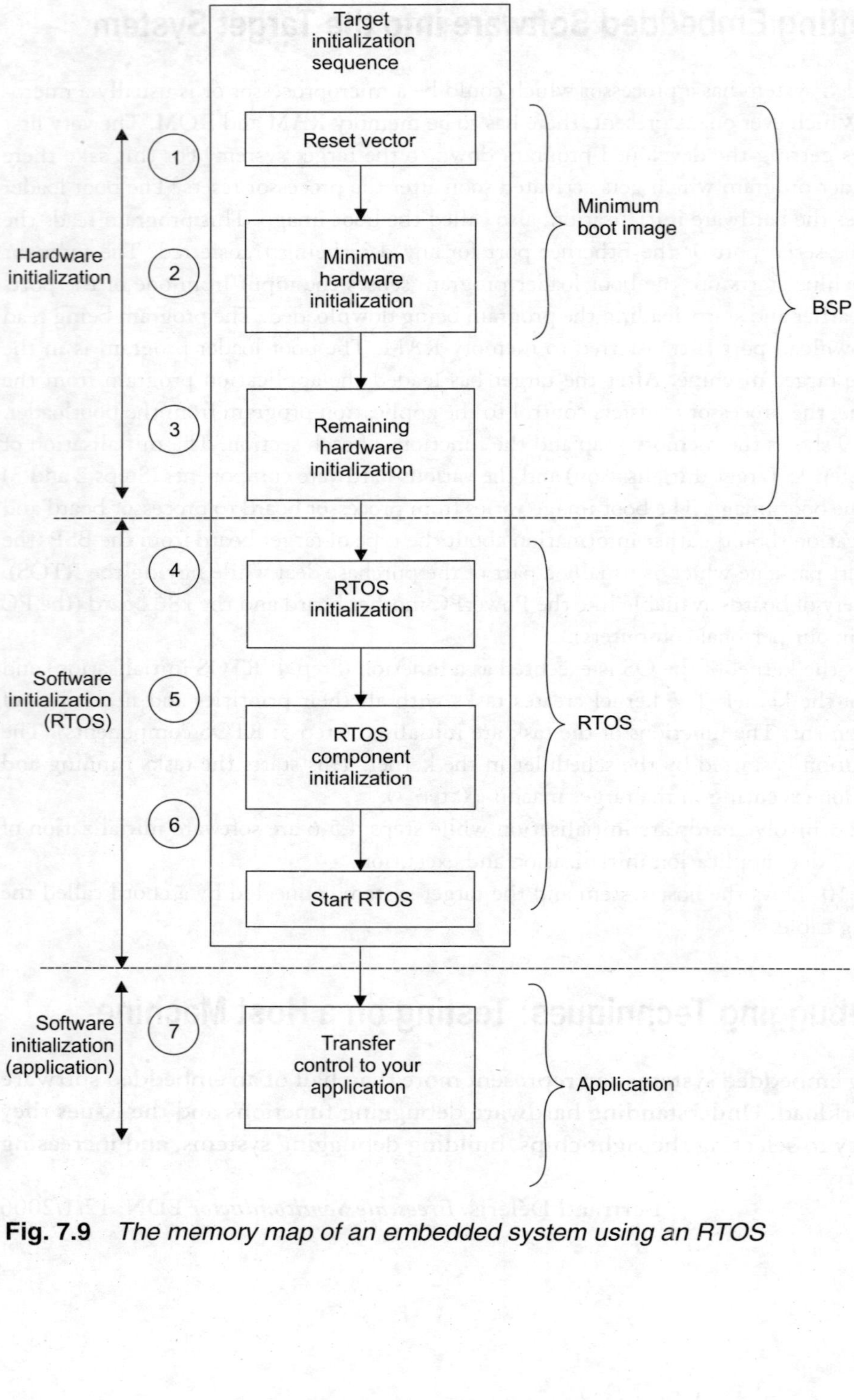

Fig. 7.9 *The memory map of an embedded system using an RTOS*

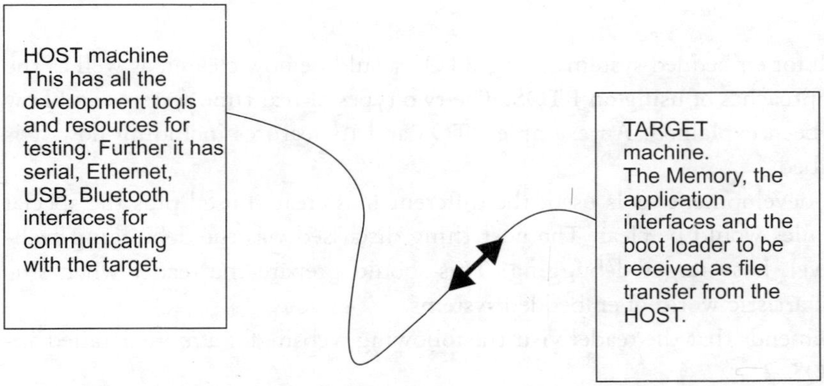

Fig. 7.10 *The host system and the target system connected by the chord called the downloading cable*

The oldest and most common method of debugging is to add print statements in the code to show information about which pieces of the software execute. They provide insight into the actual values of the registers and variables. This exercise may be a legacy of the first-year-student exercise, "hello world," in which the appearance of the two words on the screen proves that the program is alive and has executed up to a certain point. The print statement, or printf, is just one variant of logging, the process of using the processor to write important information to a "pipe" for external tracing. The pipe you use depends on the system; in the printf case, the pipe is the standard output (screen), but it can also be a UART, a USB, or even a general-purpose I/O.

There is a debug monitor in the host which can be used for debugging the application without the target and is therefore called the host level debugging. This is just a rehearsal. There is also a debug monitor which works with the code running on the target's memory. A debugger running on a host communicates with the monitor through a dedicated port to send commands and receive responses. This debugger communicating with the host's debugger is called host–target debugging. This is a dress rehearsal. After this, the transfer is done entirely to the target and the host is disconnected from the target as the downloader cable is removed.

An example system is given at the end of Chapter 8. There is no end to reading books on topics, especially when they are better learnt through practical work. Students, who have gone through a microprocessor laboratory course where a personal computer (PC) is used to transfer the machine code to a microprocessor trainer kit, would realize that the PC here is the host system and the Microprocessor Trainer Kit is the target system. The monitor program in the Microprocessor Trainer Kit has the boot loader, downloader, debugger for target level debugging.

Summary

The design approach for embedded systems using RTOS would be now clearer, as well as the need for different approaches of using an RTOS. The two types of real time systems and how they differ has also been explained. An example RTOS and its features including how it is used has been described.

The host –target development tools used, the different files created/used plus the special need for ASCII hex files would be clear. The next thing discussed was the debugging techniques like host Level, host–target debugging. This should prepare the reader when s/he enters the wonderful artistic world of embedded systems.

The author recommends that the reader visit the following website for a more detailed approach to μCOs RTOS. 2.

https://www.ee.buu.ac.th/courseweb/downloads/ebooks/embedded_system/

Self Evaluation Questions

1. What are the considerations for using real time operating systems?
2. What are the differences between RTOSes from commercial sectors and RTOSes from open source sectors?
3. Which inter-task communication objects which help in synchronisation and data transfer? How do they do so?
4. What are the steps to be taken in the design of applications using RTOS?
5. Clearly explain hard and soft real time applications.
6. What care is to be taken for saving memory and power in an embedded system?
7. What are the modes which support saving power?
8. What are the features of a typical RTOS?
9. Discuss task, memory, time management in μCOs?
10. Discuss embedded system development tools?
11. Discuss with an example the use of compilers, linkers and loaders in developing software for embedded systems. Use examples.
12. What is the need for converting an executive file to an ASCII hex file. Explain.
13. What are the two hex file formats? Discuss the fields of one of them.
14. How is the developed software transferred to a target system?
15. What does one understand about host–target development systems and its predecessors?

8 Introduction to Advanced Architectures

In this chapter two popular and sophisticated microcontrollers RM7 and SHARC are introduced, along with two very popular embedded system interface protocols, I2C and CAN. Network embedded and internet enabled systems are also discussed. An elevator design framework is presented.

8.1 ARM and SHARC

The choice of architecture type plays a key role in processor and memory organisation and in the manner in which parallelism can be implemented at the instruction level. In this chapter, the effect of using architecture efficiently is described using two examples: ARM architecture and SuperHarvar architecture (SHARC).

8.1.1 ARM TDMI (Thumb–Debugger–Multiplier–ICE)

In the following sections, this architecture is described at all levels, such as the instructions, modes, registers and so on. The main factors that contribute to efficient and fast programming are also pointed out.

8.1.1.1 Instructions

All instructions are 32 bits long.

Every instruction can be conditionally executed while most of them execute in a single cycle. This is an example of a load/store architecture.

In such an architecture, data processing instructions act only on registers, and these instructions have a three-operand format. The combined ALU and shifter ensures high-speed bit manipulation which is enhanced by specific memory access instructions with powerful auto-indexing addressing modes. The instructions are compatible with thirty-two-bit and eight-bit data types. The ARM architecture v4 also accepts sixteen-bit data types. Other significant aspects are the flexible multiple-register load and store instructions, and the capacity for instruction-set extension using coprocessors.

8.1.1.2 Modes

The following modes are used to handle different types of tasks, such as running a job; handling interrupts or handling exceptions:

- *User:* unprivileged mode under which most tasks run
- *FIQ:* entered when a high priority (fast) interrupt is raised
- *IRQ:* entered when a low priority (normal) interrupt is raised
- *Supervisor:* entered on reset and when a software interrupt instruction is executed
- *Abort:* used to handle memory access violations
- *Undef:* used to handle undefined instructions

In addition, ARM architecture v4 has a seventh mode which differs from the user mode *system*. It is called the mode and is used for running priviliged operating system tasks.

8.1.1.3 Registers

The registers in ARM architecture show the following classification:

- 37 registers (thirty-two-bits long each)
- 1 dedicated program counter
- 1 dedicated current program status register
- 5 dedicated saved program status registers
- 30 general purpose registers

In order to organise the computer better, however, these are arranged into several banks, with the accessible bank being governed by the processor mode. Each mode can access the following: a particular set of r0–r12 registers; the stack pointer (a particular r13) and the link register (r14); the program counter (r15) and the current program status register (cpsr). In addition to these, privileged modes can also access a particular saved program status register (spsr). An example of the way different modes access these registers is laid out in Fig. 8.1.

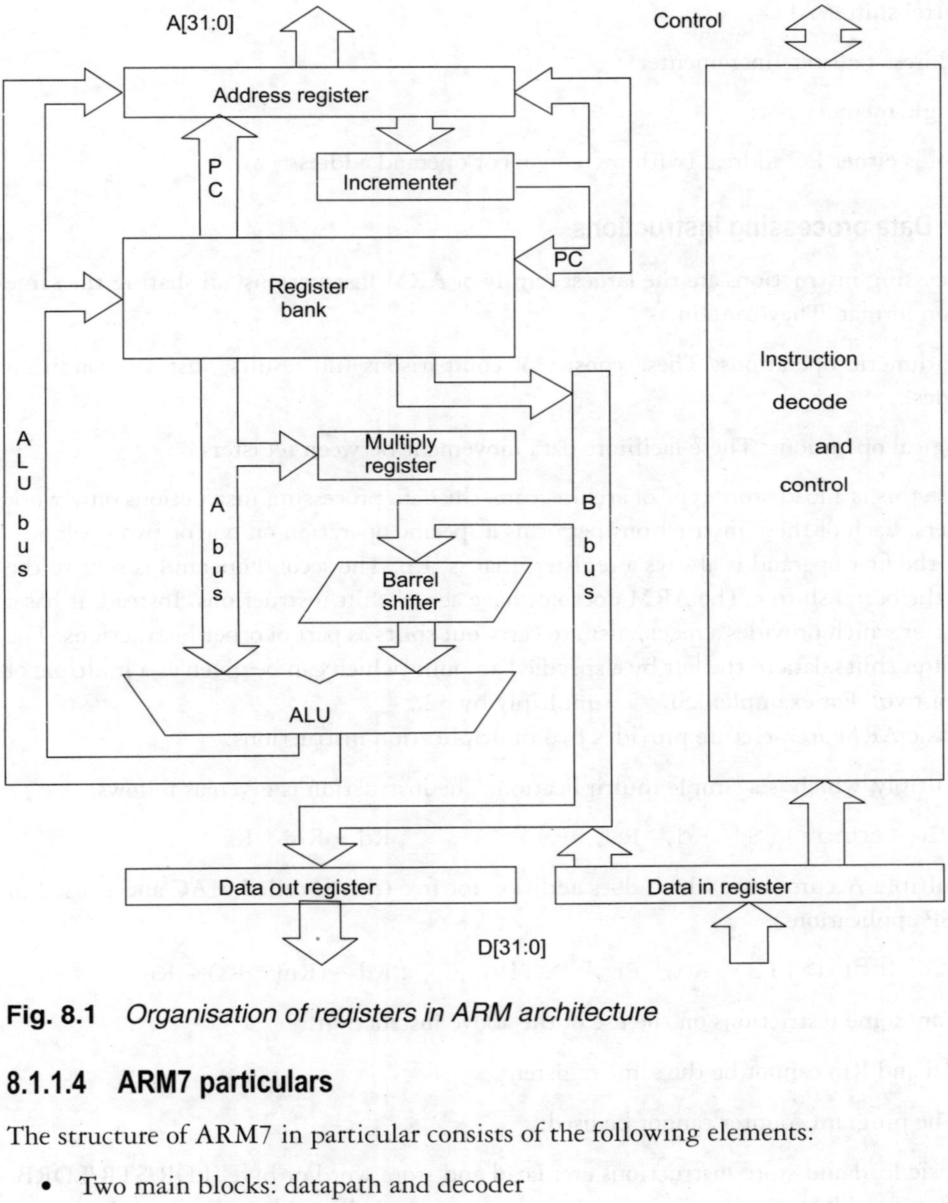

Fig. 8.1 *Organisation of registers in ARM architecture*

8.1.1.4 ARM7 particulars

The structure of ARM7 in particular consists of the following elements:

- Two main blocks: datapath and decoder
- Register bank (r0 to r15)
- Two read ports to A bus/ B bus
- One write port from ALU bus
- Additional read/write ports for program counter r15

- Barrel shifter/ALU
- Address registers/incrementer
- Single memory port
- Holds either PC address (with increment) or operand address

8.1.1.5 Data processing instructions

Data processing instructions are the largest family of ARM instructions, all sharing the same instruction format. They contain:

- Arithmetic operations: These consist of comparisons (no results, just set condition codes).
- Logical operations: These facilitate data movement between registers.

Because this is a load/store type of architecture, the data processing instructions only work on registers. Each of these instructions performs a specific operation on one or two operands. Of these, the first operand is always a register, that is, Rn. The second operand is sent to the ALU via the barrel shifter. The ARM does not have actual shift instructions. Instead, it has a barrel shifter which provides a mechanism to carry out shifts as part of other instructions. The barrel shifter shifts data to the left by a specified amount (which can be given as a multiple of a power of two). For example: LSL #5 = multiply by 32.

The basic ARM architecture provides two multiplication instructions:

- Multiply, which is a simple multiplication. The instruction is given as follows:

  ```
  MUL{<cond>}{S} Rd, Rm, Rs              ; Rd = Rm * Rs
  ```

- Multiply Accumulate, which does addition for free (this is called MAC and is used in DSP applications):

  ```
  MLA{<cond>}{S} Rd, Rm, Rs,Rn           ; Rd = (Rm * Rs) + Rn
  ```

There are some restrictions on the use of the above instructions.

1. Rd and Rm cannot be the same register.
2. The program counter cannot be used.

The basic load and store instructions are: Load and store word or byte (LDR/STR/LDRB/STRB). But the ARM architecture version 4 also supports half-words and signed data: Load and store halfword (LDRH/STRH). If the load value and sign are extended to 32 bits, the instructions are: Load signed byte or halfword (LDRSB / LDRSH). All of these instructions can be conditionally executed by inserting the appropriate condition code after STR/LDR. For example: LDREQB; or syntax:

```
<LDR|STR>{<cond>}{<size>} Rd, <address>
```

8.1.2 SuperHarvarARChitecture (SHARC)

SHARC is used often in signal-processing microcontrollers.The ADSP-21061 SHARC (Fig. 8.2) is a thirty-two-bit processor optimised for high-performance DSP applications as a complete system-on-a-chip. It has a dual ported on-chip SRAM and integrated I/O peripherals supported by a dedicated I/O bus. It is fabricated in a high-speed, low-power CMOS process, has a 20 ns instruction cycle time and operates at 40 MIPS. It has an on-chip instruction cache and executes in a single cycle i.e., the processor simultaneously fetches two operands and an instruction (from the cache), all in a single cycle.

The SHARC has thus set a new standard of integration for signal computers with high performance.

8.1.2.1 Instruction cache

The instruction cache enables three-bus operations for fetching an instruction and two data values. This allows full-speed execution of core, looped operations such as digital filter multiply-accumulates and FFT butterfly processing.

8.1.2.2 Data address generators with hardware circular buffers

Two data address generators (DAGs) implement circular data buffers in the hardware.

8.1.2.3 Flexible instruction set

The forty-eight-bit instruction word accommodates a variety of parallel operations for concise programming. It can conditionally execute a multiplication; an addition; a subtraction and a branch, all in a single instruction.

8.1.2.4 Memory and I/O interface

SHARC has a dual-ported on-chip memory that contains one megabit of on-chip SRAM, organised as two blocks of 0.5 M bits each.

Along with this there is also an off-chip memory and a peripherals interface, which consists of a 4-gigaword off-chip. The address space is unified while the separate on-chip buses for program memory, data memory and I/O are multiplexed. This creates an external system bus with a single thirty-two-bit address bus and a single forty-eight-bit (or thirty-two-bit) data bus.

The host–processor interface helps in making an easy connection to standard microprocessor buses, both sixteen- and thirty-two-bit, without much need for additional hardware. It supports asynchronous transfers at speeds that can go up to the full clock rate of the processor. SHARC has a DMA controller which allows zero overhead data transfers.

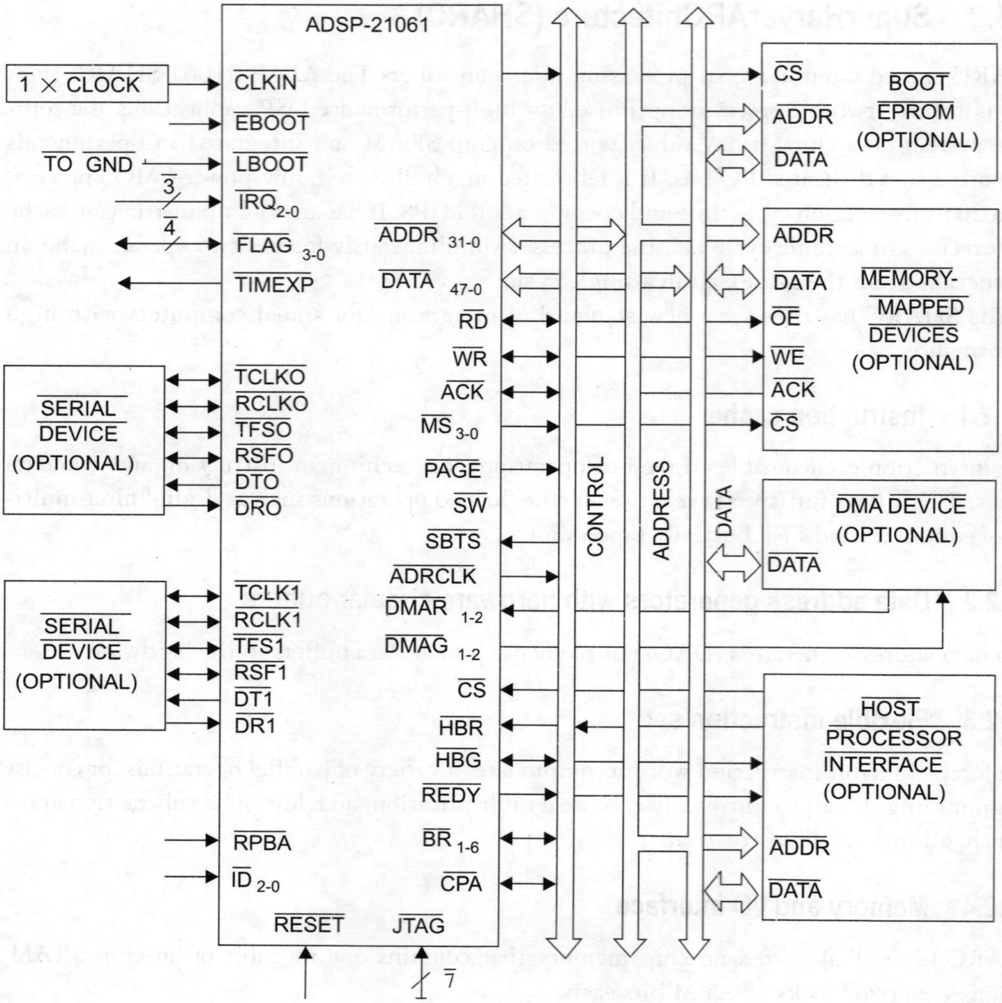

Fig. 8.2 *The ADSP-21061 SHARC architecture*

8.1.2.5 Other features

Other features included in the SHARC architecture are computation units like the ALU, multiplier (MAC), and shifter with a shared data register file. Program and data memory buses capable of supporting 4 thirty-two-bit data transfers between memory and the core at every core processor cycle are available. It also has an interval timer.

8.2 Bus Protocols: I2C Bus and CAN Bus

8.2.1 Inter-IC Communication Protocol and the I2C Bus

This protocol was first developed by the Philips Corporation. The I2C bus physically consists of two active wires and a ground connection; this is shown in Fig. 8.3. The active wires, called SDA and SCL, are both bi-directional. SDA is the serial data line, and SCL is the serial clock line. Every device hooked up to the bus has its own unique address, whether it is an MCU, LCD module, memory, real-time clock, ADC, DAC or ASIC. Each of these chips can act as a receiver and/or transmitter.

The I2C bus is a multi-master bus. This means that more than one IC which is capable of initiating a data transfer can be connected to it. The I2C protocol specification states that the IC which initiates a data transfer on the bus is considered the *bus master* at that time; all the other ICs are regarded as *bus slaves*.

Let us consider a situation where the MCU wants to send data to one of its slaves. So the MCU issues a start condition and sends an address; all slaves will listen. If the address does not match the address of the device, it has to hold back any activity until the bus becomes idle again after a stop condition.

As long as the devices monitor what is going on within the bus (start and stop) and as long as they are aware that a transaction is going on because the last issued command was not a STOP, there is no problem. If one of the devices missed the START condition or it just came out of reset and tries to start talking on the bus, this could lead to problems. The rule says that a master loses arbitration when it cannot get either SCL or SDA to go high when needed, so this problem does not exist. It is the device that sends the '0' that rules the bus.

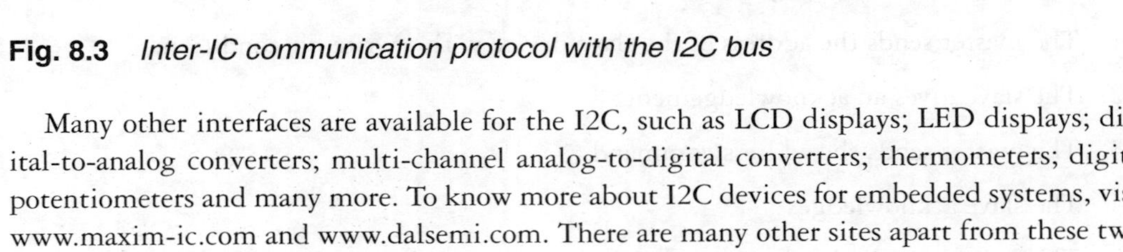

Fig. 8.3 *Inter-IC communication protocol with the I2C bus*

Many other interfaces are available for the I2C, such as LCD displays; LED displays; digital-to-analog converters; multi-channel analog-to-digital converters; thermometers; digital potentiometers and many more. To know more about I2C devices for embedded systems, visit www.maxim-ic.com and www.dalsemi.com. There are many other sites apart from these two.

8.2.1.1 Start condition

A START condition is to be issued on the bus before any transaction. This signals the other devices on the I2C bus that a transaction is being initiated. All the other devices on the bus will be in the listening state. The start condition is such that the SDA goes low and the SCL goes low after that. After this start condition, the message is transmitted by the bus master. Thus, a bus transaction is initiated by issuing a START condition. The device wishing to initiate transaction should listen to ensure an idle condition when SDA=1 and SCL=1. After that, the START condition is issued by the initiating device.

8.2.1.2 Stop condition

After a message has been completed, a STOP condition is sent. This is the signal for all devices on the bus that the bus is available again (idle). In the stop condition the SCL goes high first and then the SDA and the SCL become low. If a chip was accessed and has received data during the last transaction, it will now process this information (if not already processed during the reception of the mess.

8.2.1.3 Acknowledgement Condition

1. The SCL is low after completing transmission of bits.
2. The SDA will be pulled low by the slave.
3. The master issues a clock pulse on the SCL line.
4. The slave releases the SDA line after the clock pulse from the master is complete

8.2.1.4 Transmitting byte to slave

Once the start condition has been sent, a byte can be transmitted by the master to the slave. This first byte after a start condition will identify the slave on the bus (address) and will select the mode of operation. The meaning of all following bytes depends on the slave.

If there are slaves on the bus that can operate in the extended 10-bit addressing mode, they will all respond to the ACK cycle issued by the master.

1. The master sends the address of the slave device with a write bit condition.
2. The slave gives an acknowledgement.
3. The master sends the address/command.
4. The slave acknowledges
5. The Master sends the data and the slave writes the data at the addressed specified by the Master.
6. The master closes using stop.

8.2.1.5 Receiving byte from slave

Once the slave has been addressed and the slave has acknowledged this, a byte can be received from the slave (Fig. 8.4) if the R/W bit in the address was set to READ (set to '1').

The protocol syntax is the same as in transmitting a byte to a slave, except that now the master is not allowed to touch the SDA line. Prior to sending the eight clock pulses needed to clock in a byte on the SCL line, the master releases the SDA line. The slave will now take control of this line. The line will then go high if it wants to transmit a '1' or, if the slave wants to send a '0', it will remain low.

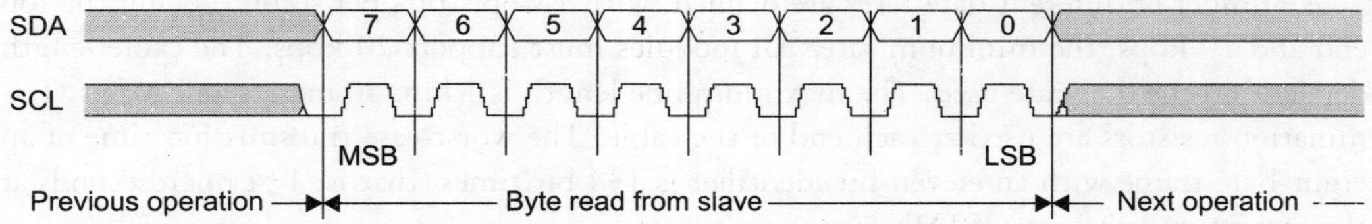

Fig. 8.4 *Reading byte from slave*

All the master has to do is generate a rising edge on the SCL line (2), read the level on SDA (3) and generate a falling edge on the SCL line (4). The slave will not change the data during the time that SCL is high. (Otherwise a start or stop condition might inadvertently be generated.)

During (1) and (5), the slave may change the state of the SDA line. In total, this sequence has to be performed 8 times to complete the data byte. Bytes are always transmitted MSB first.

The meaning of all bytes being read depends on the slave. There is no such thing as a 'universal status register'. You need to consult the data sheet of the slave being addressed, to know the meaning of each bit in any byte that is transmitted.

1. The master sends the address of the slave device with a read bit condition.
2. The slave gives an acknowledgement.
3. The master sends the address/command.
4. The slave responds with data.
5. The master closes using stop.

8.2.2 The Controller Area Network Protocol (CAN) ISO 11898 / 11519

The controller area network (CAN) specification defines the data link layer and ISO 11898 defines the physical layer. The CAN bus is a balanced (differential) two-wire interface running over either a shielded twisted pair (STP); unshielded twisted pair (UTP) or a ribbon cable. Each node uses a male nine-pin D connector.

The bit encoding used is the non-return-to-zero (NRZ) encoding (with bit-stuffing) for data on a differential two-wire bus. The use of NRZ encoding ensures compact messages with a minimum number of transitions and high resilience to external disturbance.

A number of different data rates are defined, with 1Mbps (bits per second) being the top end and 10 kbps, the minimum rate. All modules must support 20 kbps. The cable length depends on the data rate used. The maximum line length is 1 km, 40 meters at 1 Mbps. Termination resistors are used at each end of the cable. The worst-case transmission time of an eight-byte frame with an eleven-bit identifier is 134 bit times (that is, 134 microseconds at the maximum band rate of 1Mbits/sec).

Fig. 8.5 *The CAN interface*

The CAN interface (Fig. 8.5) uses an asynchronous transmission scheme controlled by start and stop bits at the beginning and end of each character, respectively. Information is passed from transmitters to receivers in a data frame. The data frame is composed of an arbitration field; control field; data field; CRC field and ACK field. The frame begins with a 'start of frame' (SOF), and ends with an 'end of frame' (EOF) space. The size of the data field may be from 0 to 8 bits. The frame check sequence is derived from a cyclic redundancy code (CRC); the coefficients are generated modulo-2: X15 + X14 + X10 + X8 + X7 + X4 + X3 + 1.

CAN implements five error-detection mechanisms: 3 at the message level and 2 at the bit level. It also incorporates error flags. These are, at the message level: cyclic redundancy checks (CRC); frame checks and acknowledgment error checks, and at the bit level: bit monitoring and bit stuffing.

8.2.2.1 CAN protocol: Electrical and mechanical

The CAN protocol can be constructed as shown in Fig. 8.6. The pin arrangement is shown in Fig. 8.7. One signal wire is the Tx signal and the other (not shown) is the common ground. The Tx line is converted to two signals CAN_L and CAN_H. This means that if there is a noise pickup on CAN_l and CAN_H it will be equal and so can be cancelled.

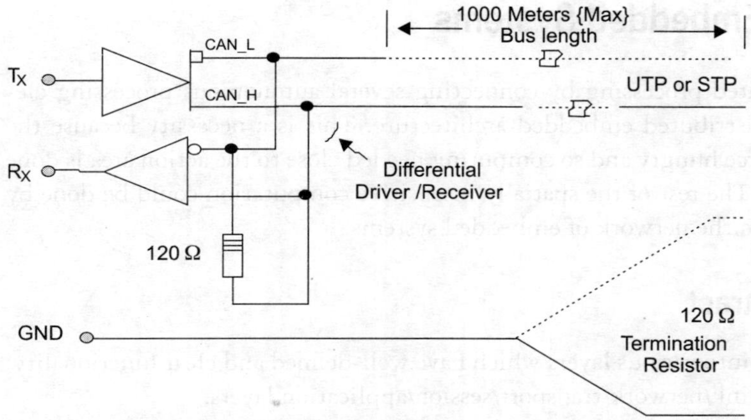

Fig. 8.6 *Constructing the CAN protocol*

A differential drive is very much noise-free. The CAN protocol is used in many control applications and was developed after the I2C protocol found wide applications. The distance for transmission was improved and the CAN protocol was made to be based on the ISO-OSI model for networking of controllers. Now the CAN protocol is widely in use.

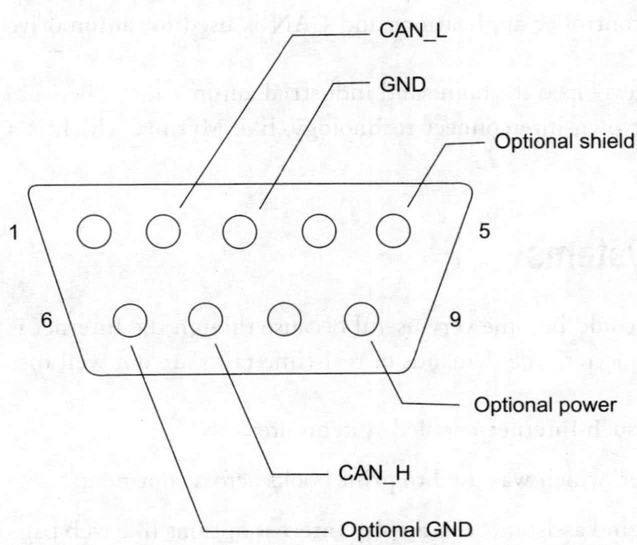

Fig. 8.7 *The CAN protocol: Pin diagram*

8.3 Networked Embedded Systems

We can achieve a distributed processing by connecting several autonomous processing elements together using a distributed embedded architecture. This is a necessity because the embedded system is resource hungry and so computing needed close to the action area is done by the embedded system. The rest of the spatially insensitive computation could be done by other embedded systems in the network of embedded systems.

8.3.1 Network Abstract

The network is abstracted into various layers which have well-defined and clear functionality: they can be physical/data link/network/transport/session/application layers.

The hardware and software are distributed over the network depending on computational or control needs. Not only the computation but also the power for controlling the system should be spatially sensitive. For example, in an electric car, the computation could be done at a central point, but the control of motors and brakes must be done locally, after receiving messages over the network.

Examples of networks for embedded systems are the MULTIBUS and VME by Intel and Motorola, respectively, for multicard systems. These use an ISA bus to support I/O cards for PC-based embedded systems; they have a PCI for high-speed interfaces in PC based applications; the I2C bus is used in microcontroller applications and CAN is used for automotive electronics.

The Echelon LON network was developed for home and industrial automation. There are many DSP sources that supply their own interconnect technology, like Myrinet which is a LAN for DSP.

8.4 Internet-Enabled Systems

Internet-enabled embedded systems could become very useful because though the Internet is well-endowed for non-real-time interaction, the demands of real-time tasks are not well met in this space.

Some of the applications that use such Internet-enabled systems are:

1. Internet-enabled Laser Printer, which was used to print books across continents.
2. Internet-enabled personal digital assistants can display internet options like web pages and so on.
3. Internet-enabled home control systems.
4. Internet-enabled flexible manufacturing systems.

8.5 Design Example: Elevator Controller

Consider a bank of N elevators in a building. The building has F floors and each elevator car moves up and down the hoistway/shaft. Each of these N elevators has a car-control panel, while each floor has a floor-control panel. Finally, each floor has a display. This is all just like the normal elevator systems that we see and use every other day except that there are a bank of N of them.

Figure 8.8 is a hoistway/shaft and it shows N elevator shafts with Floor wise Elevator control panel and floor wise displays.

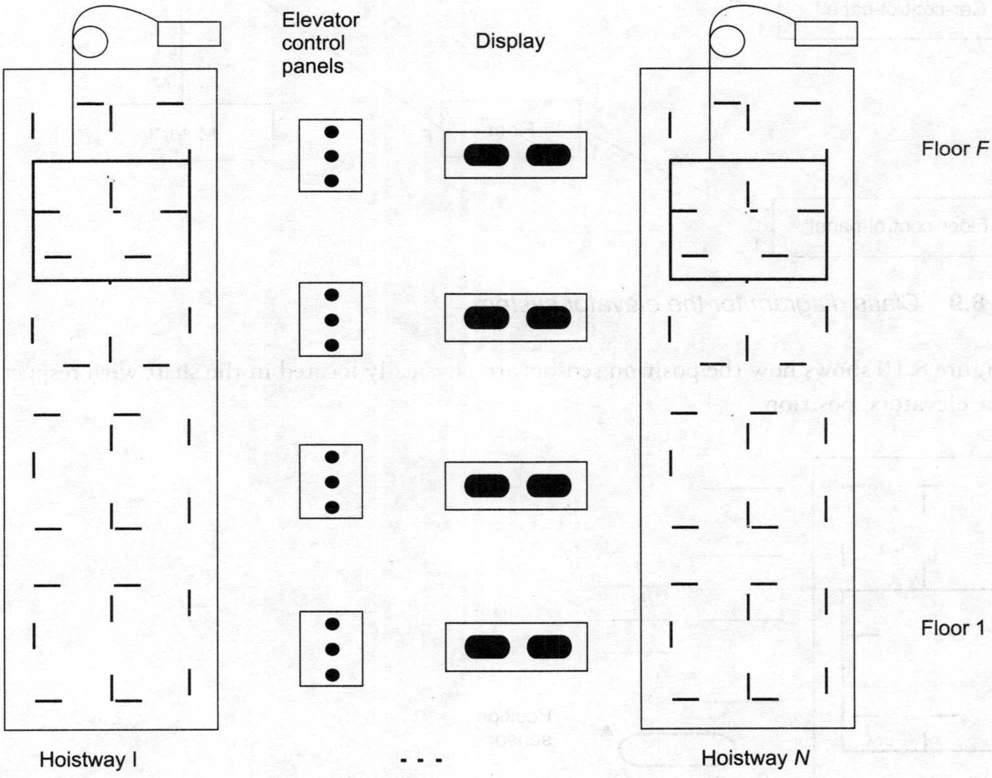

Fig. 8.8 *The elevator banks of 1 to N elevators with control panels and displays on floors*

The elevator position is sensed by position sensors located in the hoistway/shaft. There are two types of sensors—one which is not too sensitive to indicate that the lift is coming to a floor and another for accurate sensing to position it precisely onto the floor level. This is shown in Fig 8.9 as a class diagram where the classes of objects are the car control panel, the motor controller, the controller (main controller for all the lifts) and a master control panel.

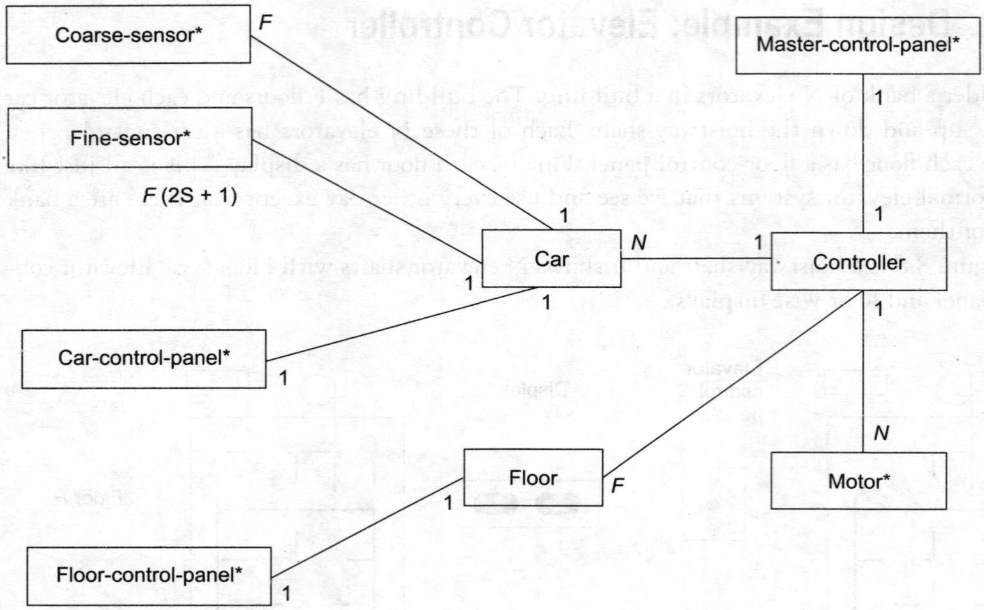

Fig. 8.9 *Class diagram for the elevator system*

Figure 8.10 shows how the position sensors are physically located in the shaft with respect to the elevators' position.

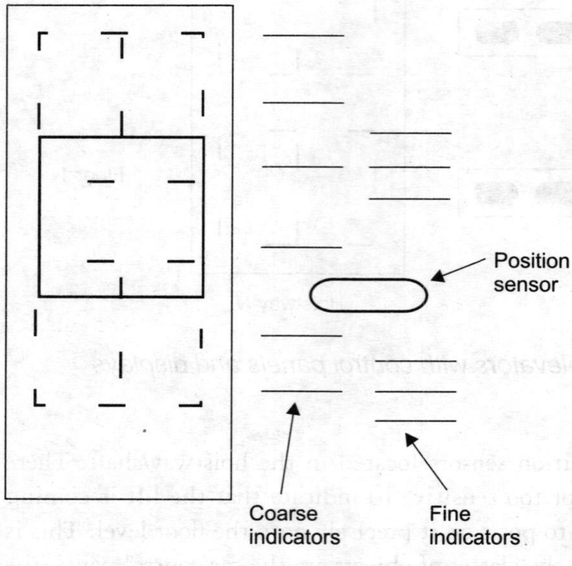

Fig. 8.10 *The floor sensors for the car showing coarse and fine position*

The working of the elevators can be broken up into smaller tasks—these are shown in Fig. 8.11. They are

- Sensor – to indicate whether it has sensed the lift or not. It takes input from the tasks of the coarse and fine sensor.
- Coarse sensor - monitors the lift position near the floor roughly manner and passes it to the task sensor.
- Fine sensor - monitors the lift position near the floor in an accurate manner and passes it to the task sensor.
- Car_Control_Panel - This task scans for the action from inside the elevator on the car control panel. It is used by the passengers already inside the elevator.
- Floor_Control_Panel - This task checks for any calls from the floor and updates the floor display panel.
- Motor - This task controls the motor direction and speed depending on the car or floor calls. The speed is changed depending on whether the coarse sensor (medium) or the fine sensor (slow) is active or inactive (fast).

The interface is designed using available motor control and keypad controls.

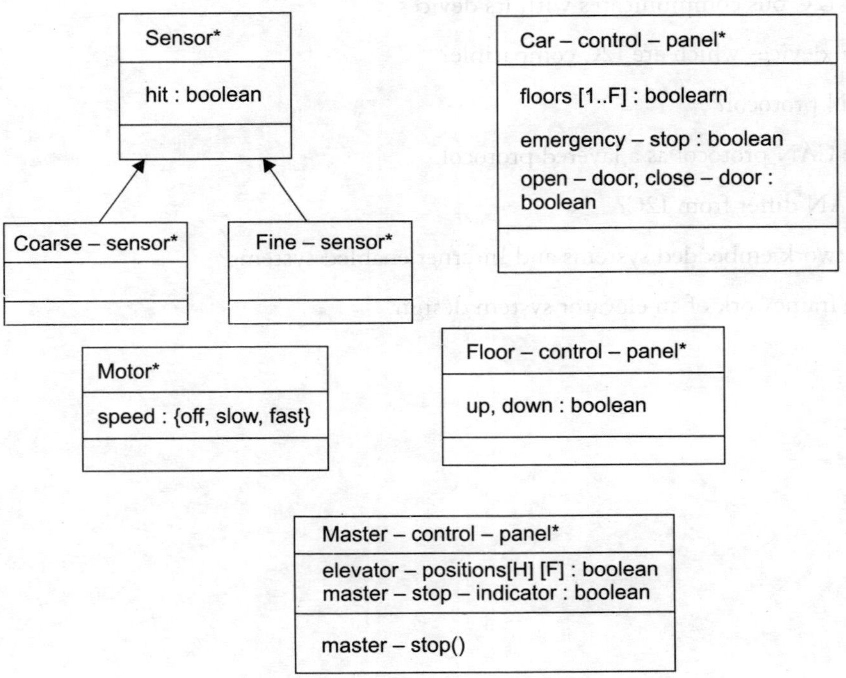

Fig. 8.11 *The tasks and the functions*

Summary

The architecture of some advanced microcontrollers like ARM7 and SHARC have been briefly described here. Network embedded systems, networks abstracts and Internet enabled systems have been highlighted. Two popular interfaces I2C and CAN have been described. For a free evaluation copy of Keil IDE please visit URLhttps://www.keil.com/demo/eval/c51.htm

Self Evaluation Questions

1. Describe the ARM 7?
2. Describe the SHARC DSP processor in analog devices.
3. How are these processors more advanced than the i8051?
4. What is the meaning of TDMI in ARM 7? Explain.
5. What is the meaning and use of MAC in ARM 7?
6. What are the bus characteristics of ARM 7?
7. What are the bus characteristics of SHARC?
8. What is I2C bus ?
9. Discuss how I2C bus communicates with its devices.
10. What are the devices which are I2C compatible?
11. What is CAN protocol?
12. Describe the CAN protocol as a layered protocol.
13. How does CAN differ from I2C?
14. What are network embedded systems and Internet enabled systems?
15. Describe the framework of an elevator system design.

Appendix A:

Instruction Set of 8051

In this appendix, the instruction set has been presented in a tabular manner. This might make what was studied in Chapter 4 clearer. It also deals with different ways of accessing the memory areas of 8051. It might appear daunting, but persevere.

A memory area block is shown and in the block a table number is given to lookup along with the access technique number. Access #1 refers to registers as memory and vice versa (register banks), Access # 2 is for bit addressed memory, Access #3 is for internal user data RAM, Access #4 is for special function registers (SFR), Access # 5 is for indirect addressable RAM access which is parallel to the SFRs. The SFRs are addressed directly from 80H to 0FFh and this Access #5 is for the indirectly accessible memory from 80H to 0FFh located in parallel with SFRs—they are distinguishable only in the way they are addressed. This is available in the upward compatible 8051s like 8052. Access #6 is for AUX RAM using DPTR, Accesses #7 and 8 are for external memory access, both ROM and RAM. The tables for internal and external accesses give the associated instructions with the accesses. The Hex to Op Code table follows. This table is useful to those who are programming their microcontroller using hex opcodes and not assembly language. It is also useful for those who have a hex source code of the program and no assembly source code—they can look up the hex opcode table and build the assembly code.

Op Code Descriptions by Function

Arithmetic

Addition

increment (none affected*)		b/c**
INC	@R0	1/1
INC	@R1	1/1
INC	a	1/1
INC	direct	2/1
INC	dptr	1/2
INC	R0	1/1
INC	R1	1/1
INC	R2	1/1
INC	R3	1/1
INC	R4	1/1
INC	R5	1/1
INC	R6	1/1
INC	R7	1/1

add (CY,AC,OV*)		b/c**
ADD	a,@R0	1/1
ADD	a,@R1	1/1
ADD	a,#data	2/1
ADD	a,direct	2/1
ADD	a,R0	1/1
ADD	a,R1	1/1
ADD	a,R2	1/1
ADD	a,R3	1/1
ADD	a,R4	1/1
ADD	a,R5	1/1
ADD	a,R6	1/1
ADD	a,R7	1/1

add with carry (CY,AC,OV*)		b/c**
ADDC	a,@R0	1/1
ADDC	a,@R1	1/1
ADDC	a,#data	2/1
ADDC	a,direct	2/1
ADDC	a,R0	1/1
ADDC	a,R1	1/1
ADDC	a,R2	1/1
ADDC	a,R3	1/1
ADDC	a,R4	1/1
ADDC	a,R5	1/1
ADDC	a,R6	1/1
ADDC	a,R7	1/1

Decimal adjust for BCD and (CY*)		b/c**
DA	a	1/1

Subtraction

decrement (None*)		b/c**
DEC	@R0	1/1
DEC	@R1	1/1
DEC	a	1/1
DEC	direct	2/1
DEC	R0	1/1
DEC	R1	1/1
DEC	R2	1/1
DEC	R3	1/1
DEC	R4	1/1
DEC	R5	1/1
DEC	R6	1/1
DEC	R7	1/1

subtract with borrow (CY,AC,OV*)		b/c**
SUBB	a,@R0	1/1
SUBB	a,@R1	1/1
SUBB	a,#data	2/1
SUBB	a,direct	2/1
SUBB	a,R0	1/1
SUBB	a,R1	1/1
SUBB	a,R2	1/1
SUBB	a,R3	1/1
SUBB	a,R4	1/1
SUBB	a,R5	1/1
SUBB	a,R6	1/1
SUBB	a,R7	1/1

Multiplication (CY,OV*)		b/c**
MUL	ab	1/4

Division (CY,OV*)		b/c**
DIV	ab	1/4

Logical

bit ops set/CLR/complement (as targeted*)		b/c**
CLR	bit	2/1
CLR	c	1/1
SETB	bit	2/1
SETB	c	1/1
CPL	bit	2/1
CPL	c	1/1

byte ops

ACC CLR/complement (none*)		b/c**
CLR	a	1/1
CPL	a	1/1

rotates (none*)		b/c**
RL	a	1/1
RR	a	1/1

rotates thru CY (CY*)		b/c**
RLC	a	1/1
RRC	a	1/1

AND (none*)		b/c**
ANL	a,#data	2/1
ANL	a,@R0	1/1
ANL	a,@R1	1/1
ANL	a,direct	2/1
ANL	direct,a	2/1
ANL	a,R0	1/1
ANL	a,R1	1/1
ANL	a,R2	1/1
ANL	a,R3	1/1
ANL	a,R4	1/1
ANL	a,R5	1/1
ANL	a,R6	1/1
ANL	a,R7	1/1
ANL	direct,#data	3/2
ANL	c,/bit	2/2
ANL	c,bit	2/2

OR (none*)		b/c*
ORL	a,#data	2/1
ORL	a,@R0	1/1
ORL	a,@R1	1/1
ORL	a,direct	2/1
ORL	direct,a	2/1
ORL	a,R0	1/1
ORL	a,R1	1/1
ORL	a,R2	1/1
ORL	a,R3	1/1
ORL	a,R4	1/1
ORL	a,R5	1/1
ORL	a,R6	1/1
ORL	a,R7	1/1
ORL	direct,#data	3/2
ORL	c,/bit	2/2
ORL	c,bit	2/2

XOR (none*)		b/c*
XRL	a,#data	2/1
XRL	a,@R0	1/1
XRL	a,@R1	1/1
XRL	a,direct	2/1
XRL	direct,a	2/1
XRL	a,R0	1/1
XRL	a,R1	1/1
XRL	a,R2	1/1
XRL	a,R3	1/1
XRL	a,R4	1/1
XRL	a,R5	1/1
XRL	a,R6	1/1
XRL	a,R7	1/1
XRL	direct,#data	3/2

*Flags affected by instruction **bc = bytes/cycles JMP: Jump CLR: Clear ACC: Accumulator

Control transfer

unconditional

jumps (none*)		b/c**
SJMP	rel	2/2
LJMP	addr16	3/2
AJMP	addr11	2/2
AJMP		2/2
AJMP		2/2
AJMP		2/2
AJMP		2/2
AJMP		2/2
AJMP		2/2
AJMP		2/2

calls (none*)		**b/c****
LCALL	addr16	3/2
ACALL	addr11	2/2
ACALL		2/2
ACALL		2/2
ACALL		2/2
ACALL		2/2
ACALL		2/2
ACALL		2/2
ACALL		2/2

returns (none*)		**b/c****
RET		1/2
RETI		1/2

table JMP (none*)		**b/c****
JMP	@a+dptr	1/2

conditional

JMP conditional on bit (none*)		**b/c****
JB	bit,rel	3/2
JC	rel	2/2
JNC	rel	2/2
JNB	bit,rel	3/2
JNZ	rel	2/2
JZ	rel	2/2

JMP on bit; CLR bit (as targeted*)		**b/c****
JBC	bit,rel	3/2

compare, JMP not equal (flags:CY)		**b/c****
CJNE	@R0,#data,rel	3/2
CJNE	@R1,#data,rel	3/2
CJNE	a,#data,rel	3/2
CJNE	a,direct,rel	3/2
CJNE	R0,#data,rel	3/2
CJNE	R1,#data,rel	3/2
CJNE	R2,#data,rel	3/2
CJNE	R3,#data,rel	3/2
CJNE	R4,#data,rel	3/2
CJNE	R5,#data,rel	3/2
CJNE	R6,#data,rel	3/2
CJNE	R7,#data,rel	3/2

decrement,JMP non-zero (none)		b/c**
DJNZ	direct,rel	3/2
DJNZ	R0,rel	2/2
DJNZ	R1,rel	2/2
DJNZ	R2,rel	2/2
DJNZ	R3,rel	2/2
DJNZ	R4,rel	2/2
DJNZ	R5,rel	2/2
DJNZ	R6,rel	2/2
DJNZ	R7,rel	2/2

Data Transfer

bit <–> carry (as targeted*)		b/c**
MOV	bit,c	2/2
MOV	c,bit	2/1

immediate data (none*)		b/c**
MOV	a,#data	2/1
MOV	@R0,#data	2/1
MOV	@R1,#data	2/1
MOV	direct,#data	3/2
MOV	dptr,#data16	3/2
MOV	R0,#data	2/1
MOV	R1,#data	2/1
MOV	R2,#data	2/1
MOV	R3,#data	2/1
MOV	R4,#data	2/1
MOV	R5,#data	2/1
MOV	R6,#data	2/1
MOV	R7,#data	2/1

ACC <–> REG, direct (none*)		**b/c****
MOV	a,R0	1/1
MOV	a,R0	1/1
MOV	a,R0	1/1
MOV	a,R0	1/1
MOV	a,R0	1/1
MOV	a,R0	1/1
MOV	a,R0	1/1
MOV	a,R0	1/1
MOV	R0,a	1/1
MOV	R1,a	1/1
MOV	R2,a	1/1
MOV	R3,a	1/1
MOV	R4,a	1/1
MOV	R5,a	1/1
MOV	R6,a	1/1
MOV	R7,a	1/1

ACC <–> REG, indirect (none*)		**b/c***
MOV	@R0,a	1/1
MOV	@R1,a	1/1
MOV	a,@R0	1/1
MOV	a,@R1	1/1

RAM <–> REG, indirect (flags:none)		b/c*
MOV	@R0,direct	2/2
MOV	@R1,direct	2/2
MOV	direct, @R0	2/2
MOV	direct, @R1	2/2

ACC <–> RAM, direct (flags:none)		b/c*
MOV	a,direct	2/1
MOV	direct,a	2/1

RAM to RAM (flags:none)		b/c*
MOV	direct,direct	3/2

REG <–> data MEM (flags: none)		b/c*
MOV	R0,direct	2/2
MOV	R1,direct	2/2
MOV	R2,direct	2/2
MOV	R3,direct	2/2
MOV	R4,direct	2/2
MOV	R5,direct	2/2
MOV	R6,direct	2/2
MOV	R7,direct	2/2
MOV	direct,R0	2/2
MOV	direct,R1	2/2
MOV	direct,R2	2/2
MOV	direct,R3	2/2
MOV	direct,R4	2/2
MOV	direct,R5	2/2
MOV	direct,R6	2/2
MOV	direct,R7	2/2

exchange ACC with RAM (none)		**b/c***
XCH	a,@R0	1/1
XCH	a,@R1	1/1
XCH	a,direct	2/1
XCH	a,R0	1/1
XCH	a,R0	1/1
XCH	a,R0	1/1
XCH	a,R0	1/1
XCH	a,R0	1/1
XCH	a,R0	1/1
XCH	a,R0	1/1
XCH	a,R0	1/1

REG: Register MEM: Memory EXT: External <–>: To/from 1cyc = 12oscillator periods

Internal data map

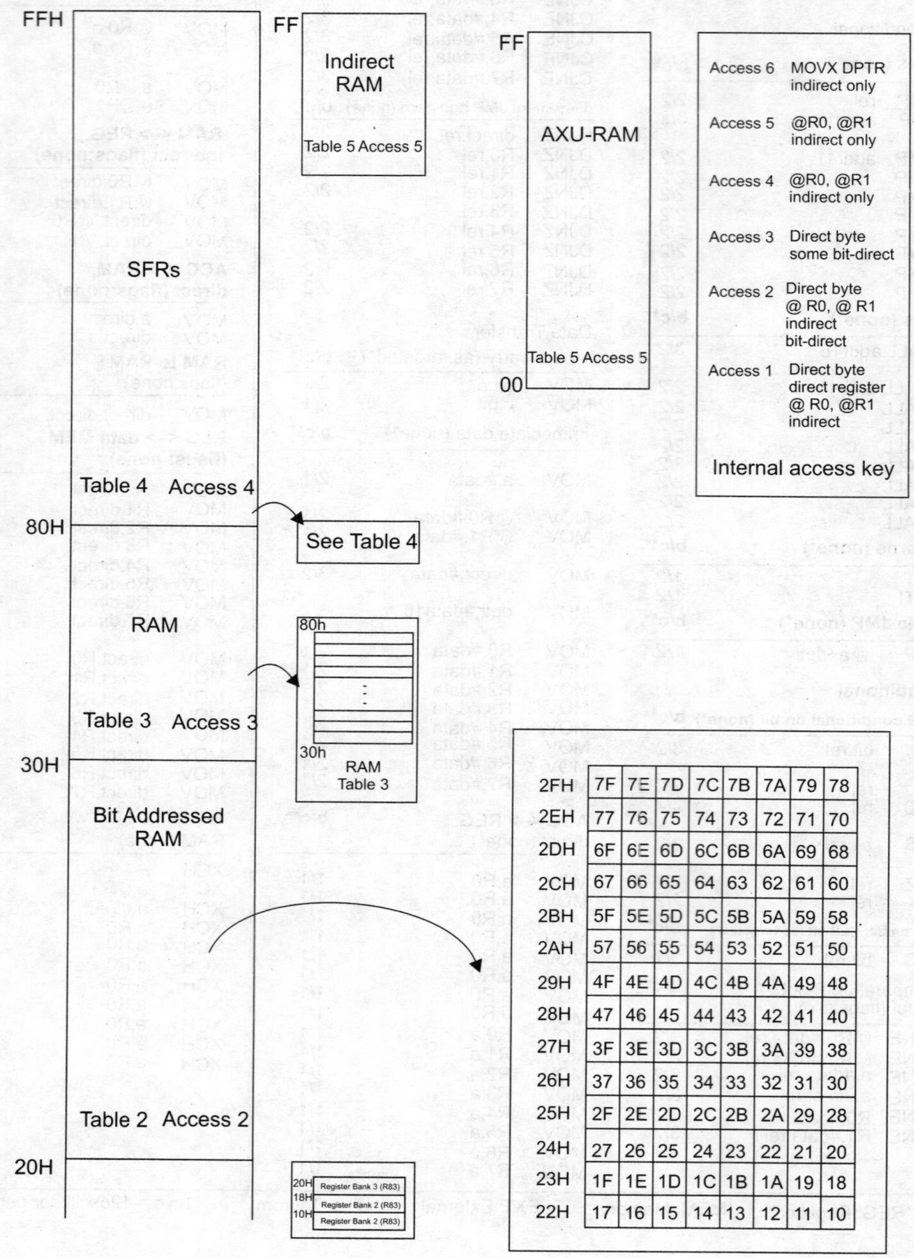

These SFRs are present on all 80C51 family members. SFR addresses not shown may be used for different purposes by derivatives. See specific data sheets for details.

Address									SFR
F0H	F7	F6	F5	F4	F3	F2	F1	F0	B
E0H	E7	E6	E5	E4	E3	E2	E1	E0	ACC
D0H	D7	D6	D5	D4	D3	D2	D1	E0	PSW
B8H	BF	BE	BD	BC	BB	BA	B9	B8	IP
B0H	B7	B6	B5	B4	B3	B2	B1	B0	P3
A8H	AF	–	–	AC	AB	AA	A9	A8	IE
A0H	A7	A6	A5	A4	A3	A2	A1	A0	P2
99H									SBUF
98H	9F	9E	9D	9C	9B	9A	99	98	SCON
90H	97	96	95	94	93	92	91	90	P1
8DH									TH1
8CH									TH0
8BH									TL1
8AH									TL0
89H									TMOD
88H	8F	8E	8D	8C	8B	8A	89	88	TCON
87H									PCON
83H									DPH
82H									DPL
81H									SP
80H	87	86	85	84	83	82	81	80	P0

Special function registers (SFRs)
Table 4

External memory map

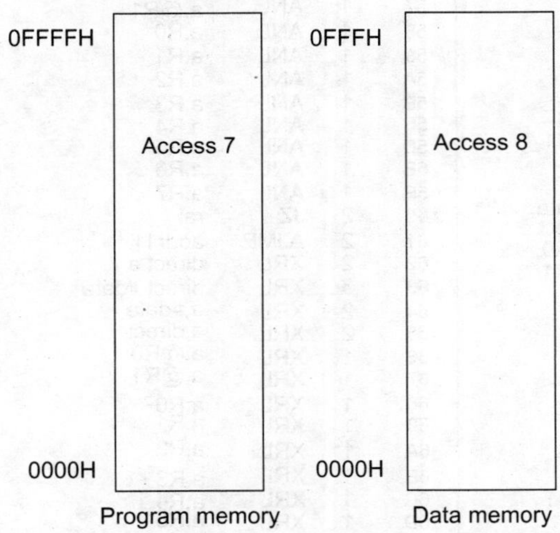

Access 7 MOVC A,@ A+DPTR
MOVC A, @A+PC

Access 8 MOVX A,@DPTR
MOVX @DPTR,A
MOVX A,@Ri
MOVX @Ri, A
Where i = 0 or 1

Hex–To–Op Code Table

Hex code	Instruction length (bytes)	Mnemonic	Operands
00	1	NOP	
01	2	AJMP	addr11
02	3	LJMP	addr16
03	1	RR	a
04	1	INC	a
05	2	INC	direct
06	1	INC	@R0
07	1	INC	@R1
08	1	INC	R0
09	1	INC	R1
0A	1	INC	R2
0B	1	INC	R3
0C	1	INC	R4
0D	1	INC	R5
0E	1	INC	R6
0F	1	INC	R7
10		JBC	bit,rel
11	2	ACALL	addr11
12		LCALL	addr16
13	1	RRC	a
14	1	DEC	a
15	2	DEC	direct
16	1	DEC	@R0
17	1	DEC	@R1
18	1	DEC	R0
19	1	DEC	R1
1A	1	DEC	R2
1B	1	DEC	R3
1C	1	DEC	R4
1D	1	DEC	R5
1E	1	DEC	R6
1F	1	DEC	R7
20	3	JB	bit,rel
21	2	AJMP	addr11
22	1	RET	
23	1	RL	a
24	2	ADD	a,#data
25	2	ADD	a,direct
26	1	ADD	a,@R0
27	1	ADD	a,@R1
28	1	ADD	a,R0
29	1	ADD	a,R1
2A	1	ADD	a,R2
2B	1	ADD	a,R3
2C	1	ADD	a,R4
2D	1	ADD	a,R5
2E	1	ADD	a,R6
2F	1	ADD	a,R7
30	3	JNB	bit,rel
31	2	ACALL	addr11
32	1	RETI	
33	1	RLC	a
34	2	ADDC	a, #data
37	1	ADDC	a,@R1
38	1	ADDC	a,R0
39	1	ADDC	a,R1
3A	1	ADDC	a,R2
3B	1	ADDC	a,R3
3C	1	ADDC	a,R4
3D	1	ADDC	a,R5
3E	1	ADDC	a,R6
3F	1	ADDC	a,R7
40	2	JC	rel
41	2	AJMP	addr11
42	2	ORL	direct.a
43	3	ORL	direct.a#data
44	2	ORL	a.#data
45	2	ORL	a.direct
46	1	ORL	a.@R0
47	1	ORL	a.@R1
48	1	ORL	a.R0
49	1	ORL	a.R1
4A	1	ORL	a.R2
4B	1	ORL	a.R3
4C	1	ORL	a.R4
4D	1	ORL	a.R5
4E	1	ORL	a.R6
4F	1	ORL	a.R6
50	2	JNC	ral
51	2	ACALL	addr11
52	2	ANL	direct.a
53	3	ANL	direct.#data
54	2	ANL	a.#data
55		ANL	a.direct
56	1	ANL	a.@R0
57	1	ANL	a.@R1
58	1	ANL	a.R0
58	1	ANL	a.R1
5A	1	ANL	a.R2
5B	1	ANL	a.R3
5C	1	ANL	a.R4
5D	1	ANL	a.R5
5E	1	ANL	a.R6
5F	1	ANL	a.R7
65	2	JZ	ral
61	2	AJMP	addr11
62	2	XRL	direct.a
63	3	XRL	direct.#data
64	2	XRL	a,#data
65	2	XRL	a,direct
66	1	XRL	a,@R0
67	1	XRL	a,@R1
68	1	XRL	a,R0
69	1	XRL	a,R1
6A	1	XRL	a,R2
6B	1	XRL	a,R3
6C	1	XRL	a,R4
6D	1	XRL	a,R5
6E	1	XRL	a,R6
6F	1	XRL	a,R7

72	2	ORL	c, bit
73	1	JMP	@a+dptr
74	2	MOV	a,#data
75	3	MOV	direct,#data
76	2	MOV	@R0,#data
77	2	MOV	@R1,#data
78	2	MOV	R0,#data
79	2	MOV	R1,#data
7A	2	MOV	R2,#data
7B	2	MOV	R3,#data
7C	2	MOV	R4,#data
7D	2	MOV	R5,#data
7E	2	MOV	R6,#data
7F	2	MOV	R7,#data
80	2	SJMP	rel
81	2	AJMP	addr11
82	2	ANL	c,bit
83	1	MOVC	a,@a+pc
84	1	DIV	ab
85	3	MOV	direct,direct
86	2	MOV	direct, @ R0
87	2	MOV	direct, @ R1
88	2	MOV	direct, R0
89	2	MOV	direct, R1
8A	2	MOV	direct, R2
8B	2	MOV	direct, R3
8C	2	MOV	direct, R4
8D	2	MOV	direct, R5
8E	2	MOV	direct, R6
8F	2	MOV	direct, R7
90	3	MOV	dptr,#data 16
91	2	ACALL	addr11
92	2	MOV	bit,c
93	1	MOVC	a, @a+dptr
94	2	SUBB	a, #data
95	2	SUBB	a, #direct
96	1	SUBB	a,@Ro
97	1	SUBB	a,@R1
98	1	SUBB	a, R0
99	1	SUBB	a, R1
9A	1	SUBB	a, R2
9B	1	SUBB	a, R3
9C	1	SUBB	a, R4
9D	1	SUBB	a, R5
9E	1	SUBB	a, R6
9F	1	SUBB	a, R7
A0	2	ORL	c,bit
A1	2	AJMP	add11
A2	2	MOV	c,bit
A3	1	INC	dptr
A4	1	MUL	ab
A5		(reserved)	
A6	2	MOV	@R0,direct
A7	2	MOV	@R1,direct
A8	2	MOV	R0,direct
A9	2	MOV	R1,direct
AA	2	MOV	R2,direct
AB	2	MOV	R3,direct
AC	2	MOV	R4,direct

AD	2	MOV	R5, direct
AE	2	MOV	R6, direct
AF	2	MOV	R7, direct
B0	2	ANL	c,/bit
B1	2	ACALL	addr11
B2	2	CPL	bit
B3	1	CPL	b
B4	3	CJNE	a#data,rel
B5	3	CJNE	a#direct,rel
B6	3	CJNE	@ R0,#data,rel
B7	3	CJNE	@ R1,#data,rel
B8	3	CJNE	@ R0,#data,rel
B9	3	CJNE	R1,#data,rel
BA	3	CJNE	R2,#data,rel
BB	3	CJNE	R3,#data,rel
BC	3	CJNE	R4,#data,rel
BD	3	CJNE	R5,#data,rel
BE	3	CJNE	R6,#data,rel
BF	3	CJNE	R7,#data,rel
C0	3	PUSH	direct
C1	2	AJMP	addr11
C2	2	CLR	bit
C3	1	CLR	c
C4	1	SWAP	a
C5	2	XCH	a,direct
C6	1	XCH	a,@R0
C7	1	XCH	a,@R1
C8	1	XCH	a,R0
C9	1	XCH	a,R0
CA	1	XCH	a,R2
CB	1	XCH	a,R3
CC	1	XCH	a,R4
CD	1	XCH	a,R5
CE	1	XCH	a,R6
CF	1	XCH	a,R7
D0	2	POP	direct
D1	2	ACALL	addr11
D2	2	SETB	bit
D3	1	SETB	c
D4	1	DA	a
D5	3	DJNZ	direct,rel
D6	1	XCHD	a, @R0
D7	1	XCHD	a, @R1
D8	2	DJNZ	R0,rel
D9	2	DJNZ	R1,rel
DA	2	DJNZ	R2,rel
DB	2	DJNZ	R3,rel
DC	2	DJNZ	R4,rel
DD	2	DJNZ	R5,rel
DE	2	DJNZ	R6,rel
DF	2	DJNZ	R7,rel
E0	1	MOVX	a,@dptr
E1	2	AJMP	addr11
E2	1	MOVX	a,@R0
E3	1	MOVX	a,@R1
E4	1	CLR	a
E5	2	MOV	a,direct
E6	1	MOV	a,@R0
E7	1	MOV	a,@R1

E8	1	MOV	a,R0
E9	1	MOV	a,R1
EA	1	MOV	a,R2
EB	1	MOV	a,R3
EC	1	MOV	a,R4
ED	1	MOV	a,R5
EE	1	MOV	a,R6
EF	1	MOV	a,R7
F0	1	MOVX	@dptr,a
F1	2	ACALL	addr11
F2	1	MOVX	@R0,a
F3	1	MOVX	@R1,a
F4	1	CPL	a
F5	2	MOV	direct,a
F6	1	MOV	@R0,a
F7	1	MOV	@R1,a
F8	1	MOV	R0,a
F9	1	MOV	R1,a
FA	1	MOV	R2,a
FB	1	MOV	R3,a
FC	1	MOV	R4,a
FD	1	MOV	R5,a
FE	1	MOV	R6,a
FF	1	MOV	R7,a

Key :

addr11	= lower 11 bits of 16-bit addresses; upper 5 bits come from current PC (after incrementing twice)
addr16	= code address in program memory
bit	= bit address (0-FF) (bit is complemented before use)
direct	= data address in internal RAM memory
im8	= immediate byte value (0-FF)
im16	= immediate word value (0-FFFF)
rel	= signed 1 byte program memory displacement

00	NUL	28	+	57	W
01	SCH	2C	,	58	X
02	STX	2D	“	59	Y
03	ETX	2E	‘	5A	Z
04	EOT	2F	/	5B	[
05	ENQ	30	0	5C	\
06	ACK	31	1	5D	]
07	BEL	33	3	5E	^
08	BS	34	4	5F	_
09	MT	35	5	60	‘
0A	LF	36	6	61	a
0B	VT	37	7	62	b
0C	FF	38	8	63	c
0D	CR	39	9	64	d
0E	SO	3A	:	65	e
0F	SI	3B	;	66	f
10	DLE	3C	<	67	g
11	DC1 (X-ON)	3D	=	68	h
12	DC2 (TAPE)	3E	>	69	I
13	DC3 (X-OFF)	3F	?	6A	j
14	DC4	40	@	6B	k
15	NAK	41	A	6C	l
16	SYN	42	B	6D	m
17	ETB	43	C	6E	n
18	CAN	44	D	6F	o
19	EM	45	E	70	p
1A	SUB	46	F	71	q
1B	ESC	47	G	72	r
1C	FS	48	H	73	s
1D	GS	49	I	74	t
1E	RS	4A	J	75	u
1F	US	4B	K	76	v
20	SP	4C	L	77	w
21	!	4D	M	78	x
22	*	4E	N	79	y
23	#	4F	O	7A	z
24	$	50	P	7A	{
25	%	51	Q	7C	|
26	&	52	R	7D	}
27	,	53	S	7E	~
28	(	54	T	7F	DEL

Appendix B:
8051 Timer Programming

B.1 Initialising a Timer

It is important to decide the mode in which the timer is to be set. This is done depending on the applications. All modes are not equally often used: Mode 0 is rarely used and the most often used modes are Mode 1 and Mode 2. Mode 1 is used for general-purpose timing and counting up to a value of 65,536. Mode 2 is an eight-bit auto-reload timer where the reloading of counts and setting of run bits is automatically done by hardware. This mode is always used for serial communications. If there is no serial communications being done then this could be used for short auto-reload/run timers. Take an example of Timer 0 being in Mode 1 and used for giving out a pulse.

1. The TMOD SFR has to be initialised:
   - the lower 4 bits of TMOD are used
   - GATE0 and C/T0 are both 0 as the timer is not dependent on pins and the function is of a timer and not a counter
   - mode is 1 so M1 = 0 and M0 = 1. MOV TMOD,#01h is the instruction and Timer 0 is now in 16-bit timer mode.
2. The timer value register TH0 and TL0 are to be loaded. Timer 0 will begin counting by incrementing once in every 12 crystal clock pulses. In case the frequency of the crystal used for the clock is 12 MHz then the timer will increment every 1 μsec. In case the timer is to be set for 1 msec, which is 1000 μ sec, then at 1 μ sec per count, the time count is to be 1000. The Timer 0 count registers are TH0 and TL0 and they are of eight-bits. So the 1000 clocks at 1 μsec should cause an overflow of the timer. The timer overflows only after the highest value it can hold is reached, that is, 0FFFFH. The equivalent of 1000D in hexadecimal system is 03E8H. The value to be loaded in TH0 and TL0 should be such that after it is incremented by 03E8H (1000D), the timer should overflow and cause an interrupt. The value to be loaded into the sixteen-bit register is

0FFFF0 – 03E8H which is 0FC17H. TH0=0FCH and TL0=17H. Use the calculator program in the start menu of the PC to get to these values.

3. The Timer 0 service routine is now to be written. Whenever the timer count exceeds 0FFFFH and causes a timer overflow, the TF0 flag is set and the PC is loaded with the interrupt service of Timer 0. The routine is to be written at this location. This location is in the ROM address area from 000BH to 0012H. These eight locations are usually insufficient to write the entire code for the Timer 0 service including a RETI. This necessitates that a long jump to the address of the service routine be made at 000BH. At 000BH, the following instruction may be put LJMP timer0_int_service. This service routine has to take care of reloading the TH0 and TL0 values and giving the start trigger (Step 5). In case it does not do it, the timing is only for one pulse.
4. Initialise the interrupt registers IE and IP. IE=10000010B, that is, EA=1 and IT0=1.
5. The timer is now to be started as it is not on auto-run. Setting the TR0 bit will start the timer to count up by using SETB TR0 instructions.

B.2 Reading the Timer

Reading the value of a timer can be done for two operations. One as an eight-bit in the case of Mode 2 auto-reload. In this mode, the eight-bit register is read and there are no other issues.

For a 16/13-bit timer reading, a problem arises called scoreboarding. The CPU being eight-bit, can read a byte at a time. This means that either the upper or lower byte has to be read first and then the other. It may happen that there may be a rollover (wrap around) of the upper byte from 0FFH to 00H. So if the value in the sixteen-bit timer was 0FFFEH, the program reads the lower byte first and after a few microseconds may read the upper byte as 00H, because it could have wrapped around to 00hH. This causes an erroneous reading to be made. To avoid this, the timer could be stopped by using the CLR TRx instruction. After reading, the timer could be started by SETB TR0. Reading the timer is usually not needed. In case stopping the timer is not desirable then this next method could be used. Read the TH0 to the accumulator and the TL0 to another register. Compare the accumulator with the current TH0 value. If it is the same, then it is correct, otherwise, deduce that a wrap around has occurred.

```
AGAIN: MOV A, TH0.
MOV R7,TL0
CJNE A,TH0,AGAIN
MOV R6,A
```

This does the job without stopping the timer.

Appendix C:

8051 Counter Programming

C.1 Limits to Reading Counters

If the C/T0 bit is set, Timer 0 will monitor the P3.4 line and count the events on the P3.4 line. Making the P3.4 pulse will cause the counter to increment on each pulse. Logic 1–0 transitions on the P3.4 line are counted. Note that the 8051 checks the P3.4 line after each instruction cycle (once every 12 clock cycles).

In case P3.4 being low is taken to high and returned to low in 6 crystal clock cycles, this will not be detected by the 8051. The counting rate is 1/24th of the crystal frequency. When crystal frequency is 12.000 Mhz, 500,000 events per second can be counted.

C.2 Frequency Measurement: Tachometers

These applications make use of both the timer and the counter. The Timer 0 could be used to gate the Timer 1 as counter. The gating could be for a period of 1 millisecond in which case the count would be the kilohertz value.

Appendix D:

8051 Serial Programming

D.1 Setting the Serial Port Baud Rate

Once the Serial Port Mode has been configured, as explained in the previous appendix, the program must configure the serial port's baud rate. This only applies to Serial Port Modes 1 and 3. The baud rate is determined based on the oscillator's frequency when in Mode 0 and 2. In Mode 0, the baud rate is always the oscillator frequency divided by 12. This means that if the crystal frequency crystal is 11.059 Mhz, the Mode 0 baud rate will always be 921,583 baud. In Mode 2, the baud rate is always the oscillator frequency divided by 64, so that a 11.059 Mhz crystal speed will yield a baud rate of 172,797.

In Mode 1 and Mode 3, the baud rate is determined by how frequently Timer 1 overflows.

The more frequently Timer 1 overflows, the higher the baud rate. There are many ways one can cause Timer 1 to overflow at a rate that determines a baud rate, but the most common method is to put Timer 1 in an eight-bit auto-reload mode (Timer Mode 2) and set a reload value (TH1) that causes Timer 1 to overflow at a frequency appropriate to generate a baud rate.

To determine the value that must be placed in TH1 to generate a given baud rate, we may use the following equation (assuming PCON.7 is clear).

TH1 = 256 – ((Crystal / 384) / Baud)

If PCON.7 is set, then the baud rate is effectively doubled, thus the equation becomes

TH1 = 256 – ((Crystal / 192) / Baud)

For example, if we have an 11.059 Mhz crystal and want to configure the serial port to 19,200 baud,

TH1 = 256 – ((Crystal / 384) / Baud)
TH1 = 256 – ((11,059,000 / 384) / 19,200)
TH1 = 256 – ((28,799) / 19,200)

TH1 = 256 – 1.5 = 254.5

As you can see, to obtain 19,200 baud on a 11.059 Mhz crystal, we would have to set TH1 to 254.5. If we set it to 254 we will have achieved 14,400 baud and if we set it to 255, we will have achieved 28,800 baud. Thus to achieve 19,200 baud, we simply need to set PCON.7 (SMOD). When we do this, we double the baud rate and utilise the second equation mentioned above. Thus we have:

TH1 = 256 – ((Crystal / 192) / Baud)
TH1 = 256 – ((11,059,000 / 192) / 19,200)
TH1 = 256 – ((57,699) / 19,200)
TH1 = 256 – 3 = 253

Here we are able to calculate a nice, even TH1 value. Therefore, to obtain 19,200 baud with an 11.059 MHz crystal we must:

1. Configure Serial Port Mode 1 or 3.
2. Configure Timer 1 to Timer Mode 2 (8-bit auto- reload).
3. Set TH1 to 253 to reflect the correct frequency for 19,200 baud.
4. Set PCON.7 (SMOD) to double the baud rate.

D.2 Writing to the Serial Port

Once the Serial Port has been properly configured as explained above, it is ready to be used to send and receive data. To write a byte to the serial port one must write the value to the **SBUF** (99h) SFR. For example, if you wanted to send the letter 'A' to the serial port, it could be accomplished by the following statement:

```
MOV SBUF,#'A'
```

Upon execution of the above instruction, the 8051 will begin transmitting the character via the serial port. Obviously, the transmission is not instantaneous—it takes a measureable amount of time to transmit. And since the 8051 does not have a serial output buffer, we need to be sure that a character is completely transmitted before we try to transmit the next character.

The 8051 lets us know when it is done transmitting a character by setting the **TI** bit in SCON. When this bit is set, we know that the last character has been transmitted and that we may send the next character, if any. Consider the following code segment:

```
CLR TI           ; Be sure the bit is initially clear
MOV SBUF,#'A'    ; Send the letter 'A' to the serial port
JNB TI,$         ; Pause until the RI bit is set.
```

The above three instructions will successfully transmit a character and wait for the TI bit to be set before continuing. The last instruction says 'Jump if the TI bit is not set to $' where $ in most assemblers means 'the same address of the current instruction'. Thus the 8051 will pause on the JNB instruction until the TI bit is set by the 8051 upon successful transmission of the character.

D.3 Reading the Serial Port

Reading data received by the serial port is equally easy. To read a byte from the serial port, one just needs to read the value stored in the **SBUF** (99h) SFR after the 8051 has automatically set the **RI** flag in SCON.

For example, if your program wants to wait for a character to be received and subsequently read it into the accumulator, the following code segment may be used:

```
JNB RI,$                ; Wait for the 8051 to set the RI flag
MOV A,SBUF              ; Read the character from the serial port
```

The first line of the above code segment waits for the 8051 to set the RI flag; again, the 8051 sets the RI flag automatically when it receives a character via the serial port. So, as long as the bit is not set, the program repeats the 'JNB' instruction continuously.

Once the RI bit is set, upon character reception, the above condition automatically fails and program flow falls through to the 'MOV' instruction which reads the value.

Appendix E: 8051 Interrupt Programming

E.1 Serial Interrupts

Serial interrupts are slightly different from the rest of the interrupts. This is due to the fact that there are two interrupt flags: RI and TI. If either flag is set, a serial interrupt is triggered. As on the serial port, the RI bit is set when a byte is received by the serial port and the TI bit is set when a byte has been sent. This means that when your serial interrupt is executed, it may have been triggered because the RI flag was set or because the TI flag was set, or because both flags were set. Thus, a program must check the status of these flags to determine what action is appropriate. Also, since the 8051 does not automatically clear the RI and TI flags, the interrupt handler must be used to clear these bits.

```
INT_SERIAL: JNB RI,CHECK_TI     ; If the RI flag is not set, we
                                ; jump to check
TI MOV A,SBUF                   ; If we got to this line, it's because
                                ; the RI bit *was* set
CLR RI                          ; Clear the RI bit after we've
                                ; processed it
CHECK_TI: JNB TI,EXIT_INT       ; If the TI flag is not set, we jump
                                ; to the exit point
CLR TI                          ; Clear the TI bit before we send
                                ; another character
MOV SBUF,#'A'                   ; Send another character to the
                                ; serial port
EXIT_INT: RETI
```

As you can see, this code checks the status of both interrupts flags. If both flags were set, both sections of code will be executed. Also note that each section of code clears its corresponding interrupt flag. If the interrupt bits are not cleared, the serial interrupt will be executed over and over until they are cleared.

Thus it is very important to clear the interrupt flags in a serial interrupt.

One very important rule applies to all interrupt handlers: Interrupts must leave the processor in the same state as it was in when the interrupt initiated. The idea behind interrupts is that the main program is not aware that they are executing in the 'background'. However, consider the following code:

```
CLR C               ; Clear carry
MOV A,#25h          ; Load the accumulator with 25h
ADDC A,#10h         ; Add 10h, with carry
```

After the above three instructions are executed, the accumulator will contain a value of 35h. But what would happen if right after the MOV instruction, an interrupt occurred? During this interrupt, the carry bit was set and the value of the accumulator was changed to 40h. When the interrupt finished and control was passed back to the main program, the ADDC would add 10h to 40h, and an additional 1h because the carry bit is set. In this case, the accumulator will contain the value 51h at the end of execution, a seemingly wrong answer. A programmer unfamiliar with interrupts would be convinced that the microcontroller is damaged in some way, provoking problems with mathematical calculations. Yet, what has happened, in reality, is that the interrupt did not protect the registers it used.

The interrupt must insure that the value of the accumulator is the same at the end of the interrupt as it was at the beginning. This is generally accomplished with a PUSH and POP sequence. For example:

```
PUSH ACC
PUSH PSW
MOV A,#0FFh
ADD A,#02h
POP PSW
POP ACC
```

At the core of the interrupt are the MOV instruction and the ADD instruction. However, these two instructions modify the Accumulator (the MOV instruction) and the value of the carry bit (the ADD instruction will cause the carry bit to be set). Since an interrupt routine must guarantee that the registers remain unchanged by the routine, the routine pushes the original values on to the stack using the PUSH instruction. It is then free to use the registers it protected.

Once the interrupt has finished its task, it pops the original values back into the registers. When the interrupt exits, the main program will never know the difference because the registers are exactly the same as they were before the interrupt executed.

In general, interrupt routines must protect the following registers:

- PSW
- DPTR (DPH/DPL)

- PSW
- ACC
- B
- Registers R0-R7

Extra care must be taken when dealing with PSW since it consists of many individual bits that are set by various 8051 instructions. It is best to protect PSW by pushing and popping it off the stack at the beginning and end of interrupts. Note also that most assemblers (in fact, ALL popular assemblers) are similar in that they will not allow execution of the instruction: `PUSH R0`. This is due to the fact that depending on which register bank is selected, R0 may refer to either internal RAM address 00h, 08h, 10h, or 18h. R0, in and of itself, is not a valid memory address that the PUSH and POP instructions can use.

Thus, if any 'R' register is used in an interrupt routine, the register's absolute address has to be pushed onto the stack instead of just saying `PUSH R0`. For example, instead of `PUSH R0`, execute: `PUSH 00h`

Of course, this only works if the default register set is selected. If an alternate register set is used, the address which corresponds to the register used has to be PUSHed.

E.2 Common Problems with Interrupts

Interrupts are very powerful tools available to the 8051 developer, but when used incorrectly they can give rise to a huge number of problems requiring hours spent in debugging programs. Errors in interrupt routines are often very difficult to diagnose and correct.

The following interrupt-related issues must be looked into.

E.2.1 Register Protection

As explained above, all registers must be protected. Unprotected registers may lead to very strange results.

E.2.2 Restore Protected Values

Another common error is pushing registers on to the stack to protect them, and then forgetting to pop them off the stack before exiting the interrupt. For example, a programmer may push ACC, B, and PSW on to the stack in order to protect them and subsequently pop only ACC and PSW off the stack before exiting. In this case, since the value of 'B', is not restored, an extra value remains on the stack. When the RETI instruction is executed, the 8051 will use that value as the return address instead of the correct value.

E.2.3 Using RET instead of RETI

Interrupts are always terminated with the RETI instruction. It is easy to inadvertently use the RET instruction instead. However, the RET instruction will not end the interrupt. Usually, using a RET instead of a RETI will cause the illusion of the main program running normally, but the interrupt will only be executed once. Simulators, such as the 8052 Simulator for Windows created by Vault Information Services, contain special features which will notify the user if the registers haven't been protected or other common interrupt-related errors.

Appendix F:

Keil IDE Project, Build, Debug

F.1 The Keil Integrated Design Environment

Click on <START>
Select <program files>
Choose <Keil µvision>
In the opening screen select <project> menu
In the pull down select <New>

A window appears asking for name of the project. Change or create a new directory and type<mfp>. "mfp" stands for "my first project". Following this a new window appears, like the one shown on the next page asking for selection of the target device.

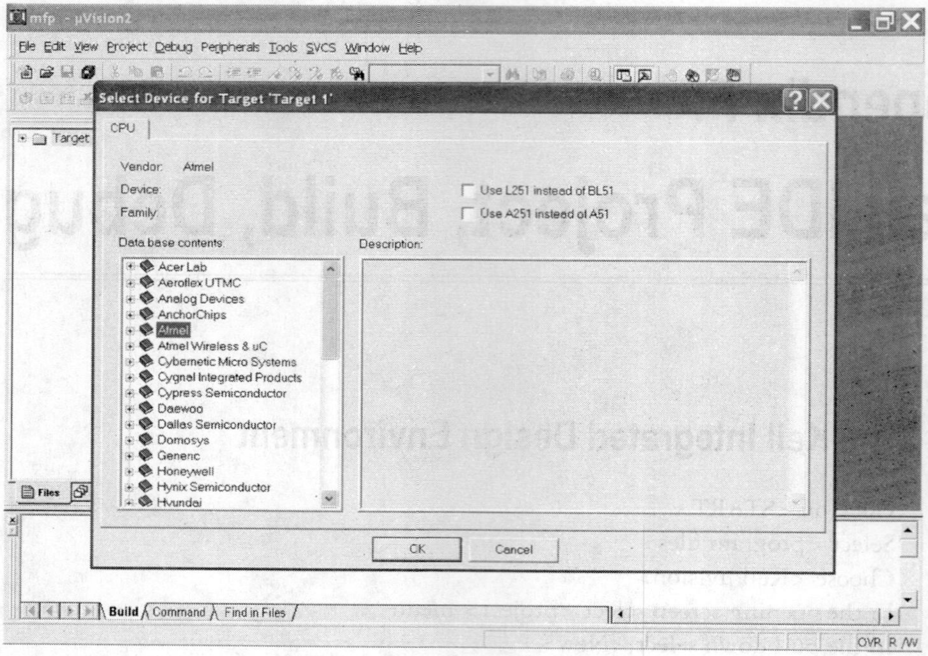
mfp - µVision2
File Edit View Project Debug Peripherals Tools SVCS Window Help
Select Device for Target 'Target 1'
CPU
Vendor: Atmel
Device:
Family:
Use L251 instead of BL51
Use A251 instead of A51
Data base contents:
Description:
Acer Lab
Aeroflex UTMC
Analog Devices
AnchorChips
Atmel
Atmel Wireless & uC
Cybernetic Micro Systems
Cygnal Integrated Products
Cypress Semiconductor
Daewoo
Dallas Semiconductor
Domosys
Generic
Honeywell
Hynix Semiconductor
Hyundai
OK
Cancel
Target
Files
Build
Command
Find in Files
OVR R /W

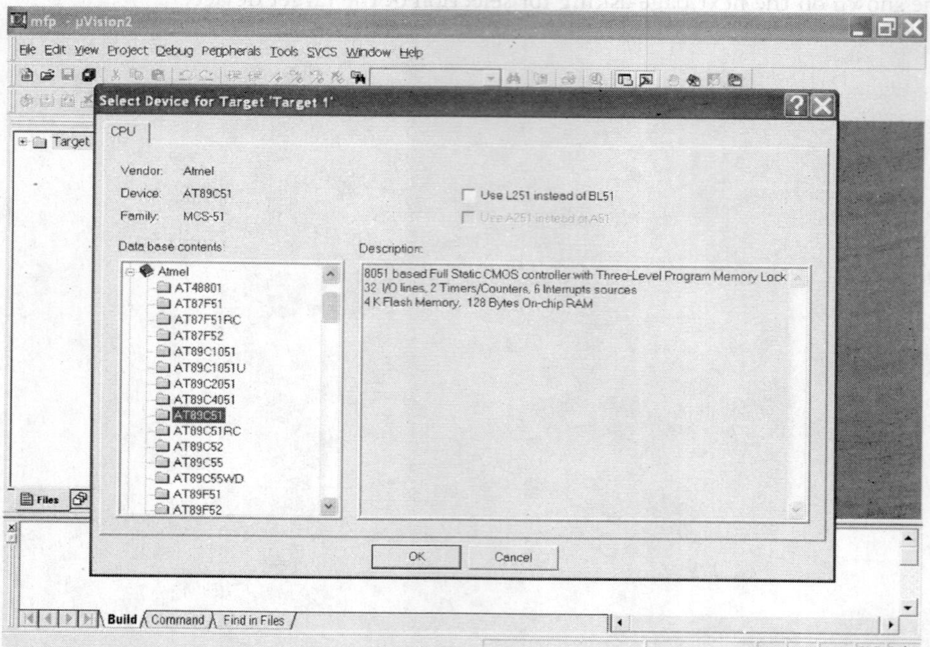
mfp - µVision2
File Edit View Project Debug Peripherals Tools SVCS Window Help
Select Device for Target 'Target 1'
CPU
Vendor: Atmel
Device: AT89C51
Family: MCS-51
Use L251 instead of BL51
Use A251 instead of A51
Data base contents:
Description:
8051 based Full Static CMOS controller with Three-Level Program Memory Lock
32 I/O lines, 2 Timers/Counters, 6 Interrupts sources
4 K Flash Memory, 128 Bytes On-chip RAM
Atmel
AT48801
AT87F51
AT87F51RC
AT87F52
AT89C1051
AT89C1051U
AT89C2051
AT89C4051
AT89C51
AT89C51RC
AT89C52
AT89C55
AT89C55WD
AT89F51
AT89F52
OK
Cancel
Target
Files
Build
Command
Find in Files
OVR R /W

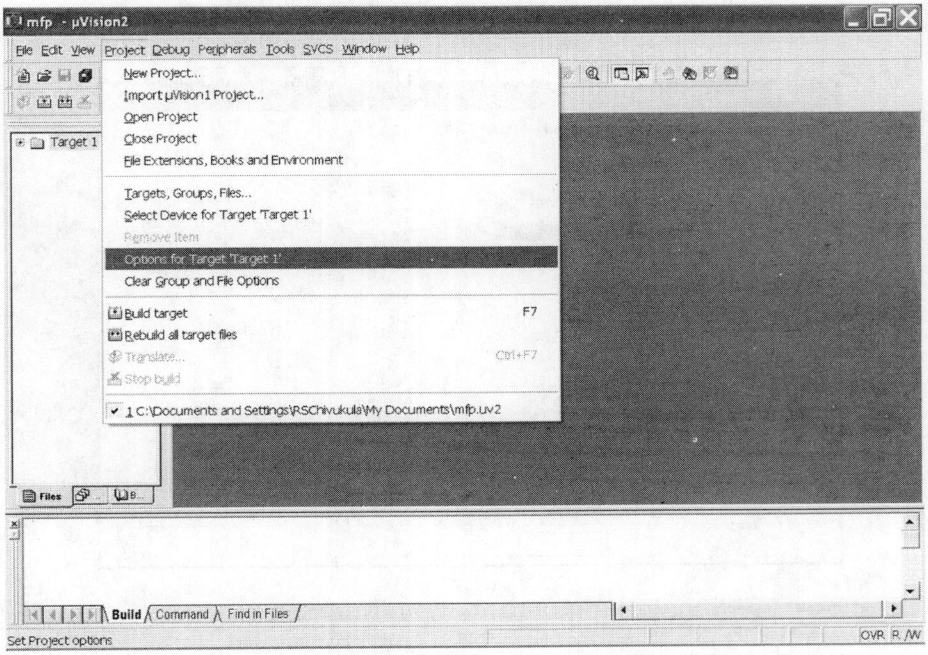
mfp - µVision2
File Edit View Project Debug Peripherals Tools SVCS Window Help
New Project...
Import µVision1 Project...
Open Project
Close Project
File Extensions, Books and Environment
Targets, Groups, Files...
Select Device for Target 'Target 1'
Remove Item
Options for Target 'Target 1'
Clear Group and File Options
Build target F7
Rebuild all target files
Translate... Ctrl+F7
Stop build
1 C:\Documents and Settings\RSChivukula\My Documents\mfp.uv2
Target 1
Files
Build Command Find in Files
Set Project options
OVR R /W

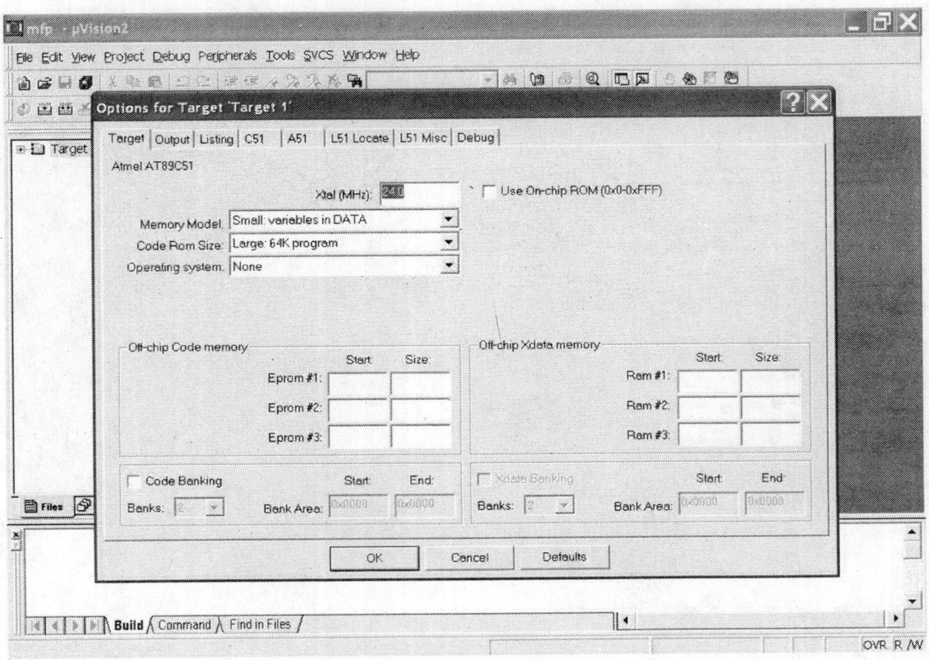
mfp - µVision2
File Edit View Project Debug Peripherals Tools SVCS Window Help
Options for Target 'Target 1'
Target Output Listing C51 A51 L51 Locate L51 Misc Debug
Atmel AT89C51
Xtal (MHz): 24.0
Use On-chip ROM (0x0-0xFFF)
Memory Model: Small: variables in DATA
Code Rom Size: Large: 64K program
Operating system: None
Off-chip Code memory
Start: Size:
Eprom #1:
Eprom #2:
Eprom #3:
Off-chip Xdata memory
Start: Size:
Ram #1:
Ram #2:
Ram #3:
Code Banking
Start: End:
Banks: 2
Bank Area: 0x0000 0x0000
Xdata Banking
Start: End:
Banks: 2
Bank Area: 0x0000 0x0000
OK Cancel Defaults
Target
Files
Build Command Find in Files
OVR R /W

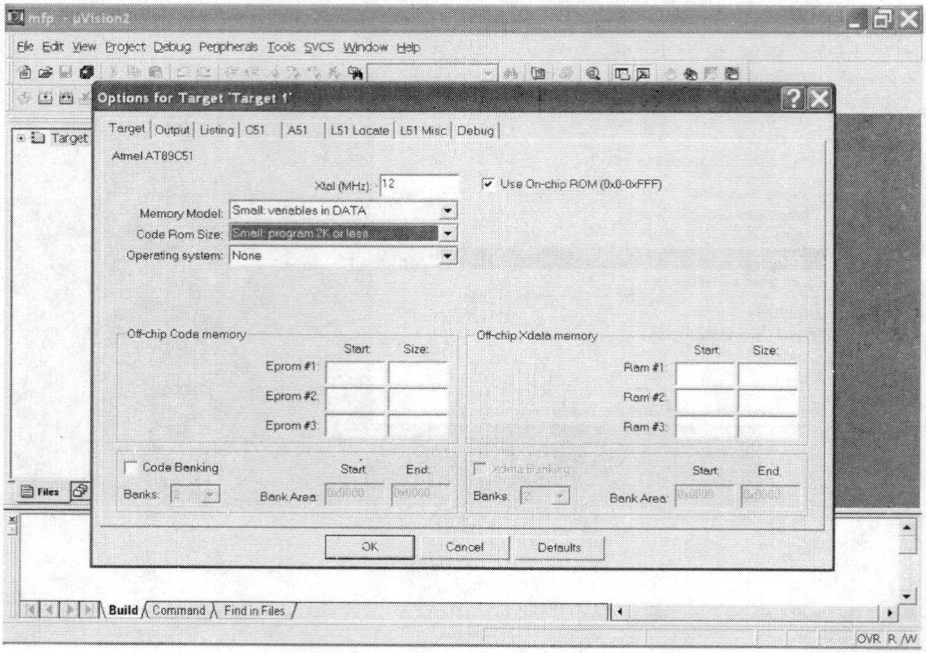
mfp - µVision2
File Edit View Project Debug Peripherals Tools SVCS Window Help
Options for Target 'Target 1'
Target | Output | Listing | C51 | A51 | L51 Locate | L51 Misc | Debug
Atmel AT89C51
Xtal (MHz): 12
Use On-chip ROM (0x0-0xFFF)
Memory Model: Small: variables in DATA
Code Rom Size: Small: program 2K or less
Operating system: None
Off-chip Code memory
Start: Size:
Eprom #1:
Eprom #2:
Eprom #3:
Off-chip Xdata memory
Ram #1:
Ram #2:
Ram #3:
Code Banking
Banks:
Bank Area:
Xdata Banking
OK Cancel Defaults
Build Command Find in Files
OVR R/W

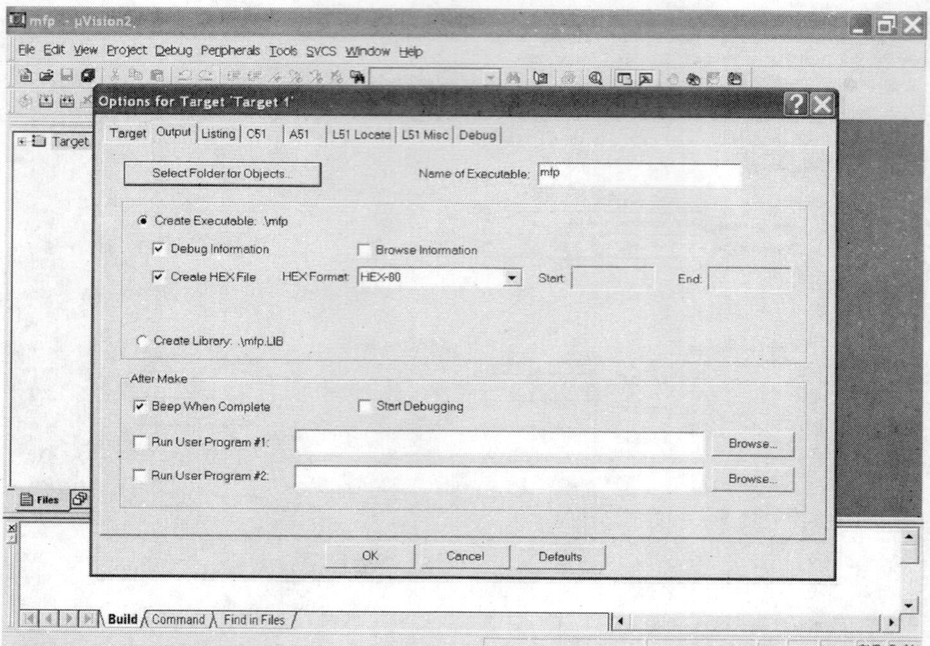
mfp - µVision2
File Edit View Project Debug Peripherals Tools SVCS Window Help
Options for Target 'Target 1'
Target | Output | Listing | C51 | A51 | L51 Locate | L51 Misc | Debug
Select Folder for Objects...
Name of Executable: mfp
Create Executable: .\mfp
Debug Information
Browse Information
Create HEX File
HEX Format: HEX-80
Start:
End:
Create Library: .\mfp.LIB
After Make
Beep When Complete
Start Debugging
Run User Program #1:
Run User Program #2:
Browse...
OK Cancel Defaults
Build Command Find in Files
OVR R/W

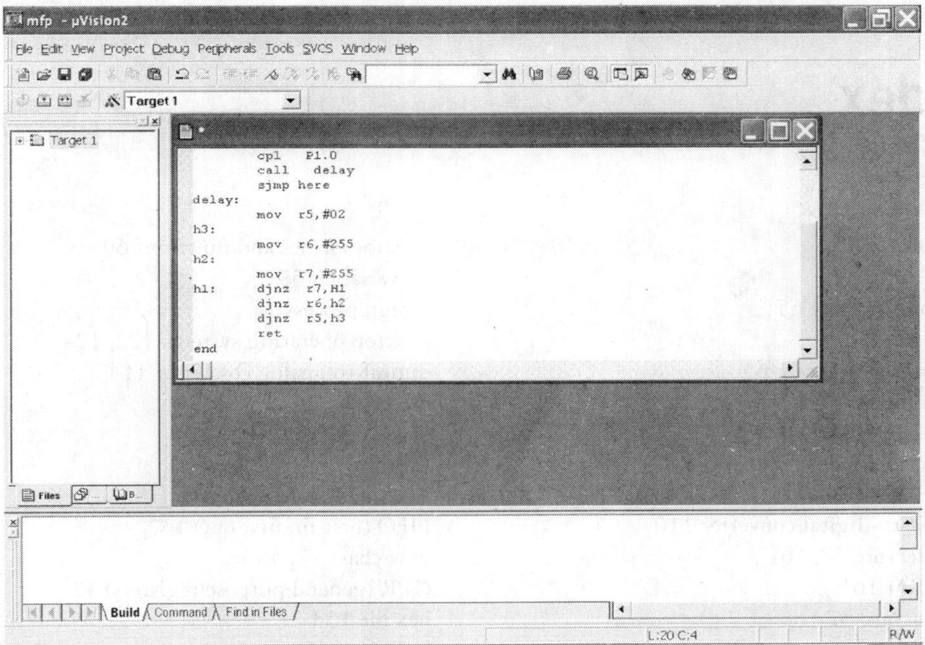
mfp - µVision2
File Edit View Project Debug Peripherals Tools SVCS Window Help
Target 1
Target 1
cpl P1.0
call delay
sjmp here
delay:
mov r5,#02
h3:
mov r6,#255
h2:
mov r7,#255
h1: djnz r7,H1
djnz r6,h2
djnz r5,h3
ret
end
Files
Build
Command
Find in Files
L:20 C:4
R/W

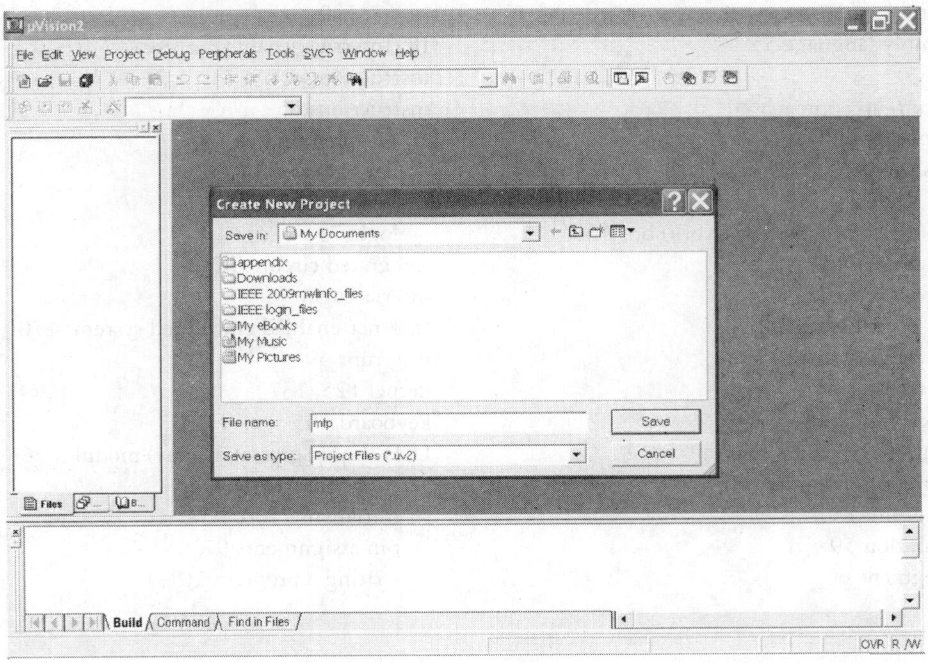
µVision2
File Edit View Project Debug Peripherals Tools SVCS Window Help
Create New Project
Save in: My Documents
appendix
Downloads
IEEE 2009mwinfo_files
IEEE login_files
My eBooks
My Music
My Pictures
File name: mfp
Save as type: Project Files (*.uv2)
Save
Cancel
Files
Build
Command
Find in Files
OVR R /W

Index

μC/OS-II 146
addressing 64
  code indirect 65
  direct 64
  external indirect 65
  immediate 64
  indirect 64
  PC relative 65
algorithm 17, 56
analog-to-digital converter 110
architecture 32, 161
  ARM 161
  Harvard 32
  SHARC 164
arithmetic operations 72, 83
ARM architecture 161
  registers 160
Assembler 61
assembly language 55
bin 63
bottom–up approach 10
bus master 165
bus slave 165
busy flag 99
CAN (controller area network) bus 168
changeability 15
code walking 72
cross compilers 151
data conversion 110
data transfer 65
  external memory 68
  internal memory 66
  program memory 68
debugging 155
declaration 59
  segment 60
  subroutines and functions 60
  variables 59
design process 7
desktop operating systems 122, 124
digital-to-analog convertor 114
directives 59
display 89
Editor 61
Enable module 96
FIFO (first in, first out) 137
flow chart 17, 56
GPR (general purpose registers) 32
hex file 153
host 124, 150
host–target development environment 10
I2C bus 165
IDE (Integrated Development Environment) 63, 122
IE (Interrupt enable register) 47
instruction set 65, 73
instructions 75
  bit manipulation 79
  flags affected by 76
  jump and call 80
  logic 75
integrated circuit (IC) 3
interfaces 88
Internet-enabled embedded systems 170
interrupt 49
kernel 125, 137
keyboard 105
LCD (liquid crystal display) modules 96
  commands table 97
  initialising 100
  pin assignments 97
  writing a program 101

LEDs (light emitting diodes) 89
Linker 62
linker/locator 151
LUT (look-up table) 115
MAKEFILE tool 63
matrix keyboard 107
memory 42
  chips 3
  code 42
  code ROM 45
  data 42
  data RAM 43
  map 152
  register addressable bank 43
  special function registers 44
microcontrollers 5
microprocessors 3
MTBF (mean time between failures) 7
multidigit multiplexed display 92
multidigit non-multiplexed display 94
multiple interrupts 117
native tools 150
non-matrix keyboard 105
OpCodes 58
PCON (power control register) 47
pin assignments 34
polled operation 106
polling 49
ports 38
pre-emptive prioritising 125
prompt lamp 89
PSW (processor status word) register 33
queue 137
registers 32
  GPR 32
  IE 47
  PCON 47
  PSW 33
  receive 47
  transmit 47
round robin 125
RTOS (real-time operating system) 123, 140
  mode of operation 125
scalability 1, 15
scheduling 140
semaphore 134,135
seven-segment LED display 90
  pin assignments 90
  segment assignments 90
SHARC architecture 164
sinking current 89
small footprint 122
sourcing current 89
special function registers 44
symbol table 62
system block diagram 19
target 150
tasks 129
  blocked 130
  states of 129
timer tick 139
timers counters 45
top–down approach 9
UART (universal asynchronous receiver
  transmitter) 47